Social and Environmental Issues in Advertising

T0359118

In the past few decades, attention has turned to the need to apply commercial marketing concepts, knowledge, and techniques to promote goods, services, and actions that enhance consumer well-being and social welfare through socially and environmentally responsible advertising, for example, recycling promotions. Critics argue, however, that for-profit advertisers who endorse social responsibility are inherently serving commercial purposes and diluting the value of socially responsible advertising. Scholars in many fields – advertising, marketing, communications, and psychology – explore ways to encourage consumers, companies, and policymakers to adopt socially responsible behaviours, and to provide theoretical and practical insights regarding effective applications of pro-social and pro-environmental marketing messages.

This book comprises 10 chapters that contribute to advertising theory, research, and practice by providing an overview of current and diverse research that compares, contrasts, and reconciles conflicting views regarding social and environmental advertising, uncovering individual differences in perception of advertising messages and their consequences for social and environmental behaviours, reconciling societal and business interests, identifying a message factor that determines eco-friendly behaviours, and identifying source factors that enhance and weaken advertising effectiveness. This book was originally published as a special issue of the *International Journal of Advertising*.

Sukki Yoon teaches marketing at Bryant University, Smithfield, RI, USA. He has been a visiting scholar at Grey Worldwide and Harvard University, and a consultant at firms and government agencies in both the United States and Korea.

Sangdo Oh teaches marketing at Yonsei University, Wonju, South Korea, and has previously taught at the University of Illinois and Ulsan National Institute of Science and Technology.

Social and Environmental Issues in Advertising

Edited by
Sukki Yoon and Sangdo Oh

LONDON AND NEW YORK

First published 2017 by Routledge

2 Park Square, Milton Park, Abingdon, Oxfordshire OX14 4RN
52 Vanderbilt Avenue, New York, NY 10017

Routledge is an imprint of the Taylor & Francis Group, an informa business

First issued in paperback 2018

Copyright © 2017 Advertising Association

All rights reserved. No part of this book may be reprinted or reproduced or utilised in any form or by any electronic, mechanical, or other means, now known or hereafter invented, including photocopying and recording, or in any information storage or retrieval system, without permission in writing from the publishers.

Notice:
Product or corporate names may be trademarks or registered trademarks, and are used only for identification and explanation without intent to infringe.

British Library Cataloguing in Publication Data
A catalogue record for this book is available from the British Library

ISBN 13: 978-1-138-22843-6 (hbk)
ISBN 13: 978-0-367-07437-1 (pbk)

Typeset in TimesNewRomanPS
by diacriTech, Chennai

Publisher's Note
The publisher accepts responsibility for any inconsistencies that may have arisen during the conversion of this book from journal articles to book chapters, namely the possible inclusion of journal terminology.

Disclaimer
Every effort has been made to contact copyright holders for their permission to reprint material in this book. The publishers would be grateful to hear from any copyright holder who is not here acknowledged and will undertake to rectify any errors or omissions in future editions of this book.

Contents

Citation Information   vii

Notes on Contributors   ix

Introduction to the special issue on social and environmental issues in advertising   1
Sukki Yoon and Sangdo Oh

1.   Pro-environment advertising messages: the role of regulatory focus   4
     Namita Bhatnagar and Jane McKay-Nesbitt

2.   How consumer knowledge shapes green consumption: an empirical study
     on voluntary carbon offsetting   23
     Yohan Kim, Sunyoung Yun, Joosung Lee and Eunju Ko

3.   'Kid tested, mother approved': the relationship between advertising
     expenditures and 'most-loved' brands   42
     Kacy K. Kim, Jerome D. Williams and Gary B. Wilcox

4.   Do bans on illuminated on-premise signs matter? Balancing environmental
     impact with the impact on businesses   61
     Charles R. Taylor and Matthew E. Sarkees

5.   Impact of fear appeals on pro-environmental behavior and
     crucial determinants   74
     Mei-Fang Chen

6.   Effort investment in persuasiveness: a comparative study of environmental
     advertising in the United States and Korea   93
     Sukki Yoon, Yeonshin Kim and Tae Hyun Baek

7.   The effect of non-stereotypical gender role advertising on consumer
     evaluation   106
     Kyounghee Chu, Doo-Hee Lee and Ji Yoon Kim

CONTENTS

8. In distrust of merits: the negative effects of astroturfs on people's
   prosocial behaviors   135
   Jungyun Kang, Hyungsin Kim, Hosang Chu, Charles H. Cho and Hakkyun Kim

9. Empowering social change through advertising co-creation: the roles of
   source disclosure, sympathy and personal involvement   149
   Davide C. Orazi, Liliana L. Bove and Jing Lei

   Index   167

Citation Information

The chapters in this book were originally published in the *International Journal of Advertising*, volume 35, issue 1 (January 2016). When citing this material, please use the original page numbering for each article, as follows:

Introduction
Introduction to the special issue on social and environmental issues in advertising
Sukki Yoon and Sangdo Oh
International Journal of Advertising, volume 35, issue 1 (January 2016) pp. 1–3

Chapter 1
Pro-environment advertising messages: the role of regulatory focus
Namita Bhatnagar and Jane McKay-Nesbitt
International Journal of Advertising, volume 35, issue 1 (January 2016) pp. 4–22

Chapter 2
How consumer knowledge shapes green consumption: an empirical study on voluntary carbon offsetting
Yohan Kim, Sunyoung Yun, Joosung Lee and Eunju Ko
International Journal of Advertising, volume 35, issue 1 (January 2016) pp. 23–41

Chapter 3
'Kid tested, mother approved': the relationship between advertising expenditures and 'most-loved' brands
Kacy K. Kim, Jerome D. Williams and Gary B. Wilcox
International Journal of Advertising, volume 35, issue 1 (January 2016) pp. 42–60

Chapter 4
Do bans on illuminated on-premise signs matter? Balancing environmental impact with the impact on businesses
Charles R. Taylor and Matthew E. Sarkees
International Journal of Advertising, volume 35, issue 1 (January 2016) pp. 61–73

Chapter 5
Impact of fear appeals on pro-environmental behavior and crucial determinants
Mei-Fang Chen
International Journal of Advertising, volume 35, issue 1 (January 2016) pp. 74–92

CITATION INFORMATION

Chapter 6
Effort investment in persuasiveness: a comparative study of environmental advertising in the United States and Korea
Sukki Yoon, Yeonshin Kim and Tae Hyun Baek
International Journal of Advertising, volume 35, issue 1 (January 2016) pp. 93–105

Chapter 7
The effect of non-stereotypical gender role advertising on consumer evaluation
Kyounghee Chu, Doo-Hee Lee and Ji Yoon Kim
International Journal of Advertising, volume 35, issue 1 (January 2016) pp. 106–134

Chapter 8
In distrust of merits: the negative effects of astroturfs on people's prosocial behaviors
Jungyun Kang, Hyungsin Kim, Hosang Chu, Charles H. Cho and Hakkyun Kim
International Journal of Advertising, volume 35, issue 1 (January 2016) pp. 135–148

Chapter 9
Empowering social change through advertising co-creation: the roles of source disclosure, sympathy and personal involvement
Davide C. Orazi, Liliana L. Bove and Jing Lei
International Journal of Advertising, volume 35, issue 1 (January 2016) pp. 149–166

For any permission-related enquiries please visit:
http://www.tandfonline.com/page/help/permissions

Notes on Contributors

Tae Hyun Baek is an Assistant Professor in the Department of Integrated Strategic Communication at the University of Kentucky, Lexington, KY, USA.

Namita Bhatnagar is an Associate Professor and F. Ross Johnson Fellow of Marketing at the I.H. Asper School of Business, University of Manitoba, Winnipeg, Canada.

Liliana L. Bove is the Deputy Head of the Department of Management and Marketing at the University of Melbourne, Australia.

Mei-Fang Chen is based in the Department of Business Management at Tatung University, Taipei, Taiwan.

Charles H. Cho is a Professor of Social and Environmental Accounting and the Director of the Centre of Excellence for Management and Society at ESSEC Business School, Paris, France.

Hosang Chu is based in the School of Business at Sungkyunkwan University, Seoul, South Korea.

Kyounghee Chu is based in the Business School at Korea University, Seoul, South Korea.

Jungyun Kang is based in the School of Business at Sungkyunkwan University, Seoul, South Korea.

Hakkyun Kim is based in the School of Business at Sungkyunkwan University, Seoul, South Korea.

Hyungsin Kim is based in the College of Education at Ewha Women's University, Seoul, South Korea.

Ji Yoon Kim is based in the Business School at Korea University, Seoul, South Korea.

Kacy K. Kim is an Assistant Professor of Marketing in the Martha & Spencer Love School of Business at Elon University, NC, USA.

Yeonshin Kim is based in the Department of Business Administration at Myongji University, Seoul, South Korea.

Yohan Kim is based in the Department of Business and Technology Management at the Korea Advanced Institute of Science and Technology, Daejeon, South Korea.

Eunju Ko is based in the Department of Clothing and Textile at Yonsei University, Seoul, South Korea.

NOTES ON CONTRIBUTORS

Doo-Hee Lee is a Professor in the Business School at Korea University, Seoul, South Korea.

Joosung Lee is based in the Department of Business and Technology Management at the Korea Advanced Institute of Science and Technology, Daejeon, South Korea.

Jing Lei is a Senior Lecturer in the Department of Management and Marketing at the University of Melbourne, Australia.

Jane McKay-Nesbitt is an Associate Professor of Marketing at Bryant University, Smithfield, RI, USA. She previously worked in the financial services industry.

Sangdo Oh teaches marketing at Yonsei University, Wonju, South Korea, and has previously taught at the University of Illinois and Ulsan National Institute of Science and Technology.

Davide C. Orazi is a Teaching Fellow and Lecturer in Marketing Strategy at the University of Melbourne, Australia.

Matthew E. Sarkees is an Assistant Professor of Marketing at St. Joseph's University, Philadelphia, PA, USA.

Charles R. Taylor is John A. Murphy Professor of Marketing in the School of Business at Villanova University, PA, USA.

Gary B. Wilcox is a Professor of Communication in the Moody College of Communication at the University of Texas at Austin, TX, USA.

Jerome D. Williams is a Professor and Prudential Chair in Business at Rutgers University, New Brunswick, NJ, USA.

Sukki Yoon teaches marketing at Bryant University, Smithfield, RI, USA. He has been a visiting scholar at Grey Worldwide and Harvard University, and a consultant at firms and government agencies in both the United States and Korea.

Sunyoung Yun is based in the Department of Business and Technology Management at the Korea Advanced Institute of Science and Technology, Daejeon, South Korea.

Introduction to the special issue on social and environmental issues in advertising

Sukki Yoon[a] and Sangdo Oh[b]

[a]Department of Marketing, College of Business, Bryant University, Smithfield, USA; [b]Management Department, School of Business Administration, Ulsan National Institute of Science and Technology, Ulsan, Republic of Korea

In the past few decades, attention has been turning to the need to apply commercial marketing concepts, knowledge, and techniques to promote goods, services, and actions that enhance consumer well-being and social welfare through socially and environmentally responsible advertising. Advertising campaigns such as recycling promotions promote socially beneficial ideas and actions, and campaigns such as anti-drunk-driving messages discourage socially detrimental ideas and actions. Critics argue, however, that for-profit advertisers who endorse social responsibility are inherently serving commercial purposes and diluting the value of socially responsible advertising.

One research thread explores ways to encourage consumers, companies, and policy-makers to adopt and encourage socially responsible behaviors (Taylor 2014), to provide theoretical and practical insights regarding effective applications of prosocial and pro-environmental marketing messages (e.g., Baek, Yoon, and Kim, 2015; Taylor 2014). Some of these articles may have appeared in various marketing, communications, and psychology journals, but advertising scholars and practitioners may lack exposure to the research and may find that it is relevant for further study or for practical managerial applications.

In this special issue, we hope to introduce *International Journal of Advertising* readers to current and diverse research that compares, contrasts, and reconciles conflicting views regarding social and environmental advertising.

This issue comprises 9 original empirical research articles that were among the best papers presented at the 2014 Global Marketing Conference in Singapore – among 1149 papers submitted, only 441 papers (39%) were accepted for the conference. The nine articles selected for the special issue are rigorously selected, as all of the articles presented here have gone through a regular IJA peer review process. These articles contribute to advertising theory, research, and practice by (1) uncovering individual differences in perception of advertising messages and their consequences for social and environmental behaviors (Bhatnagar and McKay-Nesbitt, 2016; Kim et al., 2016), (2) reconciling societal and business interests (Kim, Williams, and Wilcox, 2016; Taylor and Sarkees, 2016), (3) identifying a message factor that determines eco-friendly behaviors (Chen, 2016; Yoon, Kim, and Baek, 2016), and (4) identifying source factors that enhance and weaken advertising effectiveness (Chu, Lee, and Kim, 2016; Kang et al., 2016; Orazi, Bove, and Lei, 2016).

The authors of these articles use a wide variety of samples and methods. One article combines advertising expenditure data and survey data from two marketing research firms (Kim, Williams, and Wilcox, 2016). Two of the articles survey a nationally representative sample of advertisers and consumers (Kim et al., 2016; Taylor and Sarkees, 2016). Two articles use data collected from a consumer panel (Chu, Lee, and Kim, 2016; Orazi, Bove, and Lei, 2016), and four use experimental data collected from laboratory settings (Bhatnagar and McKay-Nesbitt, 2016; Kang et al., 2016; Chen-Fang 2016; Yoon, Kim, and Baek 2016). The use of multiple methods across studies increases the validity of overall findings reported in the issue, as strengths and weaknesses complement one another.

The first two papers focus on individual differences regarding chronic regulatory focus and environmental knowledge for determining whether consumers will be receptive to environmental advertising and will distrust non-profit organizations. Bhatnagar and McKay-Nesbitt (2016) show that chronic promotion focus is associated with environmental concerns, favorable attitudes toward pro-environment advertising recommendations, and pro-environmental behaviors, but chronic prevention focus does not generate the same positive effects. Kim et al. (2016) report that perceived behavioral control and anticipated emotion differ in their effects on green consumption. Those two papers show that individual differences play a role in determining whether consumers will comply with pro-environmental recommendations.

The next two papers address societal versus business perspectives. Kim, Williams, and Wilcox (2016) examine whether children and mothers differ in their perceptions about popular brands shown in advertising and find that advertising positively affects brand affinity for both children and mothers, while product placement influences brand affinity for children but not for mothers. Taylor and Sarkees (2016) report conflicting views on the use of lighted on-premise signs. On the one hand, governments and policymakers want to ban the signs to reduce or eliminate wasted resources and make environments more aesthetically pleasing. On the other hand, a nationally representative sample of sign users reveals that local business owners believe that the signs perform key marketing functions and that lighting restrictions harm their businesses and negatively affect the local economy. Those two papers should help policy-makers and advertisers better understand positive and negative advertising impacts.

Chen (2016) examines the impact of high and low fear appeals and demonstrates that low fear text evokes more fearful emotions and intentions to engage in pro-environmental behavior, while high fear text evokes perceptions of collective efficacy and intentions to engage in pro-environmental behavior. This research shows how fear appeals can be used to encourage pro-environmental behavior in a Chinese collectivist culture. Yoon, Kim, and Baek (2016) compare American and Korean reactions to the persuasiveness of environmental advertising campaigns that are preceded by environmental pledges. Their findings indicate that environmental advertising effectiveness depends on how much effort recipients put into making environmental pledges prior to viewing the advertisements—when environmental pledges requesting more effort precede ad messages, Americans are more persuaded but Koreans are less persuaded.

The last three papers deal with source effects in social and environmental advertising. Chu, Lee, and Kim (2016) examine what happens when a spokesperson's gender is incongruent with a product's gender image. They find that consumers who have independent self-construal and high need for uniqueness will have positive reactions to non-stereotypical novelty, but consumers who have interdependent self-construal and low need for uniqueness will show negative cognitive resistance. Kang et al. (2016) demonstrate that advertising effectiveness varies depending on whether real grassroots organizations or fake 'astroturf' organizations are sending the message. Their findings indicate that pro-environmental messages from astrotuf organizations can cause consumers to distrust non-profit organizations and to be less willing to follow prosocial requests, moderated by skepticism toward advertising. Orazi, Bove, and Lei (2016) tackle consumer-generated advertising, a newly emerging marketing trend. They show that disclosing consumer participation generates positive ad evaluations and encourages consumers to have more positive attitudes toward healthful eating, mediated by sympathy toward the ad creator. In addition, source disclosure amplifies effects on ad evaluations when the audience is highly involved with the issue being advertised. Those three studies expand advertisers' knowledge regarding how to shape advertising effectiveness by revealing message sources.

We, the guest editors, thank the authors who submitted their work and endured multiple rounds of revisions for this special issue. We also thank reviewers who provided constructive comments on the submissions. In addition, we thank Charles 'Ray' Taylor, the journal editor, Kyung Hoon Kim, the Executive Secretary of Global Alliance of Marketing and Management Associations, and Eunju Ko, the Organizing Committee Chair of 2014 GMC, for encouraging us to submit our proposal for this special issue and for trusting us to edit it.

References

Baek, T.H., S. Yoon, and S. Kim. 2015. When environmental messages should be assertive: Examining the moderating role of effort investment. *International Journal of Advertising* 34, no. 1: 135−57.

Bhatnagar, N., and J. McKay-Nesbitt. 2016. Pro-environmental advertising messages: The role of regulatory focus. *International Journal of Advertising* 35, no. 1: 4−23.

Chen, M. 2016. Impact of fear appeals on pro-environmental behavior and crucial determinants. *International Journal of Advertising* 35, no. 1: 75−93.

Chu, K., D. Lee, and J.Y. Kim. 2016. The effect of non-stereotypical gender role advertising on consumer evaluation. *International Journal of Advertising* 35, no. 1: 107−135.

Kang, J., H. Kim, H. Chu, C.H. Cho, and H. Kim. 2016. In distrust of merits: The negative effects of astroturfs on people's prosocial behavior. *International Journal of Advertising* 35, no. 1: 136−149.

Kim, K.K., J.D. Williams, and G Wilcox. 2016. "Kid tested, mother approved": The relationship between advertising expenditures and "most-loved" brands. *International Journal of Advertising* 35, no. 1: 43−61.

Kim, Y.H., S. Yun, J. Lee, and E. Ko. 2016. How consumer knowledge shapes green consumption: An empirical study on voluntary carbon offsetting. *International Journal of Advertising* 35, no. 1: 24−42.

Orazi, D., L. Bove, and J. Lei. 2016. Empowering social change through advertising co-creation: The roles of source disclosure, sympathy and personal involvement. *International Journal of Advertising* 35, no. 1: 150−168.

Taylor, C.R. 2014. Corporate social responsibility and advertising: Does it extend to taking stances on social issues? *International Journal of Advertising* 33, no. 1: 11−115.

Taylor, C.R., and M. Sarkees. 2016. Do bans on illuminated on-premise signs matter? Balancing environmental impact with the impact on businesses. *International Journal of Advertising* 35, no. 1: 62−74.

Yoon, S., Kim, Y. & Baek, T. (2016). Effort Investment in persuasiveness: a comparative study of environmental advertising in the United States and Korea. *International Journal of Advertising* 35, no. 1: 94−106.

Pro-environment advertising messages: the role of regulatory focus

Namita Bhatnagar[a] and Jane McKay-Nesbitt[b]

[a]University of Manitoba, Winnipeg, Canada; [b]Bryant University, Smithfield, RI, USA

This paper examines individuals' (promotion versus prevention) regulatory focus effects on a variety of environmentally responsible reactions. Results of two studies show that *chronic* promotion focus is associated with environmental concern, favorable attitudes towards pro-environment advertising recommendations, intentions to do what the ad recommends, and positive affect directed at the self upon adhering to ad recommendations. Conversely, chronic prevention focus while not significantly associated with environmental concern, attitudes, intentions, or positive affect – has a marginally positive association with negative affect toward the self and others who do not follow pro-environmental ad recommendations. Furthermore, *priming* promotion focus strengthens attitudes toward recommended behavior, intentions to follow through, and other-directed positive (and negative) affect. Priming prevention focus also strengthens other-directed negative (and positive) affect. No fit effects between individuals' regulatory focus and pro-environmental ads framed with recycle, reduce, or recycle and reduce orientations is found. Implications for theory and practice are discussed.

Introduction

It is widely recognized that our environment needs to be protected and that individuals can play an important role in providing that protection. For example, the United States Environmental Protection Agency reminds individuals that 'Today we realize that each thing we do can help or hurt our planet in many ways. We all need to take ownership of environmental protection' (http://www.epa.gov/gateway/learn/greenliving). Our goal is to contribute to a healthy environment by identifying factors that enhance our willingness to respond to pro-environment advertising messages and to behave in an environmentally responsible manner.

While there has been an increase in studies analyzing the association between psycho-social variables and pro-cnvironmental attitudes and behavior (e.g., Bamberg and Moser 2007; Baek, Yoon, and Kim 2015), to our knowledge none have looked at individual differences in regulatory focus (Higgins 1987) as a potential determinant of these outcomes. Thus, we first investigate the relationships between individuals' chronic regulatory focus and their environmental concern (Study 1).

Investigations of factors that contribute to pro-environmental advertising effectiveness have been reported in the literature for many years. Highly credible message sources are found to enhance the effectiveness of energy conservation messages (Craig and

MCann 1978) and message content also contributes to pro-environmental message effectiveness (e.g., Chang, Zhang, and Xie 2015). Message content that emphasizes financial advantages is effective for water conservation messages (Delorme, Hagen, and Stout 2003), whereas a message's regulatory focus influences the effectiveness of ads for environmentally friendly consumer products (Kareklas, Carlson, and Muehling 2012; Newman et al. 2012). Our research extends work that has considered factors that influence pro-environmental ads' persuasiveness by exploring message-recipient-characteristic effects on such ads. Specifically, in Study 2 we examine the effects of an individual's regulatory focus on (1) attitudes towards pro-environmental ad recommendations, (2) intentions to do what the pro-environmental ad recommends, and (3) affect directed at self and others who do or do not adhere to the ad recommendations.

Finally, given that themes pertaining to recycling and/or reduction are common in pro-environmental advertising messages (e.g., http://www2.epa.gov/recycle), we also examine the potential moderating role of such ad content in the relationship between message recipients' regulatory focus and their responsiveness to pro-environmental ads.

Background, conceptualization, and hypothesis development

Regulatory focus theory (RFT)

Regulatory focus theory suggests that although individuals may share the same goals (e.g., a desire for a healthy environment), they differ in their preferences for the means of achieving those goals (Higgins 1987). Some individuals adopt a promotion focus while others adopt a prevention focus in goal pursuit. Promotion-focused individuals are concerned with achieving an ideal state (e.g., a healthy environment), are sensitive to gains (Shah, Higgins, and Friedman 1998), and eagerly strive to reach goals (Crowe and Higgins 1997). Prevention-focused individuals are concerned with preventing problems (e.g., an unhealthy environment), are sensitive to losses (Shah, Higgins, and Friedman 1998), and proceed cautiously as they pursue goals (Crowe and Higgins 1997).

Effects of individual differences in regulatory focus on attitudes and behaviors have been extensively explored in the literature (Higgins 1987; Polman 2012), and regulatory focus theory has been applied to the investigation of a variety of social issues. For example, regulatory focus has been shown to influence an individual's (1) ability to start or maintain weight-loss or smoking-cessation programs (Fuglestad, Rothman, and Jeffery 2008); (2) perceptions of the ease or effectiveness of health behaviors (Keller 2006); and (3) thoughts and feelings about physical activity (Latimer et. al. 2008). Interestingly however, although there is evidence that individual differences are important environmentally responsible behavior determinants (e.g., turning lights off at home; Ngo, West, and Calkins 2009), to date little attention has been paid to the relationship between individual differences in regulatory focus and environmental concern or environmentally responsible behaviors.

Environmental concern and environmentally responsible behavior

Environmental concern is an attitude construct that captures an individual's views about the environment (Weigel and Weigel 1978). Environmental concern is sometimes viewed as (1) relatively enduring beliefs about the environment that could predispose an individual to act in an environmentally responsible manner (Weigel and Weigel 1978); (2) a three-dimensional construct consisting of affective, cognitive, and conative dimensions (Best and Kneip 2011; Diekmann and Preisendorfer 2003); or (3) as a worldview that emphasizes the need to balance humankind's needs with the natural environment's needs (Dunlap and VanLiere 1978).

Environmentally responsible behaviors are generally considered to be behaviors that are focused on protecting the natural environment (Cleveland, Kalamas, and Laroche 2005). Some frequently investigated environmentally responsible behaviors include actions to reduce the consumption of fossil fuels by using public transportation, riding a bicycle, walking (Ngo, West, and Calkins 2009), turning heat down, or turning off lights and appliances (Cleveland, Kalamas, and Laroche 2005; Yoon, Kim, and Baek 2015). Avoiding disposable diapers or plastic shopping bags (Polonsky, Garma, and Grau 2011), using energy efficient light bulbs (Cleveland, Kalama, and Laroche 2005), and recycling products or packaging are other examples of environmentally responsible behaviors that have been examined in the literature (Yoon, Kim, and Baek 2015).

There is evidence that environmental concern leads to a variety of environmentally responsible behaviors. Thogersen and Olander (2006) found that individuals who express higher versus lower levels of concern about various environmental issues are more likely to recycle consumer products than those who express lower levels of concern. Others have demonstrated that individuals who hold pro-environmental attitudes will pay more for green products and do not consider this to be inconvenient (Laroche, Bergeron, and Barbaro-Forleo 2001). Similarly, Joireman and his colleagues (2004) found that expressing more concern about the negative environmental impact of commuting by car leads to greater public transportation use. Ngo and her colleagues (2009) also found that green attitudes encourage indoor greenhouse gas reduction behaviors (e.g., turning off lights, recycling). Other researchers found that adolescents' pro-environmental attitudes significantly predicted their environmentally friendly product choices and explained about 22% of the variance in pro-environmental behaviors (Meinhold and Malkus 2005).

Consideration of future consequences (CFC), environmentally responsible behavior, and regulatory focus

Individuals have also been shown to differ with respect to concern for the consequences of their behavior. Some individuals are more concerned with *future or long-term* consequences whereas others are more concerned with *immediate or short-term* consequences of their current behavior (Strathman et al. 1994). This individual difference in concern for behavioral consequences has been frequently measured with a unidimensional consideration of future consequences (CFC) scale (Strathman et al. 1994). The unidimensional CFC scale assesses the extent to which an individual considers future (i.e., long term) versus immediate (i.e., short term) consequences of current behavior and the extent to which an individual's current behavior is influenced by the consideration of those consequences.

There is evidence that individuals who report high levels of concern for the future (CFC) also exhibit high levels of environmentally responsible behaviors such as recycling (Ebreo and Vining 2001; Lindsay and Strathman 1997). This finding is not surprising given that recycling makes materials available for other uses in the future and contributes to the long-term health of the environment. Similarly, high-CFC versus low-CFC individuals report greater preferences for using public versus private transportation (Joireman, Van Lange, and Van Vugt 2004).

More recently, employing a two-dimensional scale to assess CFC, Joireman and his colleagues (2012) demonstrated that individuals who consider the long-term consequences of their behavior (i.e., score high on a CFC-Future subscale) report high promotion-focus but not prevention-focus scores (Lockwood, Jordan, and Kunda 2002). Conversely, individuals who report greater concern for the short-term consequences of their behavior (i.e., score high on a CFC-Immediate subscale) score high on prevention-focus but not promotion-focus measures. Thus, while both promotion- and prevention-focused individuals consider the consequences of their actions, promotion-focused individuals appear to be concerned with more long-term consequences while prevention-focused individuals appear to be concerned with more short-term consequences of their actions. Joireman and his colleagues (2012) suggest that this relationship occurs because promotion-focused individuals, in keeping with a future orientation, adopt distal and abstract ideal self-goals (i.e., hopes and aspirations) whereas prevention-focused individuals, in keeping with a more present orientation, adopt more proximal and concrete self-goals (i.e., duties and obligations).

In summary, because it is argued that being environmentally concerned necessitates a concern for the long-term, future consequences of behavior, and because there is evidence that promotion-focused individuals have a high CFC-Future orientation (i.e., concern for long-term consequences), it is expected that as chronic promotion focus increases individuals will exhibit higher levels of environmental concern. Conversely, because prevention-focused individuals have been shown to be concerned with more immediate, short-term consequences of behavior (CFC-Immediate), it is expected that the same relationship will not be evident as prevention-focus increases.

Hypothesis 1. Chronic promotion focus will be a more important predictor than chronic prevention focus of environmental concern.

Environmental concern, pro-environmental ads, and regulatory focus

In addition to its influence on environmental behavior, environmental concern has also been found to influence consumers' responsiveness to information (Bamberg 2003) and advertising content (Bickart and Ruth 2012). Bamberg (2003) found that highly versus less environmentally concerned individuals were more interested in obtaining information about green products. In addition, highly compared to less environmentally concerned individuals indicated greater intentions to use the information they had obtained. Similarly, Bickart, and Ruth (2012) showed that when an individual's environmental concern is high, ads that feature products with an eco-seal on the package generate more purchase intentions for familiar rather than unfamiliar brands. When individuals have low levels of environmental concern however, purchase intentions are not influenced by ads that feature products with an eco-seal on the package, regardless of brand familiarity.

Environmental concern has also been shown to influence consumers' responsiveness to pro-environmental ads that employ guilt appeals (Chang 2012). Chang (2012) demonstrated that when highly environmentally concerned individuals view ads pertaining to environmental issues in a country some distance away (i.e., a low proximity issue) versus the country in which they reside (i.e., a high-proximity issue), attitudes toward the environmentally friendly brand and intentions to purchase it are more influenced by guilt- than by non-guilt appeals.

Thus, given that environmental concern has been shown to enhance message recipients' responsiveness to pro-environmental information and ad content, and given that individuals' promotion focus is a more important environmental-concern predictor than prevention focus, it is expected that individuals' regulatory focus will also influence responsiveness to pro-environmental ads. That is, we expect that promotion-focused individuals will have more positive attitudes toward pro-environmental ad recommendations as well as greater intentions to perform the behaviors recommended by the ad, than pre-vention-focused individuals. Specifically, we hypothesize the following relationships:

Hypothesis 2. Promotion focus will be a more important predictor of (a) attitudes toward pro-environmental ad recommendations, and (b) intentions to perform the behavior rec-ommended in the pro-environmental ad than prevention focus.

Regulatory focus and affect

Promotion- and prevention-focused individuals also differ with respect to their affective responses to outcomes. Promotion-focused individuals who are more sensitive to gains have been shown to experience more intense positive affect in response to gains than losses (Idson, Liberman, and Higgins 2000). Conversely, prevention-focused individuals who are more sensitive to losses have been shown to experience more intense negative affect in response to losses than gains. Similarly, promotion-focused individuals report more positive (i.e., good) and less negative (i.e., bad) feelings in response to gains whereas prevention-focused individuals report more negative (i.e., bad) and less positive feelings (i.e., good) in response to losses (Idson, Liberman, and Higgins 2004). Consistent with these findings, Sar and Anghelcev (2015) showed that positive mood enhances pro-motion-focused ad effectiveness whereas negative mood enhances prevention-focused ad effectiveness. Thus, promotion focus appears to be associated with positive affective responses whereas prevention focus appears to be associated with negative affective responses. Therefore, because promotion focus 'fits' with positive affect, as promotion focus increases, individuals are expected to feel more positively about themselves and others when environmentally responsible behaviors are evident (i.e., gains). Conversely, because prevention focus 'fits' with negative affect, as chronic prevention focus increases, individuals are expected to feel more negatively about themselves and others when environmentally responsible behaviors are not evident (i.e., losses). Thus, the fol-lowing relationships are hypothesized:

Hypothesis 3. An individual's promotion focus will be a more important predictor than his or her prevention focus of (a) positive affect toward himself or herself when he or she performs the behavior recommended in pro-environmental ads, and (b) positive affect toward others when they perform the behavior recommended in pro-environmental ads.

Hypothesis 4. An individual's prevention focus will be a more important predictor than his or her promotion focus of (a) negative affect toward himself or herself when he or she does not perform the behavior recommended in pro-environmental ads, and (b) negative affect toward others when they do not perform the behavior recommended in pro-environ-ment ads.

An individuals' regulatory focus is a stable disposition that can occur chronically and can also be primed by situational factors (Higgins 1987; Idson, Liberman, and Higgins 2000). Thus, when regulatory focus is primed via appropriately framed pro-environmen-tal ad messages, we expect the same pattern of pro-environmental responses as predicted above.

Recycle and reduce messages: Pro-environmental ad appeal types

Organizations that encourage individuals to be environmentally responsible frequently employ pro-environmental messages that encourage message recipients to recycle products, reduce consumption, or do both (e.g., http://www.epa.gov/epahome/hi-win ter.htm). Although both recycling products and reducing consumption are designed to preserve and protect the environment, recycling and reducing are two distinct strategies for achieving this goal. Recycling requires an individual to take action (i.e., an approach strategy) while reducing consumption requires an individual to stop taking action (i.e., an avoidance strategy). Therefore, it is possible that recycling products 'fits' better with a promotion than a prevention focus and that reducing consumption 'fits' better with a prevention focus. Furthermore, given evidence that regulatory fit enhances persuasion (Kees, Burton, and Tangari 2010; Koenig et al. 2009), the pro-environmental message appeal type (i.e., recycle or reduce) is expected to moderate the effects of an individual's regulatory focus on pro-environmental ad responsiveness. That is, because promotion focus 'fits' with recycling, an approach strategy, it is possible that promotion-focused individuals respond more favorably than prevention-focused individuals to pro-environmental ads that focus on recycling products. Conversely, because prevention focus 'fits' with reducing consumption, an avoidance strategy, prevention-focused individuals may respond more favorably than promotion-focused individuals to pro-environmental ads that focus on reducing consumption. Thus, the following relationships are hypothesized:

Hypothesis 5. Pro-environmental ad message framing will moderate the effect of an individual's regulatory focus on responsiveness to ad messages such that

(1) *when a **recycle** ad message is viewed, promotion focus will be a more important predictor of (a) attitudes towards pro-environmental ad recommendations and (b) intentions to perform the behavior recommended in the pro-environmental ad than prevention focus; and*
(2) *when a **reduce** ad message is viewed, prevention focus will be a more important predictor of (a) attitudes towards pro-environmental ad recommendations and (b) intentions to perform the behavior recommended in the pro-environmental ad than promotion focus.*

Study 1

In Study 1 we examined the relationship between individuals' chronic regulatory focus and general environmental concern. Specifically, we set out to test Hypothesis 1, that chronic promotion focus is a more important environmental concern predictor than chronic prevention focus.

Method

Methodology, participants, and procedure. Two hundred and forty-six undergraduate students at a major north-eastern US university participated in the study for partial course credit (59.3% male, average age = 19.78 years, 92.3% US nationals). Survey administration and data collection occurred online using the MediaLab 2010 program. Participants responded to questions to assess environmental concern and chronic regulatory focus, provided demographic information (gender, age, nationality), and then were debriefed regarding the study's purpose. Multiple linear regression was used for data analysis.

Measures

Environmental concern. Participants indicated their attitudes toward environmental issues on 12 items adapted from Weigel and Weigel's (1978) Environmental Concern scale (e.g., 'I would be willing to spend more money on products and services that are environmentally friendly'; where 1 = strongly disagree and 7 = strongly agree). The scale was reliable (Cronbach's $\alpha = .79$), and item responses were averaged to form an environmental concern index [Mean (SD) = 4.70 (.76)].

Chronic regulatory focus. Chronic regulatory focus was measured via the General Regulatory Focus Measure (GRFM; Lockwood, Jordan, and Kunda 2002) which consists of nine nine-point scale items that measure promotion focus (e.g., 'I often think about the person I would ideally like to be in the future') and nine that measure prevention focus (e.g., 'In general, I am focused on preventing negative events in my life', where 1 = not at all true of me, 9 = very true of me). Analyses revealed that the promotion and prevention scales were reliable and items were averaged to form promotion and prevention focus indices (Cronbach's $\alpha_{promotion} = .87$; Cronbach's $\alpha_{prevention} = .82$). The measures were mean centered [promotion mean (SD) = 7.28 (1.11); prevention mean (SD) = 5.21 (1.42)] to mitigate multicollinearity across predictor variables.

Results

Multiple linear regression was used to assess whether chronic promotion focus, chronic prevention focus, or the interaction between the two impacts environmental concern. The overall model explained a significant amount of environmental concern variance ($F(3, 242) = 3.28, p < .05, R^2 = .04, R^2_{Adjusted} = .03$). Neither chronic prevention focus (standardized $\beta = -.08, t(242) = -1.31$, ns) nor the interaction between promotion and prevention focus significantly impacted environmental concern (standardized $\beta = -.01, t(242) = -.16$, ns). However, as participants' chronic promotion focus increased, so did their environmental concern (standardized $\beta = .19, t(242) = 2.73, p < .01$). Thus, chronic promotion focus significantly predicted environmental concern while chronic prevention focus did not (supporting Hypothesis 1).

Discussion

This study supported our argument that environmental concern varies with chronic regulatory focus. Namely, stronger chronic promotion focus was associated with greater environmental concern, whereas there was no significant relationship between chronic prevention focus and such concerns.

Study 2

Study 2 aimed to replicate results of Study 1, and examine the effects of chronic as well as primed regulatory focus on a broader array of pro-environmental responses (described below).

Method

Methodology, participants, and procedure. As in Study 1, Hypothesis 1 was re-tested via a multiple linear regression of environmental concern on *chronic* promotion focus, prevention focus, and the interaction between these two variables. Similar multiple linear regressions were used to examine the effects of chronic regulatory focus on attitudes toward pro-environmental ad recommendations and intentions to follow the recommendation (Hypothesis 2), positive affect toward self and others that performed the ad recommendation (Hypothesis 3), and negative affect toward self and others that did not perform the ad recommendation (Hypothesis 4) in the context of plastic water bottle use. For *primed regulatory focus effects*, ANOVAs using three (regulatory focus prime: no prime, promotion prime, or prevention prime) by three (pro-environment ad frame: reduce, recycle, or reduce and recycle) between subjects designs were carried out for testing Hypotheses 2-5.

Two hundred and forty-eight undergraduate students (60.1% male, average age = 20.39 years, age range = 18-24 years, 92.3% US nationals) from the same university as in Study 1 participated for partial course credit. Participants were randomly assigned to one of the nine experimental conditions. After responding to environmental concern and chronic regulatory focus items, participants engaged in a regulatory focus priming activity followed by exposure to information about harmful environmental effects of plastic water bottle production and consumption and pro-environmental ads that advocated either (1) recycling (2) reducing, or (3) recycling and reducing plastic bottle usage. Finally, participants responded to outcome measures and provided demographic information (gender, age, nationality).

Experimental manipulations

Regulatory focus prime. Promotion focus was primed by asking participants to think about their past and current hopes, dreams and aspirations, and list three of them. *Prevention focus* was primed by asking participants to think about and list three of their past and current obligations and responsibilities (Wang and Lee 2006).

Pro-environment ad frame. Participants read one of three pro-environmental ad messages – framed with reduce, recycle, or reduce and recycle orientations – about plastic water bottle use.

Measures

Environmental concern and chronic regulatory focus. Environmental concern [mean (SD) = 4.80 (.82); Cronbach's α = 0.82], chronic promotion focus [mean (SD) = 7.48 (1.01); Cronbach's α = 0.87], and chronic prevention focus [mean (SD) = 5.31 (1.42); Cronbach's α = 0.84] were assessed in the same manner as in Study 1. Chronic promotion and prevention focus were mean-centered to reduce multicollinearity between predictor variables.

Attitude toward recommended behavior. Participants' attitudes toward doing what the pro-environment ad advocated were captured by averaging responses to three Likert scale items anchored by 1 (*unfavorable/negative/bad*) and 7 (*favorable/positive/good;* Cronbach's α = 0.93; Holbrook and Batra 1987).

Intentions to perform the recommended behavior. Consistent with others who have explored ad impact on pro-environmental intentions (Hartman at al. 2014), intentions toward performing the behaviors advocated in the ad were measured via a single item: 'I intend to do what the message advocates' (1 = not at all, 7 = very much so).

Positive affect toward self and others. Four items assessed how *proud/pleased/happy/relieved* participants would feel upon following the pro-environment ad recommendations. Items were averaged to form an index of *positive affect toward self* (1 = not at all,

7 = very much so; Cronbach's α = 0.90). Five additional item responses were averaged to form an index for *positive affect toward others* who followed the ad advice (*admiration/respect/gratitude/pleased/happy*). Items were anchored by 1(not at all) and 7 (very much so; Cronbach's α = 0.95).

Negative affect toward self and others. Two indices for negative emotions toward self and others upon not following pro-environment ad recommendations were created, using 7-point Likert scales anchored by 1(not at all) and 7(very much so). *Negative affect toward self* was assessed by averaging the extent to which participants felt *guilty, ashamed, regretful, angry, upset,* and *annoyed* (Cronbach's α = 0.95). *Negative affect toward others* was measured by averaging the degree to which respondents felt *scornful, contemptuous, disapproving, resentful, angry, upset,* and *annoyed* (Cronbach's α = 0.97). All emotion-related items were adapted from previously published scales for positive and negative emotions (Bearden and Netemeyer 1999; Weiner 2006).

Covariates. Demographic information (age, gender, nationality) was assessed as potential covariates within the analyses. Gender differences in chronic regulatory focus are found in past literature (McKay-Nesbitt, Bhatnagar, and Smith, 2013) and it is possible that cultural differences in regulatory focus and environmental perceptions exist. Individuals' *chronic regulatory focus* was also considered as a potential covariate within the ANOVAs used to test Hypotheses 2−5 that dealt with the effects of *primed promotion* and *prevention focus.* It is possible that, individual's chronic dispositions, in addition to primed orientations, continue to influence outcomes.

Manipulation check

Participants were asked to indicate whether the plastic water bottle message they viewed was a recycle, reduce, or recycle and reduce message.

Results

Manipulation check. Cross-tabulations of the *pro-environment ad frame condition* with the categorical manipulation check measure indicated that 85.37% of participants correctly identified the 'recycle and reduce'-framed ad; 46.34% correctly identified the recycle-framed ad; and 20.24% correctly identified the reduce-framed ad. The majority of participants in the reduce (73.81%) and recycle (52.44%) conditions however, incorrectly identified these ads as 'recycle and reduce'-framed ads. The ad frame manipulation was thus not successful. The cross-tabulation results suggest that recycle-, reduce-, or recycle and reduce-framed ads may trigger consumers to think about both types of pro-environmental strategies, regardless of the message frame.

Dependent measures. The means (SD) for the outcome measures were as follows − environmental concern: 4.80 (.82), attitudes toward ad recommendations: 5.78 (1.15), intentions to perform the recommended behavior: 5.41 (1.20), positive affect toward self: 4.92 (1.37), positive affect toward others when the recommendation is followed: 4.92 (1.44), negative affect toward self: 3.80 (1.47), and negative affect toward others when the recommendation is not followed: 3.87 (1.47).

Impact of chronic regulatory focus. Hypothesis 1 was tested via a multiple linear regression of environmental concern on chronic promotion focus, chronic prevention focus, and the interaction between these two variables. Similarly, multiple linear regressions examined the effects of chronic regulatory focus on attitudes toward pro-environmental ad recommendations and intentions to follow the recommendation (Hypothesis 2), positive affect toward self and others (Hypothesis 3), and negative affect toward self and others (Hypothesis 4). Age and nationality were non-significant across all dependent measures and were dropped from further analysis. Gender, where significant, was retained as a covariate.

For the impact on *environmental concern*, the model was significant overall ($F(4, 243) = 5.74, p < .001, R^2 = .09, R^2_{Adjusted} = .07$). While chronic prevention focus did not significantly influence environmental concern (standardized $\beta = -.005, t(243) = -.08$, ns), there was a significant main effect of chronic promotion focus (standardized $\beta = .14$, $t(243) = 2.17, p < .05$) and the interaction between chronic promotion and prevention focus (standardized $\beta = -.13, t(243) = -2.00, p = .046$). Multiple regressions with the predictor variables one standard deviation (1SD) before and after were conducted to further test the implications of the significant interaction term. While the analysis at higher values of the predictors (plus 1SD) indicated a significant positive effect of promotion focus on environmental concern (standardized $\beta = .23, t(243) = 3.40, p < .005$), this effect became non-significant at lower values (minus 1SD) (standardized $\beta = .06, t(243) = .67$, ns). Gender had a significant effect – environmental concern was significantly greater when participants were female as compared to male (standardized $\beta = .19, t(243) = 3.03, p < .005$). Thus Hypothesis 1 was supported for higher values of chronic promotion focus.

The overall model was significant for *attitudes toward the ad recommendation* ($F(3, 244) = 9.46, p < .001, R^2 = .10, R^2_{Adjusted} = .09$). Gender did not have a significant effect and was dropped as a covariate from the analysis. The main effect of chronic prevention focus on attitudes was not significant (standardized $\beta = -.02, t(244) = -.36$, ns). Chronic promotion focus, however, had a significant main effect (standardized $\beta = .23, t(244) = 3.64, p < .001$), and a significant interaction with chronic prevention focus (standardized $\beta = -.17, t(244) = -2.64, p < .01$). Chronic promotion focus retained a significant positive effect on attitude toward the ad recommendation at higher values of the predictors (plus 1SD; standardized $\beta = .34, t(244) = 5.25, p < .001$), but became non-significant at lower values (minus 1SD; standardized $\beta = .13, t(244) = 1.45$, ns). Hypothesis 2a was therefore supported for higher values of the predictor variables.

The overall model was also significant for *intentions to perform the recommended behavior* ($F(4, 243) = 4.40, p < .005, R^2 = .07, R^2_{Adjusted} = .05$). Gender had a significant effect and was retained in the analysis (standardized $\beta = .13, t(243) = 2.02, p < .05$) – with females reporting higher intentions than males. Chronic promotion focus had a significant main effect on intentions (standardized $\beta = .18, t(243) = 2.66, p < .01$). The main effect of chronic prevention focus was non-significant (standardized $\beta = -.06$, $t(243) = -.87$, ns) as was the interaction effect (standardized $\beta = -.10, t(243) = -1.46$, ns). Hypothesis 2b was therefore supported.

Furthermore, the overall model was significant for *positive affect toward the self* upon engaging in the recommended pro-environmental behavior ($F(4, 243) = 4.90, p < .01$, $R^2 = .07, R^2_{Adjusted} = .06$). Chronic promotion focus was found to have a significant positive effect (standardized $\beta = .19, t(243) = 2.83, p < .01$). There was no significant main effect of chronic prevention focus (standardized $\beta = .01, t(243) = .15$, ns) nor interaction effect of promotion and prevention focus (standardized $\beta = -.08, t(243) = -1.27$, ns). Gender had a significant effect (standardized $\beta = .14, t(243) = 2.29, p < .05$) – with females experiencing greater positive affect toward themselves than males. Hypothesis 3a was thus supported. No significant relationships were found for chronic promotion focus (standardized $\beta = .11, t(244) = 1.60$, ns), prevention focus (standardized $\beta = .11, t(244) = 1.60$, ns), or their interaction (standardized $\beta = .11, t(244) = 1.60$, ns) with *positive affect toward others* that engage in ad recommendations. Hypothesis 3b was therefore not supported.

For *negative affect toward the self* upon not engaging in recommended behaviors, the model overall was marginally significant ($F(4, 243) = 3.49, p = .053, R^2 = .05, R^2_{Adjusted} = .04$). There was a marginally significant main effect of chronic prevention focus (standardized $\beta = .11, t(243) = 1.77, p < .10$). Chronic promotion focus (standardized $\beta = .06, t(243) = .92$, ns) and the interaction term did not have significant effects (standardized $\beta = -.08, t(243) = -1.14$, ns). Gender had a significant effect with females displaying significantly higher negative affect toward themselves than males (standardized $\beta = .15, t(243) = 2.45, p < .05$). Partial support for Hypothesis 4a was found.

Finally, the overall model for *negative affect toward others* that do not engage in pro-environmental ad recommendations was marginally significant ($F(3, 244) = 2.67, p = .05, R^2 = .03, R^2_{Adjusted} = .02$). There was a significant main effect of chronic prevention focus (standardized $\beta = .14, t(244) = 2.16, p < .05$). Chronic promotion focus (standardized $\beta = .09, t(244) = 1.33$, ns) and the interaction term did not have significant effects (standardized $\beta = -.01, t(244) = -.18$, ns). Partial support for Hypothesis 4b was thus found.

While not formally hypothesized, additional exploratory mediation testing via analyses recommended by Baron and Kenny (1986) showed that the effect of chronic promotion focus on positive affect toward individuals' own environmental responsibility was partially mediated through environmental concern. These results are reported in Table 1A.

Similar analyses designed to test the mediating effect of promotion focus on intentions to perform the behavior advocated in the ad revealed partial mediation via environmental concern as well. These analyses are detailed within Table 1B.

Table 1. Mediating role of environmental concern in effects of chronic promotion focus on positive affect toward self, and intentions toward environmental responsibility in Study 2.

Steps	Dependent variables	Independent variables	
		Chronic promotion focus	Environmental concern
1.	Environmental concern	st $\beta = .19, t(246) = 2.99, p < .005$	
		A. Impact on positive affect toward self	
2.	Positive affect toward self	st $\beta = .22, t(246) = 3.50, p < .005$	
3.	Positive affect toward self		st $\beta = .39, t(246) = 6.80, p < .001$
4.	Positive affect toward self	st $\beta = .15, t(245) = 2.52, p = .01$	st $\beta = .37, t(245) = 6.28, p < .001$
		B. Impact on intentions	
2.	Intentions	st $\beta = .20, t(246) = 3.20, p < .005$	
3.	Intentions		st $\beta = .43, t(246) = 7.39, p < .001$
4.	Intentions	st $\beta = .12, t(245) = 2.13, p = .03$	st $\beta = .40, t(245) = 6.91, p < .001$

Note. Environmental concern *partially* mediated the impact of chronic promotion focus on *positive emotions toward the self* and *intentions* to engage in environmentally responsible behaviors. Actual *p*-values are provided to illustrate the decline in statistical significance levels.

Impact of primed regulatory focus. Univariate ANOVAs with regulatory focus prime (no prime, promotion prime, or prevention prime) and pro-environment ad frame (reduce, recycle, or reduce and recycle) as independent variables and attitudes, intentions and affect as the dependent variable (Hypotheses 2–5) were run to test the effects of primed regulatory focus. Chronic regulatory focus was added as a covariate in the analyses as prior dispositions may continue to impact individual reactions regardless of primed regulatory focus (no significant fit effects between chronic and primed regulatory focus were found). Age and nationality were dropped as covariates from further analysis as they did not have significant effects and gender was retained as a covariate where it was significant.

Significant main effects of primed regulatory focus were found for *attitudes* ($F(2, 238) = 6.29, p < .005$), *positive affect toward others* ($F(2, 238) = 4.37, p < .05$), and *negative affect towards others* ($F(2, 238) = 3.50, p < .05$). There was a marginally significant main effect of primed regulatory focus on *intentions* ($F(2, 237) = 2.97, p = .05$) with the addition of gender as a covariate. The intention to engage in recommended behaviors was greater for females than males ($F(1, 237) = 4.48, p < .05$). No main effects of primed regulatory focus were found on *positive affect toward self* ($F(2, 238) = 1.99$, ns) or *negative affect toward self* ($F(2, 238) = 2.36$, ns). Furthermore, no significant main effects of pro-environmental ad frame were found for *attitudes* ($F(2, 238) = 1.49$, ns), *intentions* ($F(2, 237) = 2.12$, ns), *positive affect toward self* ($F(2, 238) = .19$, ns), *positive affect toward others* ($F(2, 238) = 1.78$, ns), *negative affect toward self* ($F(2, 238) = .08$, ns), or *negative affect towards others* ($F(2, 238) = 1.53$, ns). Similarly, no significant interaction effects between primed regulatory focus and pro-environmental ad frame were found for *attitudes* ($F(4, 238) = .61$, ns), *intentions* ($F(4, 237) = 1.02$, ns), *positive affect toward self* ($F(4, 238) = .56$, ns), *positive affect toward others* ($F(4, 238) = .71$, ns), *negative affect toward self* ($F(4, 238) = .32$, ns), or *negative affect towards others* ($F(4, 238) = 1.38$, ns). The means (SD) for dependent variables with (full or marginal) significant main effects of regulatory focus prime are reported in Table 2.

Planned contrasts were carried out for the no-prime versus promotion-prime conditions as well as the no-prime versus prevention-prime conditions where there were (full or marginal) significant overall main effects of regulatory focus priming (extracted from the full 3 × 3 ANOVAs) – specifically, for *attitudes and intentions* (Hypotheses 2a and 2b), *positive affect toward others* (Hypothesis 3b), and *negative affect toward others* (Hypothesis 4b). Contrasts were not carried out for positive affect toward self (Hypothesis 3a not supported) and negative affect toward self (Hypothesis 4a not supported) as the overall ANOVA results did not show significant main effects for primed regulatory focus.

Table 2. Means (SD) for dependent measures with significant effects of regulatory focus prime in Study 2.

	Dependent variables			
	Attitudes	Intentions	Positive affect toward others	Negative affect toward others
Independent variable	$F(2, 238) = 6.29,$ $p < .005$	$F(2, 237) = 2.97,$ $p = .05$	$F(2, 238) = 4.37,$ $p < .05$	$F(2, 238) = 3.50,$ $p < .05$
No prime	5.47 (1.33)	5.14 (1.38)	4.54 (1.51)	3.55 (1.51)
Promotion prime	6.11 (.88)	5.63 (1.05)	5.16 (1.35)	4.10 (1.40)
Prevention prime	5.73 (1.18)	5.44 (1.12)	5.05 (1.41)	3.87 (1.47)

Contrast results showed that promotion-primed versus unprimed participants had significantly greater pro-environmental *attitudes* ($M_{\text{no prime}} = 5.47$, $M_{\text{promotion prime}} = 6.11$, $F(1, 238) = 12.72$, $p < .001$) and *intentions* ($M_{\text{no prime}} = 5.14$, $M_{\text{promotion prime}} = 5.63$, $F(1, 237) = 6.11$, $p < .05$). Prevention-primed versus unprimed participants however, showed no significant differences in *attitudes* ($M_{\text{no prime}} = 5.47$, $M_{\text{prevention prime}} = 5.73$, $F(1, 238) = 1.82$, ns), or *intentions* ($M_{\text{no prime}} = 5.14$, $M_{\text{prevention prime}} = 5.44$, $F(1, 237) = 2.35$, ns). Hypothesis 2a for attitudes was fully supported, and Hypothesis 2b for intentions was partially supported as the overall primed regulatory effect was marginally significant. Primed promotion focus was shown to be a more important predictor of attitudes toward pro-environmental ad recommendations and intentions to engage in them than primed prevention focus.

As the overall main effect of priming on *positive affect toward the self* was not significant, Hypothesis 3a was not supported. Hypothesis 3b however, was supported. Promotion-primed versus unprimed respondents were shown to have significantly greater *positive affect toward others* who followed the pro-environmental ad recommendations ($M_{\text{no prime}} = 4.54$, $M_{\text{promotion prime}} = 5.16$, $F(1, 238) = 7.86$, $p < .01$). Moreover, prevention-primed versus unprimed individuals also displayed significantly greater *positive affect towards others* ($M_{\text{no prime}} = 4.54$, $M_{\text{prevention prime}} = 5.05$, $F(1, 238) = 5.15$, $p < .05$). Thus, although priming both promotion and prevention foci increased positive affect toward others' environmentally responsible behaviors, the impact of promotion focus was more significant than that of prevention focus.

There was an overall lack of a main effect of priming on *negative affect toward the self*; Hypothesis 4a was thus not supported. A marginally significant increase in *negative affect toward others* resulting from prevention versus no priming occurred ($M_{\text{no prime}} = 3.55$, $M_{\text{prevention prime}} = 3.87$, $F(1, 238) = 3.31$, $p = .07$). Promotion versus un-primed individuals also reported significantly greater *negative affect toward others* who did not behave in an environmentally responsible manner ($M_{\text{no prime}} = 3.55$, $M_{\text{promotion prime}} = 4.10$, $F(1, 238) = 6.51$, $p < .05$). Thus, while both promotion and prevention-priming influenced negative affect, prevention priming was not a more important predictor of negative affect toward others than promotion priming.

Moderating impact of pro-environmental ad frame on regulatory focus. Hypothesis 5 was tested by examining the interaction effects of regulatory focus (both primed and chronic) and ad frame on the dependent variables. As reported above, primed regulatory focus had a significant main effect on *attitudes toward the ad recommendation* ($F(2, 238) = 6.29$, $p < .005$), and a marginally significant effect on *intentions* ($F(2, 237) = 2.97$, $p = .05$; gender as a covariate). Furthermore, no significant main effects of pro-environmental ad frame were found for *attitudes* ($F(2, 238) = 1.49$, ns) or *intentions* ($F(2, 237) = 2.12$, ns). Similarly, no significant interaction effects between primed regulatory focus and pro-environmental ad frame were found for *attitudes* ($F(4, 238) = .61$, ns) or *intentions* ($F(4, 237) = 1.02$, ns). Similar results were found when chronic promotion or prevention focus and message frame were used as the independent variables. No support for Hypotheses 5a and 5b was therefore found.

Discussion

In this study we identified important relationships between individuals' regulatory focus (chronic and primed) and several environmentally responsible responses regarding the use of plastic water bottles. Specifically, participants' *chronic* promotion (versus prevention) focus was found to be a more important predictor of general *environmental concern*.

At higher values, while chronic promotion focus positively influenced environmental concern, prevention focus did not have a significant effect.

Similar relationships between chronic or primed promotion focus (versus prevention focus) and participants' *attitudes* toward the ad recommendations and *intentions* to follow through on the ad recommendation emerged when individuals read pro-environmental messages. When promotion focus was *primed, attitudes* toward the ad recommendation rose significantly and *intentions* to engage in the ad recommendation rose marginally. Attitudes and intentions however did not significantly change when prevention focus was primed. Hypothesis 2a related to attitudes was thus supported – at higher values of chronic promotion- (versus prevention-) focus, and fully for primed promotion- (versus prevention-) focus. And, Hypothesis 2b related to intentions was supported – fully for chronic promotion- (versus prevention-) focus, and partially when promotion- (versus prevention-) focus was primed.

Chronic and primed regulatory focus had differing effects on participants' *positive affective reactions* toward themselves and others as a consequence of following through on pro-environmental ad recommendations. Participants' *chronic* promotion (versus prevention) focus was a more important predictor of positive affect toward the *self.* And, *primed* promotion (versus prevention) focus was a more important predictor of positive affect toward *others.* Specifically, higher chronic promotion focus led to significantly higher self-directed positive affect, but this was not so for prevention focus. Non-significant effects of chronic promotion or prevention-focus were found for other-directed positive affect. Interestingly, while both primed promotion and prevention-focus resulted in higher positive affect toward others, the impact of promotion focus was more significant than that of prevention focus. H3a related to positive affect toward the self was thus supported for chronic, but not primed regulatory focus. And, H3b related to positive affect toward others was supported for primed, but not chronic regulatory focus.

Partial support for Hypotheses 4a and 4b that *chronic* prevention (versus prevention) focus is a more important predictor of *negative affect* toward the self and others as a result of not engaging in pro-environmental ad recommendations was found. As participants' chronic prevention focus rose, negative affect toward both self and others marginally increased.

No support for Hypotheses 4a and 4b was found, for *primed* regulatory focus. Neither primed prevention nor promotion-focus significantly influenced negative *self-directed* affect. However, while priming prevention focus resulted in marginally higher negative affect toward *others,* priming promotion focus significantly increased negative affect toward others. Contrary to our expectations, primed promotion (versus prevention) focus was thus a more important predictor of negative *other-directed* affect.

No fit effects between chronic or primed regulatory (promotion or prevention) focus and pro-environment ads (recycle, reduce, or recycle and reduce) were found (i.e., Hypothesis 5 was not supported). Our manipulation check indicated that the majority of participants inferred that all of the pro-environment ads contained both recycle and reduce components, perhaps due to the widespread use of joint recycle, reduce, and reuse terminology within mainstream public pro-environmental messaging. Thus, ineffectiveness of our message manipulation may have contributed to the lack of support for Hypothesis 5.

Finally, exploratory analyses found that general environmental concern partially mediated the effect of chronic promotion focus on positive self-directed affect as a result of pro-environmental actions. Partial mediation via environmental concern also occurred for intentions to follow the pro-environmental ad advice.

General discussion

Significant relationships between regulatory focus and environmental concern, attitudes, intentions, and affect have been identified in this work. Results of two studies indicate the importance of intensifying *chronic* and *primed promotion focus* on a variety of pro-environmental responses. This relationship is not as evident for chronic prevention focus. As expected, promotion-focused individuals, who have higher CFC-Future than prevention-focused individuals (Joireman et al. 2012), express more concern for the environment and respond more favorably to pro-environment ads than prevention-focused individuals. We have thus found support for our view that because promotion focus is related to CFC-Future, and because CFC-Future is related to environmental responsibility (e.g., Ebreo and Vining 2001), relationships between promotion focus and pro-environmental responses will be evident.

The positive association of *chronic promotion (but not prevention) focus* with general environmental concern found in the first study was replicated in the second study for higher values of regulatory focus. This indicates the robustness of our findings, which in turn, contributes to the advancement of theory and practice.

We also found a positive association between both chronic and primed *promotion* (versus *prevention)* focus and a wider set of pro-environmental responses in the second study – namely, individuals' attitudes toward behaviors recommended in pro-environment ads (at higher promotion focus values), intentions to act on pro-environment ad recommendations, and positive affect toward themselves (but not others) as a consequence of doing so. Marginal support for a positive influence of chronic *prevention* focus on negative affect toward oneself and others as a consequence of not acting on ad recommendations was also evident. Unexpectedly, primed prevention focus yielded a significant rise in positive affect toward others, and primed promotion-focus was a more significant predictor of negative affect toward others than primed prevention-focus.

Although our work further reveals that promotion and prevention-focused individuals display no differences in responsiveness to recycle or reduce advertising messages, the lack of expected effects may have occurred because 'reduce and recycle' terminology is used together so frequently in advertising that consumers are unable to distinguish these actions even when they are presented separately in a message frame – with the presentation of one term automatically triggering thoughts of the other.

Several theoretical and managerial contributions have emerged here. First, we have extended regulatory focus theory (Higgins 1987) by demonstrating the relationship between chronic promotion focus and environmental concern. Interestingly, despite the extensive application of regulatory focus theory in various domains (e.g., Levine, Higgins, and Choi 2000; Noort, Kerkhof, and Fennis 2008) and despite calls for research to identify consumers who are most likely to be concerned for the environment (Chang 2012), little attention has been paid to the relationship between an individual's regulatory focus and their environmental concern. Our results, which show that promotion focus (chronic and primed) contributes to responsiveness to green advertising messages, also extends the literature that has focused on regulatory focus effects on advertising effectiveness (e.g., Zhao and Pechmann 2007).

Our research also provides guidance on strategies for encouraging environmentally responsible behaviors. Our work suggests that environmental concern and receptiveness to pro-environmental ads may be enhanced by encouraging individuals to adopt a promotion focus, and, that fostering a promotion focus will yield both positive and negative affect directed at others contingent on their environmentally responsible or irresponsible actions. While positive affect based on our own actions is significantly related to our dispositional chronic promotion focus, priming such a focus mainly impacts positive (as well as negative) affect resulting from others' actions. This relationship between chronic and primed promotion focus and affect is particularly important given the role that affect can play in engendering compliance with ad recommendations. Passyn and Sujan (2006) demonstrate that emotions, rather than cognitive appraisals are the fundamental drivers of behavior.

Some suggest that to the extent that broad environmental concerns determine behavior, it makes sense to apply strategies that aim directly at strengthening these broad worldviews (Thorgersen and Olander 2006). Our results suggest that priming an individual's promotion focus may be one such strategy. Given that promotion and prevention focus may be primed by reading information about promotion and prevention features (Bullard and Manchanda 2013), advertising messages may be effective vehicles for priming promotion focus and generating environmentally responsible reactions. For example, promotion-focused ads that emphasize achievements or striving for positive outcomes (e.g., creating a healthy and beautiful environment) may be more effective for promoting pro-environmental behavior than prevention-focused ads that emphasize responsibilities and preventing negative outcomes (e.g., averting environmental degradation)

Interestingly, an emphasis on responsibility and obligation toward others or future generations is often evident in pro-environment ads. Anheuser-Busch, for instance, promotes pro-environmentalism via the slogan: 'Our earth, our responsibility' (http://anheuser-busch.com). Similarly, Nintendo states 'leaving a better environment to the next generation is one of its most important responsibilities and is therefore taking positive steps to protect the environment' (http://www.nintendo.co.jp/csr/). Outcomes of our research suggest that shifting to a more promotion-focused ad frame may be effective for encouraging pro-environmental behavior.

Limitations and avenues for future research

A number of issues limit the research presented here and open up avenues for future research. While the message recipient's regulatory focus was not a factor in contributing to the persuasiveness of reduce, recycle, and reduce and recycle messages for plastic water bottles, it is possible that regulatory focus may contribute to the persuasiveness of pro-environment ads that promote other forms of environmentally responsible behavior (e.g., energy conservation). For example it is possible that owning an electric car could be viewed as an approach strategy which is more appealing to a promotion-focused individual whereas car pooling could be viewed as an avoidance strategy which is more appealing to a prevention-focused individual. Further investigation of the relationship between individuals' regulatory focus and pro-environment messages that advocate other types of environmentally responsible behavior could confirm the effects we have identified here. Similarly, while we used a widely accepted environmental concern measure, more recent measures are available (Diekmann and Preisendorfer 2003; Milfont and Duckitt 2010). Future studies using these measures could provide confirmation of the results presented here.

Our sample of university students is particularly appropriate given our study's context. Young adults have the potential to make significant differences to the health of the environment because there may be many years during which their environmentally responsible or irresponsible actions will have an impact. Thus, understanding effects of individual differences within this generation on environmental concern and actions is particularly important. Because our sample consisted mainly of US nationals however, future studies with a more diverse sample would add to the generalizability of our findings. Future studies could also consider individuals at later stages of life. For example, families with children have the potential to make a significant impact on the environment through their behaviors because they consume more than individuals in earlier stages of the family life cycle. Understanding factors that encourage these individuals to care about the environment is thus an important undertaking.

Finally, as discussed above, our results show that promotion- and prevention-focused individuals respond similarly to reduce, recycle, or reduce and recycle ad messages, possibly because these terms are frequently used together. Future studies could thus consider other ad manipulations to confirm the results we have reported here.

Conclusions

Our research has identified an important relationship between regulatory focus and environmentally responsible attitudes, affect, and intentions. Our findings thus contribute to both theory and practice. We have identified avenues for future research and provided guidance to those who endeavor to encourage environmentally responsible behavior. As such, we believe that our work has contributed to the worthy goal of preserving and protecting our environment.

Disclosure statement

No potential conflict of interest was reported by the authors.

References

Baek, T.H., S. Yoon, and S. Kim. 2015. When environmental messages should be assertive: Examining the moderating role of effort investment. *International Journal of Advertising* 34 (1): 135–57.

Bamberg, S. 2003. How does environmental concern influence specific environmentally related behaviors? A new answer to an old question. *Journal of Environmental Psychology* 23: 21–32.

Bamberg, S., and G. Moser. 2007. Twenty years after Hines, Hungerford, and Tomera: A new meta-analysis of psycho-social determinants of pro-environmental behavior. *Journal of Environmental Psychology* 27: 14–25.

Baron, R.M., and D.A. Kenny. 1986. The moderator-mediator variable distinction in social psychological research: Conceptual, strategic, and statistical considerations. *Journal Personality Social Psychology* 51 (6): 1173–82.

Bearden, W.O., and R.G. Netemeyer. 1999. *Handbook of marketing scales*. 2nd ed. Thousand Oaks, CA: Sage.

Best, H., and T. Kneip. 2011. The impact of attitudes and behavioral costs on environmental behavior: A natural experiment on household waste recycling. *Social Science Research* 40: 917–30.

Bickart, B.A., and J.A. Ruth. 2012. Green eco-seals and advertising persuasion. *Journal of Advertising* 41: 51–67.

Bullard, O., and R.V. Manchanda. 2013. Do sustainable products make us prevention focused? *Marketing Letters* 24: 177–89.

Chang, C. 2012. Are guilt appeals a panacea in green advertising? The right formula of issue proximity and environmental consciousness. *International Journal of Advertising* 31 (4): 741–71.

Chang, H., L. Zhang, and G. Xie. 2015. Message framing in green advertising: The effect of construal level and consumer environmental concern. *International Journal of Advertising* 34 (1): 158–76.

Cleveland, M., M. Kalamas, and M. Laroche. 2005. Shades of green: Linking environmental locus of control and pro-environmental behaviors. *Journal of Consumer Marketing* 22 (4/5): 198–01.

Craig, C.S., and J.M. McCann. 1978. Assessing communication effects on energy conservation. *Journal of Consumer Research* 5: 82–8.

Crowe, E., and E.T. Higgins. 1997. Regulatory focus and strategic inclinations: Promotion and prevention in decision-making. *Organizational Behavior and Human Decision Processes* 69: 117–32.

DeLorme, D.E., S.C. Hagen, and I.J. Scott. 2003. Consumers' perspectives on water issues: Directions for educational campaigns. *The Journal of Environmental Education* 34: 28–35.

Diekmann, A., and P. Preisendorfer. 2003. Green and greenback: The behavioral effects of environmental attitudes in low-cost and high-cost situations. *Rationality and Society* 15: 441–72.

Dunlap, R.E., and K.D. Van Liere. 1978. The new environmental paradigm. *The Journal of Environmental Education* 40: 19–28.

Ebreo, A., and J. Vining. 2001. How similar are recycling and waste reduction? Future orientation and reasons for reducing waste as predictors of self-reported behavior. *Environment and Behavior* 33: 424–48.

Fuglestad, P.T., A.J. Rothman, and R.W. Jeffery. 2008. Getting there and hanging on: The effect of regulatory focus on performance in smoking and weight loss interventions. *Health Psychology* 27: S260–S70.

Hartman, P., V. Apaolaza, C. D'Souza, J.M. Barrutia, and C. Echebarria. 2014. Environmental threat appeals in green advertising. *International Journal of Advertising* 33: 741–65.

Higgins, E.T. 1987. Self-discrepancy: A theory relating self and affect. *Psychological Review* 94: 319–40.

Holbrook, M.B., and R. Batra. 1987. Assessing the role of emotions as mediators of consumer responses to advertising. *Journal of Consumer Research* 14: 35–42.

Idson, L.C., N. Liberman, and E.T. Higgins. 2000. Distinguishing gains from nonlosses and losses from nongains: A regulatory focus perspective on hedonic intensity. *Journal of Experimental Social Psychology* 36: 252–74.

Idson, L.C., N. Liberman, and E.T. Higgins. 2004. Imagining how you'd feel: The role of motivational experiences from regulatory fit. *Personality and Social Psychology Bulletin* 30: 926–37.

Joireman, J.A., P.A.M. Van Lange, and M. Van Vugt. 2004. Who cares about the environmental impact of cars? Those with an eye toward the future. *Environment and Behavior* 36: 187–06.

Joireman, J.A., M.J. Shaffer, D. Balliet, and A. Strathman. 2012. Promotion orientation explains why future-oriented people exercise and eat healthy: Evidence from the two-factor consideration of future consequences-14 scale. *Personality and Social Psychology Bulletin* 38: 1272–1287.

Kareklas, I., J.R. Carlson, and D.D. Muehling. 2012. The role of regulatory focus and self-view in 'green' advertising message effectiveness. *Journal of Advertising* 41: 25–39.

Kees, J., S. Burton, and A.H. Tangari. 2010. The impact of regulatory focus, temporal orientation, and fit on consumer responses to health-related advertising. *Journal of Advertising* 39: 19–34.

Keller, P.A. 2006. Regulatory focus and efficacy of health messages. *Journal of Consumer Research* 33: 109–14.

Koenig, A.M., J. Cesario, D.C. Molden, S. Kosloff, and E.T. Higgins. 2009. Incidental experiences of regulatory fit and the processing of persuasive appeals. *Personality and Social Psychology Bulletin* 35: 1342–55.

Laroche, M., J. Bergeron, and G. Barbaro-Forleo. 2001. Targeting consumers who are willing to pay more for environmentally friendly products. *The Journal of Consumer Marketing* 18: 503–18.

Latimer, A.E., S.E. Rivers, T.A. Rench, N.A. Katulak, A. Hicks, J.K. Hodorowski, E.T. Higgins, and P. Salovey. 2008. A field experiment testing the utility of regulatory fit messages for promoting physical activity. *Journal of Experimental Social Psychology* 44: 826–32.

Levine, J.M., E.T. Higgins, and H.S. Choi. 2000. Development of strategic norms in groups. *Organizational Behavior and Human Decision Processes* 82: 88–01.

Lindsay, J.J., and A. Strathman. 1997. Predictors of recycling behavior: An application of a modified health belief model. *Journal of Applied Social Psychology* 27: 1799–23.

Lockwood, P., C.H. Jordan, and Z. Kunda. 2002. Motivation by positive or negative role models: Regulatory focus determines who will best inspire us. *Journal of Personality and Social Psychology* 83: 854–64.

McKay-Nesbitt, J., N. Bhatnagar, and M. Smith. 2013. Regulatory fit effects of gender and marketing message content. *Journal of Business Research* 66: 2245–51.

Meinhold, J.L., and A.J. Malkus. 2005. Adolescent environmental behaviors: Can knowledge, attitudes, and self efficacy make a difference? *Environment and Behavior* 37: 511–32.

Milfont, T.L., and J. Duckitt. 2010. The environmental attitudes inventory: A valid and reliable measure to assess the structure of environmental attitudes. *Journal of Environmental Psychology* 30: 80–94.

Newman, C. L., E. Howlett, S. Burton, J. C. Kozup, and A. Heintz Tangari. 2012. The influence of consumer concern about global climate change on framing effects for environmental sustainability messages. *International Journal of Advertising* 31: 511–27.

Ngo, A.T., G.E. West, and P.H. Calkins. 2009. Determinants of environmentally responsible behaviors for greenhouse gas reduction. *International Journal of Consumer Studies* 33: 151–61.

Noort, G.V., P. Kerkhof, and B.M. Fennis. 2008. The persuasiveness of online safety cues: The impact of prevention focus compatibility of Web content on consumers' risk perceptions, attitudes, and intentions. *Journal of Interactive Marketing* 22: 58–72.

Passyn, K., and M. Sujan. 2006. Self-accountability emotions and fear appeals: Motivating behavior. *Journal of Consumer Research* 32: 583–9.

Polman, E. 2012. Effects of self-other decision making on regulatory focus and choice overload. *Journal of Personality and Social Psychology* 102: 980–93.

Polonsky, M.J., R. Garma, and S.L. Grau. 2011. Western consumers' understanding of carbon offsets and its relationship to behavior. *Asia Pacific Journal of Marketing and Logistics* 23: 583–03.

Sar, S., and G. Anghelcev. 2015. Congruity between mood and message regulatory focus enhances the effectiveness of anti drinking and driving advertisements: a global versus local processing explanation. *International Journal of Advertising* 34 (3): 421–46.

Shah, J., E.T. Higgins, and R.S. Friedman. 1998. Performance incentives and means: How regulatory focus influences goal attainment. *Journal of Personality and Social Psychology* 74: 285–93.

Strathman, A., F. Gleicher, D.S. Boninger, and C.S. Edwards. 1994. The consideration of future consequences: Weighing immediate and distant outcomes of behavior. *Journal of Personality and Social Psychology* 66: 742–52.

Thogersen, J., and F. Olander. 2006. To what degree are environmentally beneficial choices reflective of a general conservation stance? *Environment and Behavior* 38: 550–69.

Wang, J., and A.Y. Lee. 2006. The role of regulatory focus in preference construction. *Journal of Marketing Research* 43: 28–38.

Weigel, R., and J. Weigel. 1978. Environmental concern: the development of a measure. *Environment and Behavior* 10: 3–15.

Weiner, B. 2006. *Social motivation, justice and the moral emotions.* Mahwah, NJ: Lawrence Erlbaum Associates.

Yoon, S., Y. Kim, and T. Baek. 2015. Effort investment in persuasiveness: A comparative study of environmental advertising in the United States and Korea. *International Journal of Advertising* 35.

Zhao, G., and C. Pechmann. 2007. The impact of regulatory focus on adolescents' response to anti-smoking advertising campaigns. *Journal of Marketing Research* 44: 671–87.

How consumer knowledge shapes green consumption: an empirical study on voluntary carbon offsetting

Yohan Kim[a], Sunyoung Yun[a], Joosung Lee[a] and Eunju Ko[b]

[a]Department of Business and Technology Management, Korea Advanced Institute of Science and Technology, KAIST, Daejeon, Republic of Korea; [b]Department of Clothing and Textile, Yonsei University, Seoul, Republic of Korea

This paper investigates how highly knowledgeable consumers differ from less knowledgeable consumers in their rational and emotional determinants of desire for green consumption, and derive distinct advertising implications for each group. We distinguish consumer knowledge into three categories (knowledge related to the environment, available action, and its effectiveness) and test them as moderating variables. A survey of 256 US consumers revealed that less knowledgeable consumers were driven primarily by their perceived behavioral control, while highly knowledgeable consumers exhibited a distinct influence from positive anticipated emotions on their desire. This distinction was brought upon only within low/high action/effectiveness knowledge groups, but not within low/high environment knowledge. Our findings highlight the importance of raising consumer's system, action-related, and effective knowledge, as well as the need for targeted advertising strategies for consumers with differing knowledge levels in green consumption.

1. Introduction

Consumers in today's global marketplace are becoming increasingly aware of environmental issues, demonstrating high levels of environmental concern (Krause 1993). This reorientation of consumer mind-set has in turn attracted researchers to seek a more comprehensive understanding of factors that influence consumer's green consumption (Pieters et al. 1998). As an essential prerequisite for consumers' behavior, consumer knowledge has been the center of attention for numerous researchers and marketers alike. It is a primary means of overcoming mental obstacles such as ignorance and misinformation, and is generally regarded as a critical requirement for taking action.

Although there is a strong theoretical support for the influence of knowledge level on green consumption (e.g. Lantermann, Döring-Seipel, and Schima 1992), the empirical support has been conflicting at best. An extensive meta-analysis by Bamberg and Möser (2007) reveals that knowledge does not clearly and sufficiently explain pro-environmental behaviour. Individual studies also report conflicting results, where studies such as Kollmuss and Agyeman (2002) report no clear correlation between knowledge and green consumption, while other studies such as Rokicka and Slomczynska (2002) report that people with high ecological knowledge exhibit much more prominent green consumption behavior.

Kaiser and Fuhrer (2003) suggest that such inconsistent result is due to the different forms of knowledge not being recognized in conjunction with the traditional measure of amount of knowledge possessed. According to Kaiser and Fuhrer, one must understand the natural state of the environment (system knowledge), know available actions to address the problem (action-related knowledge), as well as know the benefit that a given particular action brings (effective knowledge). Most studies have focused only on the awareness of environmental problem when investigating the factors affecting pro-environment behavior (Gambro and Switzky 1999; Rokicka and Slomczynska 2002).

Complicating the academic understanding of consumer knowledge and green consumption is the rising trend of a new green marketing strategy. Traditionally, green marketing consisted of promoting firm's green behaviors, where consumers are led to simply recognize firm's green efforts. Instead of simply recognizing firm's green activities, the new engagement-oriented marketing invites consumers to be an active participant in firm's green initiatives (Kim, Cheong, and Lim 2015; Ko, Hwang, and Kim 2013). Such shift in green marketing reflects upon the findings of established research, where consumer-to-business interactions were shown to positively impact consumer's propensity toward the firm (Bettencourt 1997; Matzler et al. 1996).

One of the industries to adopt such engagement-oriented green strategy is the airline industry, in particular with deployment of voluntary carbon offsetting (VCO). VCO is a relatively new consumer engagement green program that holds each passenger accountable for his or her calculated portion of harmful emissions produced during the flight. Even though airline companies pursue consumers to participate in green consumption, public awareness of carbon offsetting is still low, in addition to mass media's general lack of interest in carbon offsetting (Natural Marketing Institute 2011). The public's poor awareness of carbon offsetting and the absence of active advertising by airlines highlight the need for the development of an articulated advertising strategy for VCO, findings of which can be generalized toward advertisement of emerging engagement-oriented green consumption offerings.

Given this, our study seeks to understand how knowledge of the available actions and their effectiveness − in addition to the more conventional environmental knowledge − influence consumer's intention toward such engagement-oriented green consumption behavior. To do so, we implement the three knowledge types as a moderating factor into model of goal-directed behavior (MGB). MGB is an extension of theory of planned behavior (TPB), which is a key model in predicting behavioral dispositions. Within this framework, we observe how consumers with low and high knowledge differ in terms of significant behavioral determinants of green consumption. The research model and hypothesized patterns were empirically tested using structural equation modeling on the survey results of 256 airline consumers who have heard of VCO as a form of green airline program. An in-depth look into VCO is provided in the following chapter, followed by literature review and corresponding hypothesis in Section 2 and 3. Measurement and data collection and results are discussed proceeding Section 4 and 5, followed by discussion in Section 6 and conclusion in Section 7.

2. Voluntary carbon offsetting (VCO) and aviation market

Currently, many airlines are inviting their consumers to participate in a CO_2 (carbon dioxide) mitigation program called VCO. VCO allows airline passengers to pay the monetary equivalent of CO_2 emissions for a particular trip, where money received is donated to third-party programs that offset CO_2 by the same amount. Programs range from protection of forest areas to installation of solar panels in public buildings, with reputable programs being certified for their effectiveness. More than 35 airlines offered carbon offset programs by late 2013 (IATA 2013); however, consumer participation has been low. One of the first airlines to offer VCO, British airways, had a consumer involvement rate of just ~0.3% by 2010 (British Airways 2011). In addition, the concept of carbon offsetting is not widely recognized among the public. U.S. Department of Energy's survey of US consumers in 2011 showed very low public awareness of carbon offsetting (36%), especially when compared to other key concepts such as renewable power (71%) or carbon footprint (73%). Authors' own inquiry has shown that none of the top 10 US airlines offered VCO during checkout, nor advertised its existence. As such, customers who are aware of VCO and wish to participate must take his or her own initiative in checking VCO program availability. Only one airline, Virgin Air, set itself apart by offering VCO within the in-flight entertainment system.

Analyzing consumers' willingness to participate in such VCO programs has been a new and growing endeavor throughout various fields. Many studies analyzed aviation consumers' willingness to pay for CO_2 emissions offsetting (Brouwer, Brander, and Van Beukering 2008; Lu and Shon 2012; MacKerron et al. 2009). In addition, Lu and Shon (2012) showed that airline passengers' intentions are significantly affected by their knowledge related to emissions and offset schemes not only influenced by environmental concern (Whitmarsh and O'Neill, 2010). Existing literatures suggest consumer knowledge to be an important factor that must be assessed for its impact on green consumption behavior. Hence, this study expands upon the previous study of VCO by Kim, Yun, and Lee (2014), which addressed the differences of pro-social and pro-environmental consumption; in this paper, we address how different forms of knowledge affect pro-environmental behavior.

3. Literature review and hypothesis

3.1. Model of goal-directed behavior (MGB) and green consumption

Ajzen's TPB is the most often used construct when analyzing green consumption behavior and its behavioral antecedents (Ajzen 1991; Kalafatis et al. 1999; Chan and Lau 2002; Lam 2006). According to TPB, a person's intentions are driven by one's behavioral attitude, subjective norms, and perceived behavioral control (PBC). *Attitude* is a predisposed evaluative response when performing a particular behavior (Fazio 1995). Consistent with previous analyses of link between attitude and environmental behavior, individuals with positive attitude toward the green consumption behavior have more positive desire for green consumption (Carrus et al. 2008). *Subjective norms* is a measure of how an individual's behavior is influenced by the behavior of significant others and their perceived judgment (Ajzen 1991). Venkatesh and Davis (2000) states that a person desires to comply with societal or group norms if their influences are significant, in hopes that one will cast a positive image to the group. PBC deals with one's self-confidence in the ability to perform a particular behavior. Recent studies expanded upon this by including emotional factors in addition (Kals, Schumacher, and Montada 1999; Vining and Ebreo 2002). Perugini and Bagozzi suggest MGB to expand upon the TPB model and include anticipated emotions and desire in better explaining consumers' intention, as shown in Figure 1 (Perugini and Bagozzi 2001). Desire, as a key defining component of MGB, is defined as

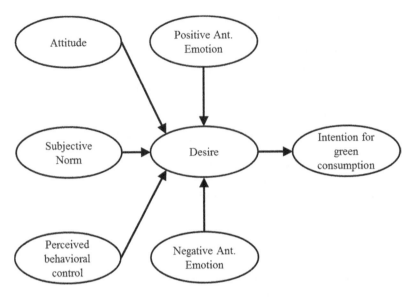

Figure 1.   Model of goal-directed behaviour (MGB).

'...a state of mind whereby an agent has a personal motivation to perform an action or to achieve a goal' (Perugini and Bagozzi 2001). Desire as such determines a persons' proclivity toward a particular action (Shiu et al. 2008). The MGB by Chen (2013) was able to account for 53% of intention to participate, which exceeded the performance of similar TPB model by van Birgelen, Semeijn, and Behrens (2011). The validity of desire as a meaningful predictor of green intentions was confirmed via numerous prior studies (Perugini and Bagozzi 2001; Sukoco 2012; Chen 2013). Thus, based on the MGB, we form hypotheses H_{1a}, H_{1b}, H_{1c}, and H_2 as follows:

H_{1a}: Attitude toward VCO has a positive influence on desire of VCO participation.
H_{1b}: Subjective norm of VCO has positive influence on desire of VCO participation.
H_{1c}: Perceived behavioral control of VCO has positive influence on desire of VCO participation.
H_2: Desire of VCO will exert a positive influence on intention to VCO participation.

MGB also expands upon conventional TPB with inclusion of positive and negative anticipated emotions. Anticipated emotions can be defined as anticipated emotional reactions toward the success or failure an action's intended goal (Bagozzi et al. 1998). Gleicher et al. (1995) state that anticipated emotions affect desires through 'pre-factual appraisals', where a person '...considers imaginary alternatives to events in terms of the implications of these events for the future', leading to a positive or negative emotion (Gleicher et al. 1995, 284). According to Chen's result (2013), desire is significantly driven by positive anticipated emotion but not by negative anticipated emotion, which is opposite of what other studies on pro-environmental behaviour have found (Carrus et al. 2008). As such, positive and negative anticipated emotions will both be considered in our research model. Based on literature, we form hypotheses 3a and 3b as follows:

H_{3a}: Positive anticipated emotion for VCO has a positive effect on desire of VCO participation.
H_{3b}: Negative anticipated emotion for VCO has a positive effect on desire of VCO participation.

3.2. Consumer knowledge of green consumption

Knowledge acts as a key factor in formation of attitude (Stutzman and Green 1982). Within green consumption, knowledge performs two distinct functions: to increase awareness of relevant environmental issues, and to empower consumer in identification and selection of best green consumption action. Information that raises consumers' level of knowledge and awareness, which in turn instigates social responsibility, is crucial in the formation of green consumption behavior (Lee, Gemba, and Kodama 2006).

However, a meta-analysis on empirical studies has shown that knowledge does not clearly and sufficiently explain pro-environmental behavior (Bamberg and Möser 2007). Studies such as Kollmuss and Agyeman (2002) report no clear correlation between knowledge and green consumption, while other studies such as Rokicka and Slomczynska (2002) report the complete opposite. Such mixed empirical findings indicate that knowledge–behavior interaction is more complex than previously thought (Chan 2001). Kaiser and Fuhrer (2003) suggest a breakdown of knowledge into three distinct categories, as described below.

For a person to take a pro-environmental action, one must first have some understanding of the current state of the environment and its problems. Such ecological knowledge under Kaiser and Fuhrer is classified as *system knowledge*. In the context of VCO, system knowledge can be attributed to knowing the current state of climate change, and how CO_2 emissions can worsen it. Parguel, Benoit-Moreau, and Russell (2015) demonstrate that 'expert' consumers (i.e. consumers with higher environmental knowledge) differ in their reactions to nature-evoking advertisements when compared to 'non-expert' consumers. A sociological model by Fietkau and Kessel posits that environmental knowledge is a necessary but insufficient antecedent of pro-environmental behavior (as cited in Kollmuss and Agyeman 2002, 10).

Second is action-related knowledge, or knowledge of available actions in addressing the given problem (Ernst 1994). Within the context of VCO, it would explain people know how to access and participate in VCO. Consumers may have appropriate system knowledge, but lacking action-related knowledge results in inability to initiate proper green consumption behavior. Results from some studies indicate action-related knowledge to be a better indicator of green consumption behavior than system knowledge (Smith-Sebasto and Fortner 1994).

Third type of knowledge deals with understanding of how an effective program like VCO is in solving environmental issues, also known as effectiveness knowledge (McEachern and Warnaby 2008). Consumers who wish to engage in green consumption, in particular green service consumption, will raise the question: is this behavior worth my sacrifice? Effective knowledge defines as people know the effectiveness of a given behavior in itself, as well as relative to others in terms of cost and benefit. From the above definition of knowledge types, we measure knowledge construct as system knowledge, action-related knowledge, and effective knowledge. Given this, we propose the following hypotheses 4a, 4b, and 4c:

H_{4a}: Consumers with higher *system knowledge* will exhibit a higher intention and other behavioral antecedents toward green consumption.

H_{4b}: Consumers with higher *action-related knowledge* will exhibit a higher intention and other behavioral antecedents toward green consumption.

H_{4c}: Consumers with higher *effective knowledge* will exhibit a higher intention and other behavioral antecedents toward green consumption.

In addition, Carrus et al. (2008) demonstrated that belief that one has control over a situation can strongly increase behavioral desires. This was found to be consistent for various green activities, such as choosing to forego private vehicle and recycling (Chan and Bishop 2013; Eriksson and Forward 2011). Alba and Hutchinson (1987) and Brucks (1985) state that consumers with lower subjective knowledge will have lower self-confidence in the ability to carry out the consumption behavior. Conversely, if a person has a strong subjective action and effective knowledge, one should have a higher confidence of his or her ability to perform a pro-environmental behavior. Chiou (1998) states that one's attitude toward behavior already reflects this confidence, which can result in attitude overshadowing the effect of PBC. Therefore, it could be stated that 'the effect of perceived behavioral control on behavioral intention will be weaker when consumers have high subjective product knowledge' (Chiou 1998).

On the other hand, if a consumer has lower action/effective knowledge, one would have reduced confidence in their ability to perform a given behavior. Thus, PBC will be the dominating antecedent of intention (Chiou 1998). Applying this general concept to pro-environmental behavior, we hypothesize the following:

H_{5a}: Perceived behavioral control will exert a stronger influence on desire when consumers have a lower level of action/effective knowledge.

In contrast, we hypothesize that although increase in system knowledge will induce positively increased intentions and other behavioral antecedents, we hypothesize that there will be no differentiation of behavioral antecedents in terms of each factor's significance. This is due to the fact that while action and effective knowledge are behavior-proximal in nature, system knowledge's function lies in setting precedence for the other two knowledge types to take hold (Martens, Rost, and Warning-Schröder 2001).

H_{5b}: Difference in levels of system knowledge will not induce differentiation of behavioral antecedents of pro-environmental behavior.

4. Measurement and data collection

Our study utilizes the modified MGB framework by Chen (2013). The survey items were developed from previous studies and validated measures. All the items were measured in a seven-point Likert scale (see Appendix 1). To test these hypotheses, a self-administering survey was developed via a thorough literature review to ensure that each question well represents relevant determinant variables. The survey was distributed to the US residents via the Internet, where each respondent first underwent a pre-screening to ensure that they are fit to take the survey, i.e. someone who flies regularly (more than once per year) and is aware of VCO program's existence. As a relatively lesser known program, it was required that respondents knew enough about VCO before taking the survey to form an opinion. In total, 256 complete and valid responses were collected. Table 1 summarizes respondent socio-demographic profiles.

5. Empirical results

A multistage model-building process was proposed by Hair et al. (2010) when utilizing structural equation model. First, the reliability and validity of measures were tested,

Table 1. Profile of respondents and flight behavior ($N = 256$).

Categories	Classification	Frequency	%
Gender	Male	157	61
	Female	99	39
Age	18–29	23	12
	30–39	160	63
	40–49	41	18
	50–59	17	7
	Over 60	8	2
Highest level of education	12th grade or less	1	0
	High school diploma	30	12
	Some college	55	21
	Bachelor' s degree	133	52
	Master's degree or higher	37	14
Income	Less than $24,999	37	14
	$25,000–$44,999	68	27
	$45,000–$64,999	53	21
	$65,000–$84,999	49	19
	$85,000–$94,999	18	7
	$95,000 or more	31	12
Main purpose of flights	Business	124	48
	Visiting friends and family	81	32
	Leisure and tourism	51	20

followed by analysis of the structural model to test the associations and overall applicability of MGB.

5.1. *Measurement reliability and validity*

To verify each construct's convergent validity, the confirmatory factor analysis was conducted. Five question items were dropped since they did not meet the minimum 0.7 value of factor loading, as shown in Table 2.

Reliability (CR > 0.7), convergent validity (AVE > 0.5), and discriminant validity (MSV < AVE, ASV < AVE, sqrt of AVE > corr.) were met by all constructs (Hair et al. 2010). The final question item set was constructed to test the relations between variables (see Table 3).

5.2. *Model fit*

Six common criteria were used for assessing overall model fit: χ^2/df, standardized root mean square residual (SRMR), root mean square error of approximation (RMSEA), comparative fit index (CFI), norm fit index (NFI), and incremental fit index (IFI). The observed norm χ^2 for the measurement model was 2.162 ($\chi^2 = 413.319$, df = 219), well within the recommended range of less than 3. Each fit indices' value is shown in Table 4.

Table 2. Results of confirmatory factor analysis for measurement model.

Construct	Questions	F.L.*
Attitude (ATT)	Overall, participating in VCO would be good for humankind	0.93
	Participating in VCO is a wise thing to do for a society	0.96
	Participating in VCO is valuable to the society	0.97
	Participating in VCO is beneficial to the humankind	0.95
Subjective norm (SN)	Most people important to me would think that I should participate in VCO	0.80
	The people in my life whose opinions I value would approve of my participation	0.85
Perceived behavioral control (PBC)	For me to successfully participate in VCO in my next flight would be easy	0.79
	It is mostly up to me whether or not I participate in VCO	0.72
	I have the resources necessary to participate in VCO	0.85
Positive anticipated emotions (PAE)	If my participation in VCO successfully achieved its goal of helping the environment, I would feel.........	
	Excited	0.74
	Happy	0.83
	Satisfied	0.91
	Proud	0.85
	Self-assured	0.81
Negative Anticipated Emotions (NAE)	If my participation in VCO did not achieve its goal of helping the environment, I would feel.........	
	Angry	0.76
	Frustrated	0.85
	Sad	0.88
	Disappointed	0.92
Desire (DES)	My desire to participate in VCO can be described as strong	0.93
	I have a passionate wish to participate in VCO	0.91
	Participating in VCO is something that I want to do	0.96
Intention (INT)	I will make an effort to participate in VCO next time I get the opportunity	0.97
	I plan to participate in VCO the next opportunity I get	0.98
	I will try to participate in VCO next time it is available	0.97

*F.R.: Factor loading value

Table 3. Measurement reliability and validity of model.

Construct	CR	AVE	MSV	ASV	1	2	3	4	5	6	7
1. DES	0.95	0.87	0.86	0.48	0.93						
2. ATT	0.97	0.90	0.65	0.45	0.81	0.95					
3. SN	0.81	0.68	0.50	0.35	0.70	0.66	0.83				
4. PBC	0.83	0.62	0.35	0.25	0.52	0.59	0.54	0.79			
5. PAE	0.92	0.69	0.54	0.38	0.68	0.73	0.51	0.54	0.83		
6. NAE	0.91	0.73	0.25	0.15	0.38	0.36	0.41	0.24	0.50	0.85	
7. INT	0.98	0.95	0.86	0.47	0.93	0.76	0.69	0.50	0.70	0.39	0.97

Table 4.   Fit indices for the measurement model and structural model.

Fit indices	Overall model	Recommended value
χ^2/df	2.051	<3
SRMR (standardized root mean square residual)	0.0429	<0.06
RMSEA(root mean square error of approximation)	0.064	<0.08
CFI (comparative fit index)	0.966	>0.9
NFI (normed fit index)	0.936	>0.9
IFI (incremental fit index)	0.966	>0.9

The SRMR, RMSEA, CFI, NFI, and IFI were 0.0435, 0.064, 0.966, 0.936, and 0.966, respectively. Considering previous studies' recommended value levels, a mix of good to adequate fit is demonstrated with the data collected.

5.3.   Full structural analysis results

The results of full structural analysis are summarized in Table 5 and graphically in Figure 2. Attitudes toward VCO (path coefficient = 0.407, $p < 0.001$), social norms (path coefficient = 0.213, $p < 0.001$), and PBC (path coefficient = 0.135, $p < 0.01$) have significant and positive influence on the desire of VCO participation. Thus, hypotheses 1a, 1b, and 1c are supported in a statistically significant level. As consistent with the results of Carrus et al. (2008), Perugini and Bagozzi (2001), and Venkatesh and Davis (2000), desire strongly influences intention (path coefficient = 0.946, $p < 0.001$). Thus, hypothesis 2 is also supported.

As for the results of anticipated emotions, while positive anticipated emotions influence to desire of VCO participation (path coefficient = 0.190, $p = 0.007$), negative anticipated emotions did not influence desire of VCO participation (path coefficient = 0.046, $p = 0.315$). That means hypothesis 3a is supported at a statistically significant level, but hypothesis 3b is not supported. Our results agree with that of Chen (2013), where only positive anticipated emotions affected desire, and not negative emotion. These findings can be explained from conjectures of Chang (2012), who states that negative emotional appeals do not work well with low-proximity issues. As the primary goal of VCO is to reduce the impact of air travel on climate change, it is classified as a relatively low-proximity issue. In fact, the 2013 March Gallup Poll within USA showed that more than 60% of population did not believe that global warming will be a tangible issue during their lifetimes.

Table 5.   Summary of testing results, full model.

Path	Path coefficient	t-value
DES → INT	0.946***	22.671
ATT → DES	0.407***	5.206
SN → DES	0.213***	3.230
PBC → DES	0.135**	2.562
PAE → DES	0.190*	2.694
NAE → DES	0.046	1.006

*$p < 0.05$, **$p < 0.01$, ***$p < 0.001$

31

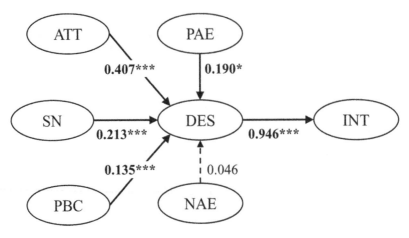

Figure 2.   Results of the structural model (dotted line represents non-significant path).
Note: Att: attitude; SN: subjective norm; PBC: perceived behavioral control; PAE: positive anticipated emotions; NAE: negative anticipated emotions; DES: desire, INT: intention (for sustainable
consumption)
$^*p < 0.05, ^{**}p < 0.01, ^{***}p < 0.001.$

5.4.   The moderating effect of knowledge level

In order to group the respondents according to their knowledge level, respondents were
asked to rate themselves for each category of knowledge (system, action-related, effective). As these are consumers' own perceptions of their knowledge level, they are not
objective but subjective knowledge. Measures of subjective knowledge differ from objective knowledge in that subjective knowledge also indicates one's level of self-confidence.
For system knowledge, respondents were asked to rate themselves on a seven-point Likert
scale from *not at all* to *very well* for the question, 'I could explain the consequences of climate change to humanity.' Similarly, for action-related knowledge, respondents were
asked: 'I could explain how I can participate in VCO,' and for effective knowledge, 'I
could explain how VCO works in addressing relevant problems.' It is also worth noting
that while three types of knowledge are interrelated with one another, consumers with
high level of action-related knowledge also tend to have high knowledge in alternative
actions, and therefore a prerequisite for effective knowledge (Frick, Kaiser, and Wilson
2004). Results reflected upon this fact, where action and effective knowledge are highly
correlated (corr. = 0.811). As such, the two knowledge types were merged as one factor
using *k*-means cluster analysis. By using cluster analysis, respondents were then catego-
rized into either low or high for (1) system knowledge, and (2) action/effective
knowledge.

An analysis of basic descriptive statistics among moderating groups show that high
knowledge groups for both action/effective and environmental knowledge had significantly higher scores across all constructs, including desire and intention to participate in
VCO. However, negative anticipated emotion, which was shown to have no significant
influence in past literatures, showed no statistically significant difference between low
and high groups (Chen 2013). As shown in Table 6, our results support hypotheses 4a,
4b, and 4c in that higher knowledge will lead to higher intention to participate in pro-
environmental behavior. The difference in intention and desire was especially strong
when comparing high system knowledge group against low system knowledge group.

Table 6.   Descriptive statistics among low/high knowledge groups.

| | Action/effective knowledge | | | | | System knowledge | | | | |
| | Low | | High | | | Low | | High | | |
	Mean	Std. dev	Mean	Std. dev	t-value	Mean	Std. dev	Mean	Stdev	t-value
INT	5.22	1.56	5.24	1.66	−1.857*	4.47	1.64	5.34	1.59	−3.72***
DES	4.52	1.65	5.10	1.62	−2.474*	4.26	1.59	5.17	1.61	−3.87***
ATT	5.11	1.51	5.54	1.41	−2.132*	4.67	1.59	5.67	1.31	−4.98***
SN	4.52	1.50	4.91	1.38	−1.967*	4.30	1.48	4.98	1.36	−3.34***
PBC	4.82	1.32	5.62	1.16	−4.694***	4.79	1.25	5.61	1.19	−4.73***
PAE	5.22	1.29	5.68	1.15	−2.694**	4.92	1.35	5.76	1.08	−5.05***
NAE	3.97	1.63	4.36	1.82	−1.542	3.91	1.54	4.37	1.83	−1.77

$^*p < 0.05, {^{**}}p < 0.01, {^{***}}p < 0.001$

In order to test the moderating effect of different knowledge types, the analysis was conducted by examining the difference between the χ^2 for a model with the structural paths constrained and one with no structural paths constrained (Byrne 2001). Results indicate that the change in χ^2 is significant for action/effective knowledge (p-value = .038), while insignificant for system knowledge (p-value = .256) supporting hypothesis 5b. From this result, we can conclude that consumers' level difference of action/effective knowledge moderates the relationship between attitude, subjective norm, PBC, anticipated emotions, desire, and intention to participate. Results of structural analysis are shown in Table 7, and summarized graphically in Figures 3 and 4.

Overall, results show a significant structural difference in behavioral antecedents for action/effective knowledge groups (low: $n = 68$; high: $n = 188$, separated via k-means clustering). First, in terms of similarities, both exhibit similar effect of desire on intention for green consumption. Negative anticipated emotions also have no influence on desire for both groups, in line with previous studies on carbon offsetting (Chen 2013). PBC had a positive and significant influence on low knowledge group's desire to participate in VCO. For low action/effective knowledge group, their perception of ease of VCO participation plays a significant role in increasing their desire for participation. However, for those who are already highly knowledgeable in what VCO is and how effective it is (high action/effective knowledge group), the perception of difficulty of participation did not

Table 7.   Summary of structural testing results, moderated by action/effective knowledge.

| | Low action/effective knowledge | | High action/effective knowledge | |
Path	Path coefficient	t-value	Path coefficient	t-value
DES → INT	0.949***	9.304	0.945***	21.578
ATT → DES	0.390***	2.062	0.449***	5.522
SN → DES	0.119	0.857	0.334***	4.352
PBC → DES	0.309**	2.929	−0.018	−0.282
PAE → DES	0.098	0.841	0.208**	2.756
NAE → DES	0.129	1.104	−0.011	−0.213

$^*p < 0.05, {^{**}}p < 0.01, {^{***}}p < 0.001$

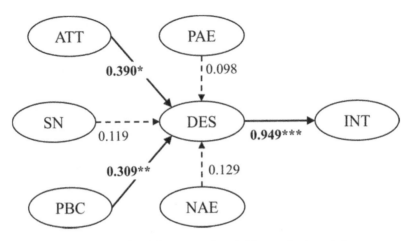

Figure 3. Results of the structural model, low action knowledge.

influence their desire to participate in VCO. Instead, the high knowledge group's desire to participate was driven by positive anticipated emotions and subjective norms, both of which were insignificant in low knowledge group. This is consistent with what was discussed in literature review, where PBC is reflective of one's confidence in ability to perform a given task, supporting hypothesis 5a. For consumers with high level of self-confidence in their ability to participate in a pro-environmental behavior, PBC would not be a factor that influences one's intention.

6. Discussions and implications for green advertising

The findings of this study should provide meaningful insights to green advertisers in promotion of new and growing green consumption programs. In particular, the findings highlight two key contributions. First, we demonstrated that increased system knowledge as well as action/effective knowledge results in increased desire and intention for green consumption. In particular, the increase in system knowledge induced a stronger impact on

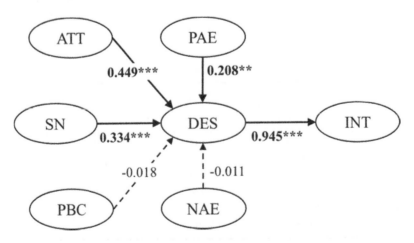

Figure 4. Results of the structural model, high action knowledge.

increasing intention and desire, when compared to action/effective knowledge. Second, the influence of behavioral antecedents (attitude, subjective norm, PBC, and anticipated emotions) on desire for green consumption shows a differing pattern when consumers have differing levels of action/effective knowledge. The above findings provide some meaningful insights to green marketers who are responsible for promoting consumer-involved green consumption programs.

Our results show that advertisements addressing all three knowledge dimensions would be effective in persuading the consumers. It implies that marketers should consider these distinct dimensions of knowledge when developing a green consumption advertisement. Given this, an effective advertisement for VCO should cover (1) the aviation's impact on environment (system knowledge), (2) what VCO is, and how it works in addressing aviation's environmental impact (action knowledge), and (3) the cost effectiveness of VCO, especially when compared to alternative methods of similar green consumption behavior (effective knowledge). In particular, the transfer of system knowledge has shown to be especially important, as it provides a credible basis for the existence of the environmental problem, upon which additional action-related and effective knowledge — what consumers can do and how it can improve the environment — can be developed. In a managerial perspective within the context of VCO, an implementation of a short, 30-second infomercial can play during the flight that explains what VCO is, and how it works in reducing the given flight's impact to the environment, followed by an easy on-screen payment system dialog is one viable option. An investigation into how such informational claims and 'virtual nature experiences' could be synergized to produce a more effective advertising experience should be done (Hartmann 2009).

Chan (2000) recognized the need for differentiated green advertising strategies based on eco-friendliness of source country. However, when advertising green products that span across globally, such as airline VCO, consumer heterogeneity must be addressed other than by localization (Koslow and Costley 2010). In light of this, our findings also recognize the need for differentiation of strategies. Instead of indiscriminate application of one style of advertisement, marketers need to recognize the differing drivers of green consumption for consumers with low and high levels of knowledge in the behavior. For consumers with low knowledge about a particular green consumption behavior, increasing their self-confidence in their ability to participate is essential. Advertisements targeted toward groups with lower action/effective knowledge, such as youth and first-time consumers, should provide a clear, concise information on how to engage in particular green consumption product to increase PBC. When targeting consumers who have higher action/effective knowledge level, such as those who have prior experience, focus instead should be made in appealing to their positive anticipated emotions and subjective norms. Advertisements emphasizing how their actions can benefit the environment should be made, as well as making it easy for their actions to be noticed by their peers. In the context of VCO, for example, a social network integrated app that posts how many tons of CO_2 one has saved through VCO, and encourages others to take part, could be an effective solution.

7. Conclusion

This study investigates how different types of knowledge influence consumer's green consumption behavior. From an academic standpoint, it broadens the current understanding of determinants that influence pro-environmental behavior by demonstrating the moderating effect of various knowledge types on MGB through empirical US data.

We suggest the future research would benefit from an international sample, considering the international nature of aviation. It should also perform a more encompassing study that investigates the interactive and procedural nature of environmental and action knowledge, as well as introducing objective measures of consumer's level of knowledge to compare against self-reported knowledge level utilized in this study.

From a practical standpoint, this study reveals the unique driving forces of green consumption for consumers with low knowledge in the behavior, as well as highlighting the need to raise their self-confidence in the ability to participate in the green consumption activity. This study shows that advertisers should not focus just on appealing the green image, but rather provide information for segmented group by knowledge level that increases consumer's knowledge of the problem, the solution, and how to participate in the solution, thereby increasing consumers' self-confidence in the ability to participate (Lee, Gemba, and Kodama 2006).

It is worth noting that negative anticipated emotions were not an effective form of appeal regardless of knowledge level in this study. This finding reinforces the academic understanding of negative emotions such as guilt as an appeal factor in green advertising, where guilt appeal loses its effectiveness when dealing with issues that have 'low proximity' to consumers such as climate change (Chang 2012). The usefulness of negative appeals as an antecedent to pro-environmental behavior remains an issue that continues to gain increasing interest in marketing academia. While our expanded MGB in this study has limited applications in capturing the varying effect of negative appeals, recent experiment-based studies that focus specifically on such guilt or fear, 'loss framed messages' have succeeded in demonstrating the conditional effectiveness of negative appeals, highlighting negative appeals as a valid research topic that needs more exploration (Chang, Zhang, and Xie 2015). In particular, the influence of action-related knowledge level on negative appeals should be further explored; results from Hartmann et al. (2014) show reduced effectiveness of fear appeals when advertising claims on the efficacy of pro-environmental behavior are introduced. Future research should also explore the moderating role of perceived issue importance, which has been shown to have a significant role in moderating pro-environmental attitude (Baek, Yoon, and Kim 2015).

Disclosure statement

No potential conflict of interest was reported by the authors.

References

Alba, J.W., and J.W. Hutchinson. 1987. Dimensions of consumer expertise. *Journal of Consumer Research* 13, no. 4: 411–54.

Ajzen, I. 1991. The theory of planned behavior. *Organizational Behavior and Human Decision Processes* 50, no. 2: 179–211.

Baek, T.H., S. Yoon, and S. Kim. 2015. When environmental messages should be assertive: Examining the moderating role of effort investment. *International Journal of Advertising* 34, no. 1: 135–57.

Bagozzi, R.P., and R. Pieters. 1998. Goal-directed emotions. *Cognition & Emotion* 12, no. 1: 1–26.

Bamberg, S., and G. Möser. 2007. Twenty years after Hines, Hungerford, and Tomera: A new meta-analysis of psycho-social determinants of pro-environmental behavior. *Journal of Environmental Psychology* 27, no. 1: 14–25.

Bettencourt, L.A. 1997. Customer voluntary performance: Customers as partners in service delivery. *Journal of Retailing* 73, no. 3: 383–406.

British Airways. 2011. Corporate responsibility report 2010/11. http://d2zax00nj39hb2.cloudfront. net/wp-content/uploads/CR-Report-2010-11.pdf.

Brouwer, R., L. Brander, and P. Van Beukering. 2008. 'A convenient truth': Air travel passengers' willingness to pay to offset their CO_2 emissions. *Climatic Change* 90, no. 3: 299–313.

Brucks, M. 1985. The effects of product class knowledge on information search behavior. *Journal of Consumer Research* 12, no. 1: 1–16.

Byrne, B.M. 2001. Structural equation modeling with AMOS, EQS, and LISREL: Comparative approaches to testing for the factorial validity of a measuring instrument. *International Journal of Testing* 1, no. 1: 55–86.

Carrus, G., P. Passafaro, and M. Bonnes. 2008. Emotions, habits and rational choices in ecological behaviors: The case of recycling and use of public transportation. *Journal of Environmental Psychology* 28, no. 1: 51–62.

Chan, L., and B. Bishop. 2013. A moral basis for recycling: Extending the theory of planned behavior. *Journal of Environmental Psychology* 36, 96–102.

Chan, R.Y. 2000. The effectiveness of environmental advertising: The role of claim type and the source country green image. *International Journal of Advertising* 19, no. 3: 349–75.

Chan, R.Y. 2001. Determinants of Chinese consumers' green purchase behavior. *Psychology & Marketing* 18, no. 4: 389–413.

Chan, R.Y., and L.B. Lau. 2002. Explaining green purchasing behavior: A cross-cultural study on American and Chinese consumers. *Journal of International Consumer Marketing* 14, no. 2–3: 9–40.

Chang, C.T. 2012. Are guilt appeals a panacea in green advertising? The right formula of issue proximity and environmental consciousness. *International Journal of Advertising* 31, no. 4: 741–71.

Chang, H., L. Zhang, and G. Xie. 2015. Message framing in green advertising: The effect of construal level and consumer environmental concern. *International Journal of Advertising* 34, no. 1: 158–76.

Chen, F.Y. 2013. The intention and determining factors for airline passengers' participation in carbon offset schemes. *Journal of Air Transport Management* 29: 17–22.

Chiou, J.S. 1998. The effects of attitude, subjective norm, and perceived behavioral control on consumers' purchase intentions: The moderating effects of product knowledge and attention to social comparison information. *Proceedings of National Science Council, Republic of China (C)* 9, no. 2: 298–308.

Eriksson, L., and S.E. Forward. 2011. Is the intention to travel in a pro-environmental manner and the intention to use the car determined by different factors? *Transportation Research Part D: Transport and Environment* 16, no. 5: 372–6.

Ernst, A.M. 1994. *Soziales Wissen als Grundlage des Handelns in Konfliktsituationen* [Social knowledge as basis of a person's action in conflict situations]. Frankfurt/M: Peter Lang.

Fazio, R.H. 1995. Attitudes as object-evaluation associations: Determinants, consequences, and correlates of attitude accessibility. *Attitude Strength: Antecedents and Consequences* 4: 247–82.

Frick, J., F.G. Kaiser, and M. Wilson. 2004. Environmental knowledge and conservation behavior: Exploring prevalence and structure in a representative sample. *Personality and Individual Differences* 37, no. 8: 1597–613.

Gambro, J.S., and H.N. Switzky. 1999. Variables associated with American high school students' knowledge of environmental issues related to energy and pollution. *The Journal of Environmental Education* 30, no. 2: 15–22.

Gleicher, F., D.S. Boninger, A. Strathman, D. Armor, J. Hetts, and M. Ahn. 1995. With an eye toward the future: The impact of counterfactual thinking on affect, attitudes, and behavior.

Hair, J.F., W.C. Black, B.J. Babin, and R.E. Anderson. 2010. Multivariate data analysis. 7th ed. Upper Saddle River, NJ: Prentice Hall.

Hartmann, P., and V. Apaolaza-Ibáñez. 2009. Green advertising revisited conditioning virtual nature experiences. *International Journal of Advertising* 28, no. 4: 715–39.

Hartmann, P., V. Apaolaza, C. D'Souza, J.M. Barrutia, and C. Echebarria. 2014. Environmental threat appeals in green advertising: The role of fear arousal and coping efficacy. *International Journal of Advertising* 33, no. 4: 741–65.

IATA. 2013. Airlines expect 31% rise in passenger demand by 2017. http://www.iata.org/press room/pr/pages/2013-12-10-01.aspx (accessed January 20, 2014).

Kaiser, F.G., and U. Fuhrer. 2003. Ecological behavior's dependency on different forms of knowledge. *Applied Psychology* 52, no. 4: 598–613.

Kalafatis, S.P., M. Pollard, R. East, and M.H. Tsogas. 1999. Green marketing and Ajzen's theory of planned behavior: A cross-market examination. *Journal of Consumer Marketing* 16, no. 5: 441–60.

Kals, E., D. Schumacher, and L. Montada. 1999. Emotional affinity toward nature as a motivational basis to protect nature. *Environment and Behavior* 31, no. 2: 178–202.

Kim, K., Y. Cheong, and J.S. Lim. 2015. Choosing the right message for the right cause in social cause advertising: Type of social cause message, perceived company – cause fit and the persuasiveness of communication. *International Journal of Advertising* 34, no. 3: 473–94.

Kim, Y., S. Yun, and J. Lee. 2014. Can companies induce sustainable consumption? The impact of knowledge and social embeddedness on airline sustainability programs in the US. *Sustainability* 6, no. 6: 3338–56.

Ko, E., Hwang, Y.K., and Kim, E.Y. 2013. Green marketing functions in building corporate image in the retail setting. *Journal of Business Research* 66, no 10: 1709–15.

Kollmuss, A., and J. Agyeman. 2002. Mind the gap: Why do people act environmentally and what are the barriers to pro-environmental behavior? *Environmental Education Research* 8, no. 3: 239–60.

Koslow, S., and C. Costley. 2010. How consumer heterogeneity muddles the international advertising debate. *International Journal of Advertising* 29, no. 2: 221–44.

Krause, D. 1993., Environmental consciousness: An empirical study. *Journal of Environment and Behavior* 25, no. 1: 126–42.

Lam, S.P. 2006. Predicting intention to save water: Theory of planned behavior, response efficacy, vulnerability, and perceived efficiency of alternative solutions 1. *Journal of Applied Social Psychology* 36, no. 11: 2803–24.

Lantermann, E.-D., E. Döring-Seipel, and P. Schima. 1992. Werte, Gefühle und Unbestimmtheit: Kognitiv-emotionale Wechselwirkungen im Umgang mit einem ökologischen System [Values, emotions, and indetermination: Cognition–affect interaction while dealing with ecological systems]. In *Umwelt und Verhalten: Perspektiven und Ergebnisse ökopsychologischer Forschung*, ed. K. Pawlik, and K.H. Stapf, 129–44. Bern: Huber.

Lee, J.J., K. Gemba, and F. Kodama. 2006. Analyzing the innovation process for environmental performance improvement. *Technological Forecasting and Social Change* 73, no. 3: 290–301.

Lu, J.L., and Z.Y. Shon. 2012. Exploring airline passengers' willingness to pay for carbon offsets. *Transportation Research Part D: Transport and Environment* 17, no. 2: 124–8.

MacKerron, G.J., C. Egerton, C. Gaskell, A. Parpia, and S. Mourato. 2009. Willingness to pay for carbon offset certification and co-benefits among (high-) flying young adults in the UK. *Energy Policy* 37, no. 4: 1372–81.

Martens, T., J. Rost, and H. Warning-Schröder. 2001. Strategies for environmental education based on the action generating process. Paper presented at the 82nd annual meeting of the American Educational Research Association, April, in Seattle, WA.

Matzler, K., H.H. Hinterhuber, F. Bailom, and E. Sauerwein. 1996. How to delight your customers. *Journal of Product & Brand Management* 5, no. 2: 6–18.

McEachern, M.G., and G. Warnaby. 2008. Exploring the relationship between consumer knowledge and purchase behavior of value–based labels. *International Journal of Consumer Studies* 32, no. 5: 414–26.

Natural Marketing Institute. 2011. *Consumer attitudes about renewable energy: Trends and regional differences.* Harleysville, PA: National Renewable Energy Laboratory. apps3.eere. energy.gov/greenpower/pdfs/50988.pdf

Parguel, B., F. Benoit-Moreau, and C.A. Russell. 2015. Can evoking nature in advertising mislead consumers? The power of 'executional greenwashing'. *International Journal of Advertising* 31, no. 1: 107–34.

Perugini, M., and R.P. Bagozzi. 2001. The role of desires and anticipated emotions in goal-directed behaviors: Broadening and deepening the theory of planned behavior. *British Journal of Social Psychology* 40, no. 1: 79–98.

Pieters, R., T. Bijmolt, F. Van Raaij, and M. De Kruijk. 1998. Consumers' attributions of pro-environmental behavior, motivation and ability to self and others. *Journal of Public Policy and Marketing* 17, no. 2: 215–25.

Rokicka, E., and J. Słomczyńska. 2002. Attitudes toward natural environment: A study of local community dwellers. *International Journal of Sociology* 32, no. 3: 78–90.

Shiu, E.M.K., L.M. Hassan, J.A. Thomson, and D. Shaw. 2008. An empirical examination of the extended model of goal-directed behavior: Assessing the role of behavioral desire. *European Advances in Consumer Research* 8: 66–71.

Smith-Sebasto, N.J., and R.W. Fortner. 1994. The environmental action internal control index. *Journal of Environmental Education* 25, no. 4: 23–9.

Stutzman, T.M., and S.B. Green. 1982. Factors affecting energy consumption: Two field tests of the Fishbein–Ajzen model. *The Journal of Social Psychology* 117, no. 2: 183–201.

Sukoco, B.M. 2012. Individual differences in participations of a brand community: A validation of the goal-directed behavior model. *The South East Asian Journal of Management* 5, no. 2: 119–33.

van Birgelen, M., J. Semeijn, and P. Behrens. 2011. Explaining pro-environment consumer behavior in air travel. *Journal of Air Transport Management* 17, no. 2: 125–8.

Venkatesh, V., and F.D. Davis. 2000. A theoretical extension of the technology acceptance model: Four longitudinal field studies. *Management Science* 46, no. 2: 186–204.

Vining, J., and A. Ebreo. 2002. Emerging theoretical and methodological perspectives on conservation behavior. In *Handbook of environmental psychology*, ed. R. B. Bechtel and A. Churchman, 2nd ed., 541–58. New York: Wiley.

Whitmarsh, L., and S. O'Neill. 2010. Green identity, green living? The role of pro-environmental self-identity in determining consistency across diverse pro-environmental behaviors. *Journal of Environmental Psychology* 30, no. 3: 305–14.

Appendix 1. Measurements for each constructs

Construct	Questionnaires	Source
Attitude	(Strongly agree - - - - Strongly disagree) • Overall, participating in VCO would be good for humankind • Participating in VCO is a wise thing to do for a society • Participating in VCO is valuable to the society • Participating in VCO is beneficial to the humankind	Perugini and Bagozzi (2001)
Subjective norm	(Not at all - - - - - Absolutely) • Most people important to me would think that I should participate in VCO • The people in my life whose opinions I value would approve of my participation • It is expected of me that I participate in VCO	Perugini and Bagozzi (2001)
Perceived behavioral control	(Not at all - - - - - Absolutely) • For me to successfully participate in VCO in my next flight would be easy • It is mostly up to me whether or not I participate in VCO • I have the resources necessary to participate in VCO	Venkatesh et al. (2003)
Positive anticipated emotions	(Strongly agree - - - - Strongly disagree) If my participation in VCO successfully achieved its goal of helping the environment, I would feel......... • Excited, happy, satisfied, proud, self-assured	Perugini and Bagozzi (2001)
Negative anticipated emotions	(Strongly agree - - - - Strongly disagree)	Perugini and Bagozzi (2001)

(continued)

Construct	Questionnaires	Source
	If my participation in VCO did not achieve its goal of helping the environment, I would feel..........	
Desire	• Angry, frustrated, guilty, sad, disappointed	Carrus et al. (2008)
	(Not at all - - - - - Absolutely)	
	• I desire to participate in VCO to help the environment	
	• My desire to participate in VCO can be described as strong	
	• I have a passionate wish to participate in VCO	
	• Participating in VCO is something that I want to do	
Intention	(Not at all - - - - - Absolutely)	Carrus et al. (2008)
	• I intend to participate in VCO next time it is available	
	• I will make an effort to participate in VCO next time I get the opportunity	
	• I plan to participate in VCO the next opportunity I get	
	• I will try to participate in VCO next time it is available	

'Kid tested, mother approved': the relationship between advertising expenditures and 'most-loved' brands

Kacy K. Kim[a], Jerome D. Williams[b] and Gary B. Wilcox[c]

[a]Department of Marketing & Entrepreneurship, Elon University, USA; [b]Management and Global Business Department, The Center for Urban, Entrepreneurship & Economic Development (CUEED), Rutgers Business School-Newark and New Brunswick, USA; [c]Department of Advertising & Public Relations, The University of Texas at Austin, USA

In this research, we examine the relationship between advertising expenditures and perceptions regarding popular brands as held by children and mothers in the United States. Our findings show that traditional media advertising expenditures positively relate with brand affinity for children and mothers, while product placement relates positively with children's brand affinity but not with mothers' brand affinity. A closer examination of advertising budgets reveals that marketers for the top children's brands devote most of their advertising to TV and magazine advertisements, indicating that they still believe that traditional media play a key role in reaching the youth market. Additionally, the advertisers spend disproportionately higher amounts to reach Hispanic and African American populations.

Kid tested, mother approved
From the TV commercial for *Kix*

The *Kix* cereal advertising slogan reflects a marketer's conundrum. On one hand, advertisers targeting children must appeal to the primary *users* – children. Simultaneously, marketers must persuade the primary *buyers* – mothers. Tackling these two distinct challenges with a single brand is as challenging as trying to kill two birds with one stone: children go for tasty and flashy brands; mothers choose brands that have socially responsible images. From a marketer's point of view, it is important to assess and manage a brand by considering how both audience groups – children and mothers – similarly and differently view the brand.

Escalating childhood obesity is increasing, alarming public health policymakers in the United States. During the last 30 years, the number of overweight children and adolescents has more than doubled. Advertisers are often blamed for having a part in this public health crisis. They are accused of taking advantage of children who lack the experience needed to interpret persuasive methods, and making them desire unhealthy foods (Macklin 1994). Although advertisers mostly target adults, when they target children and adolescents, controversy arises (i.e., Livingstone & Helsper 2006; Roedder John 2008; Charry 2014). Although the topic is growing in importance, however, no prior study has examined the link between advertising spending and brand popularities among children and mothers in the United States. The current research fills this gap.

Gaining a better understanding of the link between advertising expenditures and brand popularities is important from both a theoretical and practical perspective. Considering the theoretical perspective first, brand popularity, or 'brand liking,' is a critical step in one of the fundamental models of advertising effectiveness, namely, the hierarchy-of-effects (HOE) model (Lavidge and Steiner 1961). This model, like most advertising theories/models, attempts to explain and describe, at the individual buyer or consumer level, the process by which advertising effectively persuades individuals to take action (e.g., Barry & Howard 1990; Yoo, Kim, and Stout 2004). Ultimately, one would like to assess the direct connection between advertising expenditures and sales, typically at the top of the hierarchy. However, recognizing the effectiveness of advertising on the intermediate steps up the hierarchy, such as on 'liking,' or 'brand popularity,' is a critical step in better understanding the interconnection between increasing rates of childhood obesity, advertising expenditures on food and beverage brands, and the popularity/liking of those brands by children and moms.

From a practical perspective, this work complements existing government data on advertising expenditures directed at children, but which currently does not extend to assessing the effectiveness of those expenditures. Because of growing concerns regarding the effects of food and beverage advertising on children and parents, we chose to examine the relationship between advertising expenditures and children/mother perceptions of popular brands in the United States to provide deeper understandings of this controversial issue. Meanwhile, minority children are showing steep and increasing levels of obesity as compared with White children, so we additionally analyze advertising expenditures on media platforms and devices targeted toward minority populations.

We focus on the correlation between advertising expenditures and popular food and beverage brands that children and mothers rank most highly in terms of what we call 'likability.' We gathered 2009, 2010, and 2011 survey results from Smarty Pants, a marketing research firm that annually surveys children and mothers to isolate brands likeability for all brands, not just foods and beverages. A representative sample of 4500 US families with children aged 6–12 revealed more than 270 popular consumer brands in 20 categories. From that list, they generated a list of the 'Top 100 Kids' Most Loved Brands.'

We also purchased annual advertising expenditure data for the brands from Kantar Media, a commercial source. The data revealed that most advertising expenditures went to 17 media outlets: network TV, stop TV, Spanish Language Network TV, cable TV, syndicated media, national radio, network radio, national spot radio, national newspapers, Hispanic newspapers, magazines, Sunday magazines, local magazines, Hispanic magazines, business-to-business magazines, Internet display, and Outdoor. In addition, product placements in aforementioned media – i.e., the duration of product exposure measured in second – from the same source, Kantar Media, were analyzed.

We begin by looking at the role of advertising in the marketplace and how it might affect perceptions of popular brands by children and mothers. Next, we develop and present our analytical scheme. We then empirically test our conceptualization by aggregating data from multiple sources: how advertising spending, product placements, and mother/children's preference jointly influence the popularity of 'most-loved' food and beverage brands by children and mothers. In addition, we take a closer examination of the top five children's brands as to how much they spend on traditional media and those media that specifically target Hispanic and African American populations.

Research background

Childhood obesity and food marketing toward children

Advertising primarily strives to inform, persuade, and stimulate consumers. Intentions, however, can have unplanned consequences. Incidental results are most controversial when they impact children and adolescents, particularly when research shows that advertising can lure children into unhealthful food and beverage consumption and when critics observe the rise of childhood obesity (i.e., Stutts and Hunnicutt 1987; Nairn and Fine 2008; Biro and Wien 2010; Rifon et al. 2014).

Children and adolescents in the United States are more than twice as likely to be overweight than they were 30 years ago. From 1963 to 1970, 4% of children 6−11 years old and 5% of adolescents 12−19 years old were defined as being overweight. By 1999, the percentage of overweight children more than tripled, reaching 13%. In the same period, adolescents had almost tripled their chances of being overweight, reaching 14% (Ogden et al. 2002). The rising rates of childhood obesity may be specifically related to the increased availability of highly palatable convenience foods.

This trend is particularly pronounced among children in communities of color. Health researchers generally acknowledge that people of color in the United States have unconscionably lower health statuses in comparison with Whites, the largest ethnic group (Flora, Schooler, and Pierson 1997; Williams and Kumanyika 2002), especially in the context of obesity. Although the obesity epidemic cuts across various demographic categories, some groups remain chronically high-risk. For example, lower-income persons from racial/ethnic minority groups including African Americans, Hispanics/Latinos, American Indians, Pacific Islanders, and populations from the southern part of the United States carry substantially greater risk for obesity. Whites or non-Hispanics and higher income groups have a lower risk (Kumanyika et al. 2011; Wang and Beydoun 2007). Racial/ethnic health disparities are not equally pronounced for every intersecting sub-comparison. For example, some race-by-gender and race-by-gender-by-age comparisons evidence low or no disparities (Flegal et al. 2010; Ogden et al. 2010). Obesity levels have generally increased more steeply among African American and Mexican American children than among White children (Freedman et al. 2006). For those reasons, it is especially important for academics and researchers in public health to investigate, where data are available, whether commercial marketing plays a role in the obesity epidemic, especially as it relates to children from communities of color.

Food marketing and brand perception

Some evidence indirectly suggests the link between advertising spending and brand perception and food consumption (Aaker, Carmen, and Jacobson 1982; Hitchings and Moynihan 1998; Kwoka 1992; Peles 1971; Wilcox, Kim, and Schulz 2012). According to the Federal Trade Commission (2012), 44 reporting companies spend more than $1.6 billion annually to promote food and beverages to children and adolescents in the United States. They spend $870 million marketing foods to children under 12 years old, more than $1 billion marketing to adolescents 12−17 years old, and about $300 million to both age groups. Carbonated beverages, fast food, and breakfast cereals account for 63% of the total food, and beverages marketing expenditure. In terms of promotional strategies, they spent 46% of the $1.6 billion on television advertising, 7% on other traditional media such as radio and print advertising, and 5% on new media − company websites, Internet, word-of-mouth, and viral appeals. Because critics point to marketing advertisements for fatty, sugary, non-nutritious fast food and beverages as a factor influencing childhood obesity (Dietz and Gortmaker 1985; Hancox, Milne, and Poulton 2004; Kunkel et al. 2004), it is critical to analyze whether such advertising and product placements indeed influence children, especially when the advertising might be negatively affecting public health.

Some have argued that young children have limited memory capacity, and thus will be relatively immune to advertisements because they may easily forget them (Macklin 1994). Others argue that young children have undeveloped cognitive ability, so that they cannot easily interpret and understand persuasive advertisements. In one examination examining television advertisements and their impacts on children 4−7 years old (Pine and Nash 2002), the researchers divided the children into two groups, English children with considerable television access and Swedish children, who are legally protected from television advertising. The children were asked to list what they wanted for Christmas. The English children named specific brand name products marketed under proprietary trademarks or registered names rather than using generic terms, such as *Barbie doll*, rather than *doll*. Swedish children named 'significantly fewer items' and 'more generalized products.' The study also highlighted that children in this age group are likely to have higher trust, lower recall, and lower understanding of commercial messages than older children, supporting expectations that children are highly vulnerable to advertising, but may have lower recall of brand names.

Researchers have suggested that product placement plays an influential role in shaping brand perception (Choi, Yoon, and Lacey 2013; Yoon, Choi, and Song 2011), yet little is known about how product placement affects the food and beverage preferences and choices of children. In a descriptive study, Sutherland et al. (2015) found a large number of product placements for low-quality food and beverages in movies targeted specifically to children: 58.5% of PG-raged movies and 73.2% of PG 13-rated movies had brand appearances, and six companies – PepsiCo, Coca-Cola, Nestlé USA, McDonald's, Dr. Pepper/Snapple Group and Burger King – accounted for almost half of all brand placements. As Sutherland et al.'s (2015) study calls for more research on how product placement affects the food and beverage choices of children, we incorporate the product placement variable in the current research.

If brands evoke different degrees of recall and preference, advertisers may feel they must concentrate on influencing one or the other. Although high recall and high preference and low recall and low preference tend to be associated, they have similarities and differences. In their attempts to promote their brands and counter competitors' claims, advertisers often use puffery and exaggeration as persuasive tools. They may use generally irrational superlatives, exaggerated statements, and fabricated claims that attract adults' attention (Starek 1997; Nairn and Fine 2008). Although adults may understand that the appeals are made to be persuasive, children are less able to distinguish coercive techniques from reality, theorized to increase brand awareness and chances of future purchasing behavior. Thus, child advocates often explain that parents rather than advertisers must choose what children consume (Sykora 2003).

Because of growing concerns regarding the effects of food and beverage advertising on children and parents, we chose to examine the relationship between advertising expenditures and perceptions of popular brands among children and mothers in the United States. Our findings will provide further insight into the controversial role of advertising effects on children's brand perceptions. In addition, the results will investigate whether mothers' favorite brands have a positive relationship with children's popular ones and vice versa.

Data analysis

We used advertising expenditure data for the most popular brands of products for children and mothers in a regression model to determine advertising impact on how children and mothers ranked the brands. The database included advertising expenditure from several media, product/brand placement values, and child/mother brand affinity scores from the 'Kids' Top-100 Most-Loved Brands' and the 'Moms' Top-100 Most-Loved Brands' as listed by Smarty Pants. The analysis included three years of data – 2009, 2010, and 2011 – for both advertising expenditures and brand affinity scores.

Brand selection

Smarty Pants, a market-research firm, conducts an annual online survey called 'Young Love.' They poll a representative sample of 4,500 US families with children ages 6 to 12 to evaluate more than 270 consumer brands in 20 categories. They then compile a list of the top-100 most-loved brands, and provide *brand affinity scores* for mothers and children regarding the most-loved brands. Smarty Pants calculates scores for each brand using a proprietary formula that we used as the dependent variable our analyses (Smarty Pants 2012).

We compared brand data to create a composite list of brands appearing in 2009, 2010, and 2011 in the food and beverage categories of the children's and mothers' lists for the top-100 most-loved brands. Thirty-three food and beverage brands appeared on the lists (Exhibit 1).

While the brand affinity scores measure is a proprietary formula that the market-research firm, Smarty Pants, does not share with clients or purchasers of their data, firm research personnel did discuss certain components of the formula with the co-authors of this study. For example, based on these discussions, we know that there are three key drivers of the brand popularity measure for children and two key drivers of the brand popularity measure for moms. These drivers relate to constructs such as brand awareness, brand appeal (e.g., liking/loving the brand), and brand popularity on an individual level (e.g., how the individual child views the brand in terms of its popularity). While the researchers on this study were not privy to the proprietary formula of brand affinity, the Smarty Pants researchers shared enough insight to establish that the measure is conceptually sound and is closely related to the concepts of brand awareness/brand liking as intermediate steps typically identified in the HOE model of advertising effectiveness, as descried above.

Advertising expenditure and product placement data

We reported advertising media variables by brand in 17 categories of annual expenditures – network TV, Stop TV, Spanish language network TV, cable TV, syndicated media, national radio, network radio, national spot radio, national newspapers, Hispanic newspapers, magazines, Sunday magazines, local magazines, Hispanic magazines, business-to-business magazines, Internet display, and outdoor advertising. Individual brands widely differed in the use of the various media, creating a large number of missing values for many brands. To solve the missing values problem, we aggregated advertising expenditures from the 17 media channels. Table 1 specifies which media we combined to create the aggregated advertising expenditure variable. The data transformation greatly reduced the missing values problem.

Exhibit 1:   Food and beverage in most loved brands for children.

	Brand	2009 score	2010 score	2011 score
1	CapriSun	833	827	823
2	Cheetos	849	825	828
3	Cinnamon Toast Crunch	777	767	787
4	Coca-Cola	794	805	801
5	Doritos	844	870	847
6	Drumstick	849	843	859
7	Easy Mac	780	775	750
8	Eggo	837	819	832
9	Froot Loops	782	795	785
10	Frosted Flakes	807	797	787
11	Fruit Roll-ups	784	812	763
12	Go-GURT	763	781	792
13	Goldfish	853	869	867
14	KFC	773	786	763
15	Kraftmac/cheese	841	850	832
16	M&M	893	894	876
17	McDonalds	796	796	792
18	Minute Maid	844	854	826
19	Oreo	860	860	858
20	Pepsi	777	786	787
21	Pizza hut	837	794	807
22	Popsicle	809	861	838
23	Pringles	845	819	842
24	Reeses	873	860	889
25	Skittles	809	811	796
26	Snickers	818	799	830
27	Sprite	794	790	773
28	Starburst	823	833	783
29	Subway	852	873	856
30	Totino's	763	782	750
31	Tropicana	851	819	837
32	Twix	846	847	828
33	Wendy's	800	789	800

Additionally, advertising expenditures for the brands included brand extensions. For example, M&Ms expenditures included all related expenditures such as licensing services, vignettes, dark chocolates, and holidays. We summed the data to produce an aggregated value that would incorporate all reported 17 media expenditures.

We also considered product placements – another important form of marketing communications – in the analyses. In 2009, 2010, and 2011, the 33 'most-loved' food and beverage brands invested consistently in product placement. Kantar Media reported product placement exposure times in seconds for each promoted program.

Table 1. Summary of data sources (from 2009 to 2011).

Variables	Data description	Sources of data
Kids Brand Affinity Scores	Children's top-100 most-loved brands	Smarty Pants, LLC
Moms Brand Affinity Scores	Mothers' top-100 most-loved Brands	
Advertising Expenditure	Network TV	Kantar Media
	Spot TV	
	Spanish Language Network TV	
	Cable TV	
	Syndicated Media	
	National Radio	
	Network Radio	
	National Spot Radio	
	National Newspapers	
	Hispanic Newspapers	
	Magazines	
	Sunday Magazines	
	Local Magazines	
	Hispanic Magazines	
	B-to-B Magazines	
	Internet display	
	Outdoor advertising	
Product Placement	Seconds of product placements	Kantar Media

We recognize that the literature indicates that there are several methods that typically are employed to capture and measure product placement such as visual, auditory, and plot connection. Those are three identified in the Tripartite Typology of Product Placement developed by (Russell 1998). In this study, we focused on the 'visual' dimension of product placement as measured by total duration, or length of time, on screen. There are limitations to measuring product placement based solely on the visual element and length of time on screen, as noted by Russell (2002). For example, just counting seconds does not capture the number of appearances on the screen, the style of camera shot for the product, and so forth. Also, length of time does not indicate the context in which the brand is mentioned, the frequency with which it is mentioned, and the emphasis placed on the brand name (tone of the voice, place in the dialogue, character speaking at the time, etc.). Finally, as noted by Russell (2002), length of time does not capture the degree to which the brand is integrated in the plot of the story. Despite these limitations, though, the visual dimension of product placement as measured by seconds on screen was used in our study since it was the best measure available through Kantar Media as a secondary data source. Typically the other aspects of product placement, such as auditory and plot connection, are captured as primary data in experimental studies and content analyses. For our type of analysis, we felt the availability of secondary product placement data obtained through Kantar Media was sufficient for our model, and which matched well with our secondary Kantar Media advertising expenditure data, which likewise did not include creativity, effectiveness, or other dimensions.

Empirical model specification

Our development of the empirical model was guided by the question: What forces mainly drive children and mothers to form brand affinity? We constructed two empirical models using (1) *children's brand-affinity score* and (2) *mothers' brand-affinity score* as dependent variables. We controlled for several idiosyncratic factors that the literature has identified as influencing brand perception: children's brand perceptions as they influence mothers' favorite brands and mothers' brand perceptions as they influences children's favorite brands, and advertising investment (Johnson 1985; Duffy 1996; Pollay, Siddarth, and Siegel 1996; Wilcox 2001; Wilcox, Kim, and Schulz 2012).

To aid our interpretation, we used log-transformation for advertising expenditure variables. Log transformation converts the relationship into a linear form for empirical estimation. Moreover, log transformation smoothes the distribution of variables in the linear regression, and the estimated coefficient of the log-linear form directly reflects the elasticity of independent and dependent variables. We aggregated the advertising expenditure variables to minimize potential multicollinearity problems. To examine the relationship between the dependent variable (children's and mothers' brand perceptions) and the host of independent variables (advertising expenditures, product placements, and mother/children brand perceptions), we estimated the following models:

Children's brand affinity equation

$$(B_{\text{Kids}})_{\text{it}} = \text{CONST} + \alpha_1 \log(\text{ADV})_{\text{it}} + \alpha_2 (\text{PPL})_{\text{it}} + \alpha_3 (B_{\text{Moms}})_{\text{it}} + \varepsilon_{\text{it}}$$

Mothers' brand affinity equation

$$(B_{\text{Moms}})_{\text{it}} = \text{CONST} + b_1 \log(\text{ADV})_{\text{it}} + b_2 (\text{PPL})_{\text{it}} + b_3 (B_{\text{Kids}})_{\text{it}} + \varepsilon_{\text{it}}$$

- B_{Kids}: Kids Brand Affinity Score
- B_{Moms}: Moms Brand Affinity Score
- ADV_{it}: Aggregated Advertising Expenditure
- PPL_{it}: Seconds of Product Placement
- where $i (= 1, 2, ..., 33)$: The most-loved food and beverage brands
- $t (= 2009, 2010, 2011)$: Time of the year

for each year separately ($t = 2009, 2010, 2011$), where i indicates the most-loved food and beverage brands by children and mothers ($i = 1, 2, ..., 33$). The covariates include media spending (*ADV*), product placement (*PPL*), and *brand affinity scores*.

Data analysis procedures

We used multiple regression analysis to determine which variables significantly predicted brand scores. We used the variables described above in two generalized least-squares regression equations with *kids brand affinity score* as the dependent variable. We performed another analysis using *moms brand affinity* as the dependent variable. We conducted two separate analyses for each dependent variable to determine whether the advertising expenditure, product placement, and brand perception variables affected the *brand affinity scores*. First, we regressed the advertising expenditure, product placement, and *moms brand affinity scores* against *kids brand affinity scores*. Next we regressed the

Table 2. OLS estimation results for *kids brand affinity scores*.

Year (t)	2009	2010	2011
CONST	375.00**	269.805**	320.687**
Log ADV$_t$	1.263**	5.466**	7.409**
PPL$_t$	2.857e$-$05**	0.025**	0.026**
B$_{Moms}$	0.373**	0.601**	0.696**
Model fit F (p-value)	14.81** (.000)*	21.75** (.000)*	18.20** (.000)*
Adjusted R^2	.605**	.748**	.722**

Note: $^{**}p < 0.01$; $^{*}p < 0.05$

advertising expenditure, product placement, and *kids brand affinity scores* against *moms brand affinity scores*.

Findings

We conducted three pairs (i.e., *kids* and *moms brand affinity scores* predicted by the models) of separate analyses for 2009, 2010, and 2011, respectively, to examine the relationship between marketing communication activities – advertising expenditures and product placements – and *brand affinity scores* for children and mothers. As specified in the models, we also factored in whether children's (mothers') brand preferences are associated with mothers' (children's) brand preferences. Tables 2 and 3 present, respectively, the parameter estimates and model fits for *kids brand affinity scores* and *moms brand affinity scores*.

Children's brand affinity scores

As shown in Table 2, the positive coefficients of ADV for 2009, 2010, and 2011 revealed that advertising expenditure on traditional media – TV, radio, magazines, and newspapers – significantly predicts *kids brand affinity score* for all three years (p's < .05). This pattern suggests that investment in traditional media advertising is associated with increased brand popularity among children.

Similarly, the coefficient of PPL significantly predicts *kids brand affinity score* for the same period – 2009, 2010, and 2011 – (p's < .05), suggesting that the more product placements, the higher the *kids brand affinity score*.

Table 3. OLS estimation results for *mothers' brand affinity scores*.

Year (t)	2009	2010	2011
CONST	422.400**	109.438**	4.323**
Log ADV$_t$	10.050**	4.460**	9.864**
PPL$_t$	1.061e$-$04**	0.021**	0.017**
B$_{Kids}$	0.382**	0.861**	0.877**
Model fit F (p-value)	12.73** (.000)*	11.41** (.000)*	17.76** (.000)*
Adjusted R^2	.536**	.609**	.717**

Note: $^{**}p < 0.01$; $^{*}p < 0.05$

In addition, the coefficients of *moms brand affinity score* for 2009, 2010, and 2011 were significant (p's < .05) suggesting that mothers' brand perceptions were positively related to children's brand preferences for all three years.

In sum, the regression analyses of *kids brand affinity score* revealed that both advertising expenditure on traditional media and product placements, along with *moms brand affinity score*, are positively related to children's brand preferences.

Mothers' brand affinity scores

As shown in Table 3, the positive coefficients of ADV for 2009, 2010, and 2011 again showed that advertising expenditures on traditional media – TV, radio, magazines, and newspapers – significantly predicted *moms brand affinity scores* for all three years (p's < .01). The results were similar to those from the *kids brand affinity score* analysis: increased advertising spending on traditional media heightened the popularity of the brands among mothers. However, we found that the effects, reflected in the coefficient sizes, are greater on the *moms brand affinity score* (10.05, 4.46, and 9.86 for 2009, 2010, and 2011, respectively; Table 3) than the effects on the *kids brand affinity score* (1.26, 5.45, and 7.41, for 2009, 2010, and 2011, respectively; Table 2). In other words, although ad spending on traditional media is effective for both audience groups, it may have stronger effects on mothers' brand perceptions than it has on children's brand perceptions.

Much in the same way as mothers' brand preferences influenced children's brand preferences in *moms brand affinity score*, *kids brand affinity score* significantly predicted *moms brand affinity score* (p's < .01). This suggests that children's brand preferences influence mothers' brand preferences. When comparing the magnitude of the coefficients of *kids brand affinity score* in Table 2 (i.e., *Moms → Kids*; .37, .60, and .69, for 2009, 2010, and 2011, respectively) to that of *moms brand affinity score* in Table 3 (i.e., *Kid →* *Moms*: .38, .86, and .87, for 2009, 2010, and 2011, respectively), children seem to have a greater influence on mothers' brand preferences and mothers seem to have less influence on children's brand preferences.

However, unlike *kids brand affinity score*, PPL did not significantly predict *moms brand affinity score* in 2009 and 2010, although it did in 2011. The reduced coefficients of PPL for *moms* (vs. *kid's*) *brand affinity score* suggest that product placements may sizably influence children's brand preferences, but may fail to influence or may have less influence on mothers' brand preferences. Yet the findings require cautious interpretation because we aggregated the sub-brand data at the highest brand level; for example, all M&Ms sub-brands such as M&Ms ice cream cakes, candies, and pretzels were aggregated to create a single M&Ms brand index in the current data set.

In sum, the regression analyses of *moms brand affinity score* revealed that advertising expenditures on traditional media may positively impact mothers' brand perceptions, but product placements may not cause such visible effects, or they may have weaker effects than they have on children's brand perceptions.

Top-five children's brands

After completing the statistical analysis, we selected the top-five children's brands and examined the data from a more qualitative perspective. Table 4 shows the children's top-five most-loved food brands and shows brand expenditures on various media – TV, radio, newspapers, magazines, Internet display, and outdoor advertising. (Table 5 shows advertising breakdown details.) Notably, most brands spent the largest portion of their

Table 4. Children's most-loved beverage and food brands from 2009 to 2011 (in thousands of dollars).

Brand	TV	Radio	Newspaper	Magazines	Internet	Others
McDonald's	277,597 (84.8%)	17.286 (0.5%)	4,287 (0.1%)	84,561 (2.6%)	99,388 (3.0%)	293,303 (9.0%)
Coca-Cola	386,513 (70.2%)	5,627 (1.0%)	30,067 (5.5%)	19,891 (3.6%)	21,669 (3.9%)	86,479 (15.7%)
Oreo	125,405 (73.4%)	2,812 (1.6%)	751 (0.4%)	37,561 (22.0%)	4,061 (2.4%)	265 (0.2%)
M&Ms	242,228 (68.7%)	523 (0.1%)	476 (0.1%)	97,105 (27.5%)	11,927 (3.4%)	543 (0.2%)
Pringles	21,021 (36.4%)	–	–	36,207 (62.6%)	495.9 (0.9%)	89.4 (0.2%)

Source: Kantar Media.

advertising budget on TV advertising, except for Pringles (36.4%). The other four brands — McDonald's (84.8%), Coca-Cola (70.2%), Oreo (73.4%), and M&Ms (68.7%) — allocated more than half of their total ad budget to TV. Overall, the top-five companies allocated more than 90% of their ad budget to TV and magazines. This pattern of spending may reflect advertisers' ongoing belief that traditional media play a key role in reaching the youth market.

On the other hand, product placement data give a somewhat different picture of advertising effects. As we reported in the regression analyses, investing in traditional advertising may have significant effects on both children and mothers, yet product placements may not yield the same effects — that is, certain product placements may significantly affect only children but not mothers. The product placement data for two brands — Coca-Cola and Oreo — illustrate this point. As shown in Table 6, Coca-Cola heavily placed its

Table 5. Advertising breakdown by media channels.

Data description	Channels
TV Advertising	Network TV
	Spot TV
	Spanish Language Network TV
	Cable TV
	Syndicated Media
Radio	National Radio
	Network Radio
	National Spot Radio
Newspaper	National Newspapers
	Hispanic Newspapers
Magazines	Magazines
	Sunday Magazines
	Local Magazines
	Hispanic Magazines
	B-to-B Magazines
Internet	Internet Display
Outdoor	Outdoor Advertising

Source: Kantar Media.

Table 6. Product placement for Coca-Cola.

2009		2010		2011	
Program (age)	Sec	Program (age)	Sec	Program (age)	Sec
American Idol	85570	American Idol	92402	American Idol	89005
Undercover Boss	1689	Biggest Loser	649	Biggest Loser	455
Jimmy Kimmel Live	811	Celebrity Apprentice	495	Jimmy Kimmel Live	308
Big Brother	551	True Beauty	317	Late Show	236
Tonight Show/Jay Leno	244	Big Brother	243	Undercover Boss	221

Source: Kantar Media.

products for long exposure durations in reality shows such as American Idol (89,005 seconds = 24.72 hours in 2011). As shown in Table 7, Oreo, another of the top-five most-loved brands by children and mothers, showed a similar trend.

To better understand whether children or mothers will be more likely to be exposed to product placements, we used Common Sense Media data (https://www.commonsensemedia.org) to examine who watches the shows. Table 8 lists the TV programs that appear in Tables 6 and 7 and provides the ratings for the programs by parents and children regarding appropriateness of viewer age and scores on educational values for violence, sex, language, positive role models, consumerism, drinking, taking drugs, and smoking. For 2009–2010, Coca-Cola and Oreo placed their products in TV programs specifically geared toward children and watched by children ages 8 to 14. The findings provide a complementary explanation for our primary findings from the regression analyses – why product placements have more effect on children and less effect on mothers for influencing brand preferences.

We recognize that there are some limitations we must acknowledge in drawing conclusions from the data in Tables 6–8 and providing an explanation about the differential effect of product placement on children versus mothers. Primarily, our brand affinity measures are for children aged 6–12, and based on the Common Sense Media data from Table 8, ratings for many of the programs containing food and beverage product placement are for older children (e.g., aged 8–14). Therefore, one could easily argue that such programs could easily be blocked by parents through v-chip or other TV program settings, such that children wouldn't be watching those programs. While we recognize this

Table 7. Product placement for Oreo.

2009		2010		2011	
Program (age)	Sec	Program (age)	Sec	Program (age)	Sec
Biggest Loser	189	Tonight Show/Jay Leno	487	NCIS: Los Angeles	195
Tonight Show/Jay Leno	128	Late Show	144	Million Dollar Money Drop	177
Jimmy Kimmel Live	111	Jimmy Kimmel Live	211	Tonight Show/Jay Leno	113
Celebrity Apprentice	97	Parenthood	85	30 Rock	34
Big Brother	84	America's Next Top MD	62	Big Bang Theory	24

Source: Kantar Media.

Table 8.   Rating for product placement programs — Coca-Cola and Oreo Cases.

Program	Parents rating (age)	Kids rating (age)	Violence	Sex	Language	Positive role models	Consumerism	Drinking drugs and smoking
American Idol	9	9	N/A	1/5	2/5	0/5	4/5	N/A
Big Bang Theory	12	11	1/5	3/5	3/5	1/5	1/5	3/5
Big Brother	11	11	0/5	4/5	3/5	0/5	3/5	3/5
Biggest Loser	10	9	1/5	N/A	3/5	2/5	3/5	N/A
Celebrity Apprentice	12	11	1/5	2/5	4/5	0/5	4/5	2/5
Jimmy Kimmel Live	13	13	1/5	3/5	3/5	0/5	4/5	2/5
Late Show	14	12	2/5	2/5	3/5	3/5	2/5	2/5
Million Dollar Money Drop	10	8	N/A	1/5	1/5	1/5	1/5	N/A
NCIS: Los Angeles	14	10	3/5	2/5	2/5	1/5	2/5	1/5
30 Rock	12	12	0/5	3/5	3/5	3/5	3/5	3/5
Tonight Show	14	8	1/5	3/5	2/5	1/5	1/5	1/5
Undercover Boss	9	8	N/A	0/5	2/5	2/5	2/5	N/A

Source: Common Sense Media.

limitation, we also acknowledge that without actual exposure data for this particular study, we really cannot conclusively say what programs the children watched.

This is similar to the problem we encounter with the analysis of our advertising data, where we focus on advertising expenditures, when in fact advertising exposure (i.e., what ads children actually see), as opposed to how many dollars are spent to advertise certain brands, might present a slightly different story. Researchers have pointed out that advertisers could comply with requirements to reduce ad expenditures of unhealthy products in programs with a large share of children in the audience, while still reaching a significant share of the children audience who actually are exposed to these ads while watching programs not falling within "child-directed advertising (Powell et al. 2013). The same can be said for product placement. We recognize that all studies have some limitations, and teasing out the differential effects of advertising expenditures versus exposure, and product placements actually seen despite program ratings, is one of the limitations we encounter in the type of research we conduct in looking at the effects on children.

Additional findings: advertising targeting minority segments

Substantial research has highlighted that minority children spend different amounts of time with media as compared with nonminority children. Using 2009 and 2010 data from Kantar Media, we analyzed the top-five-rated brands' media expenditure for Hispanic and African American segments. We filtered Hispanic-targeting advertising expenditure data on media such as Hispanic newspapers and magazines and Spanish language network TV, and African American-targeting expenditure data on media such as Black Enterprise, Ebony, and BET (Table 9).

McDonald's was the top-rated brand for children (Table 10), and M&Ms was the top-rated brand for mothers (Table 11). M&Ms ranked third with children, but both top-rated brands have considerably higher shares of media devoted to the two populations, expressed as a percentage of all media expenditure spent on the specified media targeting

Table 9.   Summary of Hispanic and African American Media.

Ethnicity	Media
Hispanic	Hispanic Newspapers
	Hispanic Magazines
	Spanish Language Network (SLN) TV
	Hispanic Business
	Washington Hispanic
African American	BET, BET.com, BET.com Video
	Black Enterprise, Blackenterprise.com
	Blackamericaweb.com
	Blackplanet.com
	Ebony, EbonyJET.com
	JET
	Essence

Source: Kantar Media.

Table 10.   African American/Hispanic media expenditure for children's average top-five most-loved beverage and food brands in 2009 and 2010.

Ranking	Brand	African American Media Share (%)	Hispanic Media Share (%)	Combined Media Share of African American and Hispanic (%)
1	McDonald's	7.0	10.4	17.4
2	Oreo	0.8	8.7	9.5
3	M&Ms	7.5	10.3	17.8
4	Doritos	1.2	0	1.2
5	Popsicle	0	11.8	11.8

Hispanic and African American populations. Also, the children's top-five most-loved food brands spend a higher percentage of total media expenditures on media targeting Hispanic and African American populations, as compared with the mothers' top-five most-loved food brands.

Table 11.   African American/Hispanic media expenditure for mother's average top-five most-loved beverage and food brands in 2009 and 2010.

Ranking	Brand	African American Media Share (%)	Hispanic Media Share (%)	Combined Media Share of African American and Hispanic (%)
1	M&Ms	7.5	10.3	17.8
2	Reese's	2.0	0	2.0
3	Subway	3.9	4.0	7.9
4	Coca-Cola	1.5	17.9	19.4
5	Oreo	0.8	8.7	9.5

Discussion

In this study, we conduct a statistical analysis to examine the relationship between advertising expenditure and perceptions of popular brands by children and mothers in the United States. We find that traditional advertising has a positive and significant relationship with brand affinity scores in both children and their mothers. We also examine the relation between children's and mothers' *brand affinity scores*, and find results very similar to advertising expenditure analysis. Mothers' *brand affinity scores* positively influenced children's *brand affinity scores* and children's *brand affinity scores* positively influenced mothers' *brand affinity scores*, respectively. Interestingly, we find that mothers' scores have greater effects on children's scores than children's scores have on mothers' scores.

Another interesting observation is that product placements seem to affect children but not to affect mothers. A closer examination of the children's top-ranked brands partially explains why: companies place their products heavily on TV shows that children mostly watch. Rather than mere exposure, however, a more fundamental perhaps complementary explanation is that children may be less able to detect persuasive intents of product placements, and thus more susceptible to product placement influences (Sykora 2003). In addition, the top-brand analysis further highlights that the higher ranked 'most-loved' brands, such as McDonald's and M&Ms, generally spend much more on traditional advertising, in particular on media targeting Hispanic and African American populations.

Further extending the position that children may be more susceptible to product placement influences in accounting for the greater effect on children compared to mothers, we can draw upon the Persuasion Knowledge Model (PKM) (Friestad and Wright 1995) as another explanation. Previous product placement research suggests that hybrid 'advertisements,' such as product placements, may prove more powerful than traditional advertisements if they are not perceived as persuasive messages (Russell 2002, Yoon, Choi, and Song 2011), especially when the viewer engages in less counterarguing as they do with traditional advertising messages, according to PKM. Using a PKM framework, previous research has suggested that certain viewers, such as subsistence consumers, low-literate consumers, etc., may be more vulnerable and susceptible to the persuasive influence when they are not aware of the persuasive intent of the message (Viswanathan et al. 2010; Williams, Qualls, and Ferguson 2007). It seems reasonable to include children in this vulnerable category, and hence they too might be more susceptible to the persuasive influence of hybrid 'advertisements' such as product placements. Therefore, this too might account to some degree for the differences we found in our research of the effect of product placement on mothers versus children.

We conducted this research to investigate relationships between food and beverage brands children and mothers 'most love' and advertising expenditures for those brands. However, the advertising expenditures in our model do not include promotions, public relations, or other integrated marketing communications (IMC) strategies.

A caveat is that the children's and mothers' affinity scores are imperfectly timed with the media expenditure and product placement data. For example, the affinity scores are collected over a three-to-four month period beginning in early summer and ending in early fall, but the media data are reported on a calendar-year basis.

Our analysis does not include creative appeals or consumer psychological variables, although those factors critically interact with expenditure levels to generate highly influential advertising that can create brand preferences (e.g., Kim, Han, and Yoon 2010; Yoon and Vargas 2010).

The relationships observed in this research are correlational, not necessarily causal. In relating advertising expenditures to consumer attitudes, it is difficult to show that advertising alone is responsible for attitudes. Other factors omitted in the analysis such as changing attitudes toward brands, personal preference shifts in brand choice, or creative appeals doubtlessly impact brand evaluations.

Also, because the relationships observed in this research are correlational, and not causal, we recognize that one could assume that advertising is driving consumption, or one could assume that consumption is driving advertising (e.g., when in some cases practitioners set up their advertising budgets based on the previous year's sales). That being the case, rather than making the case that higher advertising expenditures on certain brands are causing them to become more popular among children and moms, it is certainly possible to hypothesize that our analysis shows that the most popular brands in the marketplace are subsequently advertised at a higher rate due to the fact that more consumers possess a more positive attitude towards these brands. However, this argument is tantamount to the proverbial 'chicken and egg' dilemma of what comes first (i.e., advertising or demand, and this research is not designed to address that question).

It should be noted that this question is not restricted to just issues related to advertising and children. The same applies to other segments; researchers have identified a similar dilemma when examining the differential effects of advertising and target marketing of fast food to racial/ethnic minority consumer segments. In one study, the researchers concluded that the data did not allow for precise causal ordering between demand by African Americans for a particular type of fast food and its prevalence in a given setting that may be more reflective of cultural eating practices and a genuine preference for certain types of foods compared to other types of foods (Williams et al. 2012). In the present study dealing with children, while it may be possible to explore in greater detail the causal order of advertising versus demand, this would require additional data over more years and additional analyses looking at lagged effect models, we will have to pursue that in future research endeavors.

Although we seek to offer as much insight as possible, the advertising expenditure data we used in this analysis fail to capture other types of promotion methods such as toys, cartoons, movies, and contests. To our best knowledge, information is unavailable regarding those types of marketing expenditures that we could match with brands for the period examined.

Further research is needed to provide a more in-depth understanding of the relationship of advertising/promotion to the formation of attitudes and perceptions in young people. One way to extend the current work would be to examine how various marketing budget allocation influence brand perception in different domains of social marketing. For example, future research might explorer how advertising budget correlates with brand perception in advertising that encourages environmentally responsible consumption (Baek, Yoon, and Kim 2015; Yoon, Kim, and Baek 2015) or physical activities (McKay-Nesbitt and Yoon 2015). Other social science approaches might provide additional insight into the role of advertising and promotion on the formation of brand attitudes and perceptions.

Furthermore, in terms of future research, the Kantar advertising media expenditure data fail to consider expenditures targeted toward children, such as specific expenditures reported by the FTC (2012). Instead the data include all media expenditures for the specified brands, whether adult-oriented or child-oriented. Further research is needed to provide a more in-depth understanding of the relationship of advertising/promotion to the formation of attitudes and perceptions of preferred brands in young people. For example, using data revealing exposure to children rather than data revealing media expenditure for each 'most-loved' brand might be a next step in advancing our understanding of the relationship between advertising and brand attraction among children.

Disclosure statement

No potential conflict of interest was reported by the authors.

Funding

The authors wish to acknowledge partial funding for this research from the University of Minnesota, Robert Wood Johnson Foundation Healthy Eating Research Program, Grant #3001-11176-00017177.

References

Aaker, D.A., J.M. Carman, and R. Jacobson. 1982. Modeling advertising-sales relationships involving feedback: a time series analysis of six cereal brands. *Journal of Marketing Research* 19 (February): 116–25.

Baek, T., S. Yoon, and S. Kim. 2015. When assertive language enhances environmental advertising persuasion: the moderating role of effort investment. *International Journal of Advertising* 34, no. 1: 135–57.

Barry, T.E. and D.J. Howard. 1990. A review and critique of the hierarchy of effects in advertising. *International Journal of Advertising* 9, no. 2: 121–35.

Biro, F.M. and M. Wien. 2010. Childhood obesity and adult morbidities. *American Journal of Clinical Nutrition* 91, no. 5: 1499–505.

Charry, K.M. 2014. Product placement and the promotion of healthy food to pre-adolescents. When popular TV series make carrots look cool. *International Journal of Advertising* 33, no. 3: 599–616.

Choi, Y., S. Yoon, and H.P. Lacey. 2013. Online game characters' influence on brand trust: self-disclosure, group membership, and product type. *Journal of Business Research*, 66, no. 8: 996–1013.

Dietz, W.H. and S.L. Gortmaker. 1985. Do we fatten our children at the television set? Obesity and television viewing in children and adolescents. *Pediatrics* 75, no. 5: 807–12.

Duffy, M.H. 1996. An econometric study of advertising and cigarette demand in the United Kingdom. *International Journal of Advertising* 15, no. 3: 262–84.

Federal Trade Commission. 2012. *A review of food marketing to children and adolescents: Follow-up reports*. Washington, DC: Federal Trade Commission.

Flegal, K.M., M.D. Carroll, C.L. Ogden, and L.R. Curtin. 2010. Prevalence and trends in obesity among US adults, 1999–2008. *The Journal of the American Medical Association* 303: 235–41.

Flora, J.A., C. Schooler, and R.M. Pierson. 1997. Effective health promotion among communities of color: the potential of social marketing. In *Social marketing: Theoretical and practical perspectives*, ed. M. E. Goldberg, M. Fishbein, and S. E. Middlestadt. Mahwah (NJ): Lawrence Erlbaum Associates, Inc.

Freedman, D.S., L.K. Khan, M.K. Serdula, C.L. Ogden, and W.H. Dietz. 2006. Racial and ethnic differences in secular trends for childhood BMI, weight, and height. *Obesity* 14, no. 2: 301–8.

Friestad, M. and P. Wright. 1995. The persuasion knowledge model: how people cope with persuasion attempts. *Journal of Consumer Research* 22 (June): 62–74.

Hancox, R.J., B. Milne, and R. Poulton. 2004. Association between child and adolescent television viewing and adult health: a longitudinal birth cohort study. *The Lancet* 364, no. 9430: 257–62.

Hitchings, E. and P.J. Moynihan. 1998. The relationship between television food advertisements recalled and actual foods consumed by children. *Journal of Human Nutrition and Dietetics* 11: 511–7.

Johnson, L.W. 1985. Alternative econometric estimates of the effect of advertising on the demand for alcoholic beverages in the United Kingdom. *International Journal of Advertising* 4, no. 1: 19–25.

Kim, B., S. Han, and S. Yoon. 2010. Advertising creativity in Korea: scale development and validation. *Journal of Advertising* 50, no. 2: 93–108.

Kumanyika, S. S.A. Grier, K. Lancaster, and V. Lassiter. 2011. *Impact of sugar-sweetened beverage consumption on Black American's health.* Philadelphia. PA: African American Collaborative Obesity Research Network.

Kunkel, B.L., J.C. Wilcox, P.S. Edward, S. Linn, and P. Dowrick. 2004. *Report of the APA task force on advertising and children.* Washington (DC): American Psychological Association.

Kwoka, J.E. 1992. Market segmentation by price-quality schedules: some evidence from automobiles. *Journal of Business* 65: 615–28.

Lavidge, R. and G.A. Steiner. 1961. A model for predictive measurements of advertising effectiveness. *Journal of Marketing* 25, no. 6: 59–62.

Livingstone, S. and E.J. Helsper. 2006. Does advertising literacy mediate the effects of advertising on children? A critical examination of two linked research literatures in relation to obesity and food choice. *Journal of Communication* 56, no. 3: 560–84.

Macklin, C. 1994. The effects of an advertising retrieval cue on young children's memory and brand evaluations. *Psychology and Marketing* 11, no. 3: 291–311.

McKay-Nesbitt, J. and S. Yoon. 2015. Social marketing communication messages: how congruence between source and content influences physical activity attitudes. *Journal of Social Marketing* 5, no. 1: 40–55.

Nairn, A. and C. Fine. 2008. Who's messing with my mind? The implications of dual process models for the ethics of advertising to children. *International Journal of Advertising* 27, no. 3: 440–70.

Ogden, C.L., K.M. Flegal, M.D. Carroll, and C.L. Johnson. 2002. Prevalence and trends in overweight among US children and adolescents, 1999–2000. *JAMA* 288, 1728–32.

Ogden, C.L., M.D. Carroll, L.R. Curtin, M.M. Lamb, and K.M. Flegal. 2010. Prevalence of high body mass index in US children and adolescents, 2007–2008.*The Journal of the American Medical Association* 303: 242–9.

Peles, Y. C. 1971. Rates of amortization of advertising expenditures. *Journal of Political Economy* 79: 1032–58.

Pine, J.K. and A. Nash. 2002. Dear Santa: the effects of television advertising on young children. *International Journal of Behavioral Development* 26, no. 6: 529–39.

Pollay, R.A., S. Siddarth, and M. Siegel. 1996. The last straw? Cigarette advertising and realized market shares among youth and adults 1979–1993. *Journal of Marketing.* 60: 1–16.

Powell, L.M., R.M. Schermbeck, G. Szczypka, and F.J. Chaloupka. 2013. Children's exposure to food and beverage advertising on television: tracking calories and nutritional content by company membership in self-regulation. In *Advances in communication research to reduce childhood obesity,* ed. J. D. Williams, K. E. Pasch, and Collins, 179–95. New York: Springer.

Rifon, N.J., E.T. Quilliam, H. Paek, L.J. Weatherspoon, S. Kim, and K.C. Smreker. 2014. Age-dependent effects of food advergame brand integration and interactivity. *International Journal of Advertising* 33, no. 3: 475–508.

Roedder, J.D. 2008. Stages of consumer socialization: the development of consumer knowledge, skills, and values from childhood to adolescent. In *Handbook of consumer psychology,* ed. C. P. Haugtvdt, P. M. Herr, and F. R. Kardes, 221–46. New York: Taylor & Francis Group, LLC.

Russell, C.A. 1998. Toward a framework of product placement: theoretical propositions. In *Advances in consumer research.* Vol. 25, ed. Joseph W. Alba and J. Wesley Hutchinson, , 357–62. Provo, UT: Association for Consumer Research.

Russell, C.A. 2002. Investigating the effectiveness of product placements in television shows: the role of modality and plot connection congruence on brand memory and attitude. *Journal of Consumer Research* 29, no. 3: 306–18.

Smarty Pants, LLC. 2012. Top 100 kids' most loved brands. http://184.168.85.192/index.php/about-the-family-business-entry/C8 (accessed June 14, 2011).

Starek, R.B. 1997. *The ABCs at the FTC: Marketing and advertising to children.* US FTC.

Stutts, M.A. and G.G. Hunnicutt. 1987. Can young children understand disclaimers in television commercials? *Journal of Advertising* 16 (Spring): 41–6.

Sutherland, L.A., T Mackenzie, L.A. Purvis, and M. Dalton. 2015. Prevalence of food and beverage brands in movies: 1996–2005. *Pediatrics* 125, no. 3: 468–74.

Sykora, A. 2003. *Our approach. Presentation on behalf of Coca Cola New Zealand to Childhood Obesity Symposium.* 2003, 2 September. Albany, New Zealand: Massey University.

Viswanathan, M., C. Torelli, S. Yoon, and H. Riemer. 2010. 'Fish out of water': understanding decision making and coping strategies as second language consumers through a situational literacy perspective. *Journal of Consumer Marketing* 27, no. 6: 524–33.

Wang, Y. and M.A. Beydoun. 2007. The obesity epidemic in the United States – gender, age, socioeconomic, racial/ethnic, and geographic characteristics: a systematic review and meta-regression analysis. *Epidemiologic Reviews* 29: 6–28.

Wilcox, G.B. 2001. Beer brand advertising and market share in the United States: 1975 to 1998. *International Journal of Advertising* 20, no. 2: 49–168.

Wilcox, G.B., K.K. Kim, and H.M. Schulz. 2012. Liquor advertising and consumption in the United States: 1971–2008. *International Journal of Advertising* 31, no. 4 8: 819–34.

Williams, J.D., D. Crockett, R.L. Harrison, and K.D. Thomas. 2012. The role of food culture and marketing activity in health disparities. *Preventive Medicine* 55, no. 5: 382–6.

Williams, J.D. and S.K. Kumanyika. 2002. Is social marketing an effective tool to reduce health disparities? *Social Marketing Quarterly* 8: 14–31.

Williams, J.D., W.J. Qualls, and N. Ferguson. 2007. Potential vulnerabilities of U.S. subsistence consumers to persuasive marketing communication. In *Product and market development for subsistence marketplaces: Consumption and entrepreneurship beyond literacy and resource barriers*, ed. J. Rosa and M. Viswanathan, 87–100. London, UK: Elsevier.

Yoo, C.Y., K. Kim, and P.A. Stout. 2004. Assessing the effects of animation in online banner advertising: hierarchy of effects model. *Journal of Interactive Advertising* 4, no. 2: 49–60.

Yoon, S., Y. Choi, and S. Song. 2011. When intrusive can be likable: product placement effects on multitasking consumers. *Journal of Advertising* 40, no. 2: 63–75.

Yoon, S., S. Kim, and T. Baek. 2015. Effort investment in persuasiveness: a comparative study of environmental advertising in the United States and Korea. *International Journal of Advertising*. doi: 10.1080/02650487.2015.1061963

Yoon, S. and P. T. Vargas. 2010. Feeling happier when paying more: dysfunctional counterfactual thinking in consumer affect. *Psychology & Marketing* 27, no. 12: 1075–100.

Do bans on illuminated on-premise signs matter? Balancing environmental impact with the impact on businesses

Charles R. Taylor[a] and Matthew E. Sarkees[b]

[a]Department of Marketing, Villanova School of Business, Villanova University, Villanova, USA;
[b]Department of Marketing, Haub School of Business, St. Joseph's University, Philadelphia, USA

Recent years have seen some US municipalities implementing restrictions on lighted on-premise signs, often based on environmental arguments. At the same time, sign companies and sign users argue that restrictions are harmful to businesses. To date there has not been any research on the degree to which restrictions on illuminated signs are harmful to businesses. To this end, this study reports the results of a nationally representative sample of on-premise sign users which explores the degree to which sign users: (1) rely on the signs to help them perform key marketing functions; and (2) report that these signs impact their bottom line. Findings indicate that respondents strongly agree that lighted on-premise signs perform key marketing functions for them and a majority of respondents believe that restrictions on lighting harm their profitability.

Introduction

In recent years, some United States (US) municipalities have implemented restrictions on the illumination of on-premise signs. Those in favor of such restrictions do not view the lighting of on-premise signs as playing any necessary role (e.g., International Dark-Sky Association 2014; Flagstaff Dark Skies 2014). Critics of illuminated signs also argue that they are aesthetically displeasing, waste energy, and do not provide benefits to any stake-holder group. Some critics have blamed on-premise signs for light pollution, defined as 'light that is either too bright for its intended purpose' or 'that shines where it is not needed or wanted' (RASC 2003; c.f., Garvey 2005, 8). While available evidence docu-ments that the vast majority of on-premise signs do not meet photometric levels associ-ated with light pollution (e.g., Garvey 2005), controversy still remains. Some examples of restrictions on lighting of signs include the following:

- Pima County, Arizona, mandates a shut-off time of 10:00 pm unless the business remains open. If the business remains open after 10:00 pm, illumination must be turned off between closing time and sunrise.
- Hilton Head, South Carolina, bans all internally illuminated signs.
- Winston Salem, North Carolina, mandates that illuminated signs shall be so shielded so as not to cast direct light onto any residential district.

- Arlington County, Virginia, provides lighting standards for illumination of traditional signage.
- Mendham Borough, New Jersey, prohibits neon signs.

Such restrictions have been growing in recent years, and, in many cases, 'grandfather clauses' in local codes that exempt existing (but not new) businesses from signage regulations may expand the impact exponentially for communities. In contrast, sign companies argue that illumination of signage plays an important role in allowing companies to communicate information about their business and ultimately draw interested consumers into their stores.

Despite these competing public policy perspectives, there has been no research on the impact of restrictions on illuminated signage for businesses that employ these marketing techniques. This is unfortunate, as it has been documented by prior research that many businesses use on-premise signs to perform important marketing functions (Taylor, Claus, and Claus 2005; Taylor, Sarkees, and Bang 2012). Moreover, an increasingly wide variety of issues related to the environment have been studied recently (e.g., Hartmann et al. 2014; Baek, Yoon, and Kim 2015; Chang, Zhang, and Xie 2015). Thus, it is particularly important to examine the degree to which illumination of on-premise signs impacts businesses subject to such regulation. If illumination of on-premise signs is found to have a negative impact on businesses, this is a factor that should be weighed in public policy debates. On the other hand, if academic research demonstrates that lighted, on-premise signs do not negatively impact businesses, such findings would also be relevant to policy-makers.

To provide some insight into this question, we draw a nationally representative sample of on-premise sign users. In conducting the analysis, we place emphasis on the impact of these restrictions on small businesses versus larger businesses. Almost half of the US gross domestic product is generated from small businesses (U.S. Small Business Administration 2012). Second, approximately half of all Americans working in the private sector are employees of small businesses (U.S. Small Business Administration 2009). Third, small businesses also contribute to the tax base of the local community in which they operate. The failure rates of these types of business are very high, making visibility an even higher priority. Restrictions may cause damage not only to thousands of businesses but also to communities across the US. Interestingly, the signage issue for small businesses may be a global one. For example, in the European Union, most non-financial businesses are small or mid-size and a staggering two out of every three employees are employed by these organizations (European Commission 2014).

Through a US survey of a nationally representative sample of on-premise sign users, we explore how illuminated signage impacts business. Specifically, the study examines the degree to which lighted on-premise signs: (1) help businesses perform four key marketing functions; and (2) impact the financial performance of the businesses that use them. In addition, the study explores whether factors such as size of business, number of years in business, type of business, and geographic location play a role in the degree to which companies hold the above beliefs. In particular, we find that smaller businesses face a larger sales loss if illuminated on-premise signs are subject to regulation. For communities that rely on businesses to draw consumers and to provide government with tax revenue, these restrictions become an important policy issue.

Conceptual background and hypotheses

Businesses invest in on-premise signs because of the communication role they play. Prior research indicates that on-premise signs play four key marketing functions: (1)

communicating the location of the business; (2) reinforcing advertisements and other marketing variables as part of integrated marketing communications (IMC); (3) enhancing the image of the store or business; and (4) branding the site. As propositions pertaining to these variables will be put forward, they will be discussed in more detail below. First, however, the rationale for how restrictions on illumination could inhibit the effectiveness of on-premise signs is discussed.

Extant literature cites several aspects of signage that contribute to on-premise signs' general effectiveness (U.S. Small Business Administration 2003). A sign's ability to be read is a fundamental prerequisite to success. In addition to size and proper placement, two key issues to a sign's effectiveness are visual conspicuity and its level of visibility. Visibility refers to the physical attributes of a sign that allow for its detection at a given distance. Visual conspicuity (hereafter, conspicuity) refers to the capacity of a sign to stand out or be distinguishable from its surroundings and thus be readily discovered by the eye (Taylor, Claus, and Claus 2005). As observed by Taylor, Claus, and Claus (2005, 8.2):

> One way to think of conspicuity, as opposed to visibility, legibility, or readability, is that the term relates to a sign's surroundings. A sign in isolation may meet all the criteria for visibility (or detectability at some distance), legibility (letters and/or graphics can be easily differentiated), and readability, (the legend in totality conveys a meaningful or understandable message to the viewer). However, when that sign is placed in the urban environment where it competes with other signs, utility poles, traffic control devices, bus shelters, and right of way landscaping, it can become essentially invisible.

A conspicuous sign is one that stands out from its visual surroundings and has a high probability of being noticed. If the sign does not stand out from its surroundings, it is much less likely to get noticed. Under certain weather conditions and during dark hours of the day, illumination enhances both the visibility and conspicuity of on-premise signs. Thus, we would expect that such restrictions would have the potential to inhibit the ability of on-premise signs to perform key marketing functions.

Lighting affects both the visibility and conspicuity of signage, particularly at night or under bad weather conditions. As a result, the on-premise sign industry needs to adapt to several illumination needs, including accurate color rendering, readability, energy efficiency, cost, and local weather conditions (see Taylor, Claus, and Claus 2005). Moreover, visibility and conspicuity, as well as the sign's readability, can be affected by lighting, in some instances, even under relatively good daytime weather conditions. As a result, it is plausible to believe that restrictions on illumination inhibit a sign's ability to fully perform marketing functions. In the following sections, we develop hypotheses that predict that lighted on-premise sign users will report that restrictions harm the ability of the sign to generate sales based on prior literature on the marketing functions of signage. Additionally, we hypothesize that based on consumer information processing theory, the reported effects of the ability of signage to inhibit marketing functions and sales will be perceived to be higher by companies who actually face these restrictions. Thus, for each of the marketing functions of signs and their sales impact we propose both a proposition pertaining to overall impact and a hypothesis based on responses of businesses that face regulation versus those who do not.

Communicating the location of the business

A business' on-premise sign normally plays a critical role in identifying where the business is located. For new businesses or those being patronized by a customer for the first time, the sign plays a key role both in wayfinding and in 'getting the word out' that the business exists at a particular location. Signage also plays an important wayfinding role for established businesses, both in terms of new customers finding the business and triggering associations in the minds of existing customers. For example, a customer that sees the Starbucks logo or the McDonald's arches instinctively knows that a location is near. The visual triggers a mental association with the brand (Keller 2005). Equally important, a potential customer, at the very least knows that seeing these signs means food and beverages are available at these locations and can choose to stop on impulse or commit the location to memory for possible future visits. For some businesses, especially those that rely on impulse purchases, or serve immediate needs, the sign may often directly lead to a customer purchase. According to the U.S. Small Business Administration, impulse stops account for 15%–45% of sales, depending on the type of business (c.f., U.S. Small Business Administration 2003).

Sign visibility and conspicuity closely relate to the ability to know where the store is (Berman and Evans 2007; Dunne and Lusch 1993). Thus, restrictions on illumination, especially during evening hours or poor weather conditions, would harm signage's identification function. As a result, we propose that on-premise sign owners will report that their illuminated on-premise sign is helpful to them in communicating the location of the business:

Proposition 1: Illuminated on-premise signs enhance a company's ability to communicate the location of the business.

To draw hypotheses based on level of government regulations on illuminated signage on firms, we draw on consumer perception theory. For most communications objectives, including communicating the location of the business, companies rely on delivering a consistent message. One of the reasons why variations in the messaging may occur is due to restrictions on the communications. Restrictions create situations where the consumers may have trouble receiving or processing the information they are receiving from the firm (Ahluwalia, Burnkrant, and Unnava 2000). In this context, a consumer receives messages from a firm and attempts to make a decision. The decision could be to enter a store, purchase a product, contact the company, or disregard the message all together, among other options. Thus, clear communications, whether visually or verbally, from a firm are important in consumer information processing both in terms of the customer receiving the message and being able to process the message in the intended manner. In the case of communicating the location of the business, the signage can either lead to a new customer receiving a message for the first time or reinforcing previously received information on the location of the business (including prior exposure to the sign). As companies will have heighted awareness of the interference with messages being received in an environment characterized by restrictions, we hypothesize:

H1: Businesses who face restrictions on illuminated on-premise signs are more likely to believe that those signs enhance the ability to communicate the location of the business than those that face no restrictions.

Reinforcing advertisements and other marketing variables as part of integrated marketing communications (IMC)

It is well accepted by promotion theorists that marketers must carefully communicate a consistent message to consumers because consumer perceptions of a company or brand are a synthesis of messages received from the company, as well as every point of contact with the business (Belch and Belch 2007; Kerr et al. 2008; Taylor 2010). Inconsistent or incongruent messaging can confuse the consumer and harm brand equity (Duncan 2005; Garretson and Burton 2005). Every point of contact a company should be coordinated (e.g., Duncan 2005; Hackley and Kelly 2010; Kliatchko and Schultz 2014). Belch and Belch (2004) note the way a consumer perceives a company is the result of a synthesis of the bundle of messages they receive and the points of contact they have with the business. Because it clearly involves a point of contact with the consumer, exposure to on-premise signage must be considered part of IMC (Taylor, Sarkees, and Bang 2012). If lighting restrictions prevent a business from communicating and displaying its message, such as an identifiable logo or character (e.g., Target, Wendy's), other marketing communications and associations that have built up from those communications are not reinforced if the sign cannot be seen. Thus:

Proposition 2: Businesses who face restrictions on illuminated on-premise signs report a higher level of agreement with the statement that illuminated signage enhances a company's ability to reinforce advertisements and other marketing variables as part of integrated marketing communications.

Retailers employ signs on their premises to help reinforce other marketing communications. Customers (or potential customers) may have received a flyer in the mail, seen the company's logo on a website or television advertisement, or received an email promotion. The signage reinforces the messaging the customer has received. If there are restrictions on the signage, then customers' expectations are not reinforced, causing additional mental process to connect previous communications to this incident at the location. This can potentially cause harm to the business. As with communicating the location of the business, we predict that those businesses actually facing restrictions will have heightened awareness of these potential impacts and, thus, propose the following:

H2: Businesses that face restrictions on illuminated on-premise signs are more likely to believe that those signs reinforce the advertising and integrated marketing communications of the business than those that face no restrictions.

Branding the site

Branding, and in particular, brand equity or the value of a brand is becoming more paramount in today's business environment. A brand equity mindset is reinforced by academic studies (e.g., Mizik 2014) as well as by industry assessments (e.g., Interbrand, Forbes). The on-premise sign contributes to brand equity through the unique capability to brand the business' physical site (Taylor, Claus, and Claus 2005). Moreover, the visual appearance of the sign, including trademarks, can help both to enhance recall of the business and to build positive associations with the brand (Kopp and Langenderfer 2014). For example, a customer sees a Nordstrom sign or that of the local restaurant, and instantly feels a connection, and may commit its location to memory. The expectation of a good customer experience, and thus a stronger relationship, becomes evident at the sight of the sign. It may even create an emotional desire in the consumer to stop and transact business. For example, the lighted sign at a favorite restaurant may trigger the desire to eat, thus financially benefitting the business while satisfying the customer.

A key point is that the on-premise sign can help to brand the site even when the store is closed. Even though a business may be closed, the illuminated sign can create top-of-mind awareness, which means the consumer may not need the product or service at that time, but they will remember the location for a subsequent time when they might. Thus, at night, an illuminated sign can still provide value to the business via the exposure it provides to consumers. A sign that is not visible or cannot be read cannot help brand the site, whether the business is open or not, and, again, companies facing restrictions are likely to have heightened awareness of this. Thus:

Proposition 3: Businesses that face restrictions on illuminated on-premise signs report a higher level of agreement with the statement that illuminated signage enhances a company's ability to brand its site.

H3: Businesses that face restrictions on illuminated on-premise signs are more likely to believe that those signs help to brand the site location than those that face no restrictions.

Enhancing the image of the store or business

Retailing experts have long emphasized the importance of brick-and-mortar stores creating a clear store image in order to be successful (Golden, Albaum, and Zimmer 1987; Pessemeir 1980). Signage can play a key role in building and reinforcing store image, because it both attracts attention and can give clear signals about the store's image and atmosphere (Berman and Evans 2007). For example, some stores seek prestige via expensive signage, coupled with an elegant storefront. Old Navy returned to its original logo in order to be consistent with the family-oriented environment inside its stores (Fredrix 2010). The on-premise sign should consistently demonstrate the store's image. Lighting an on-premise sign allows this image to be communicated at all hours.

If a sign is not illuminated and cannot be seen, or is not easily visible at certain hours, its effectiveness in building store image will be either reduced or eliminated altogether. Again, we also predict that businesses that actually face these restrictions will have heightened attention to these issues. Thus:

Proposition 4: Businesses that face restrictions on illuminated on-premise signs report a higher level of agreement with the statement that illuminated signage enhances a company's ability to enhance the image of the store or business.

H4: Businesses that face restrictions on illuminated on-premise signs are more likely to believe that those signs enhance the image of the store than those that face no restrictions.

Sales impact of on-premise signs

Many academic and practitioner studies from various perspectives (for the most part, legal) suggest businesses would lose sales if on-premise signs were altered, restricted, or removed (e.g., Taylor, Claus, and Claus 2005). Additionally, Taylor, Sarkees, and Bang (2012) found that 85% of a representative US sample of on-premise sign users would lose sales if they did not have an on-premise sign. Additionally, the average reported loss of sales across the sample was 34.5%.

The on-premise-sign debate includes arguments that without adequate signage customers will not know a business' location or enter the store, and thus sales will suffer. Related marketing studies support this theory. An on-premise sign, as a 'feature' notification method, may drive customer foot traffic and sales (e.g., Lohse 1997; Zhang, Wedel, and Pieters 2009). This suggests a business could lose first-time customers and potentially longer term revenue without an on-premise sign. Additionally, limiting the on-premise sign's ability to perform marketing functions hinders longer term consumer perceptions, such as branding the site, enhancing image, and reinforcing other marketing communications. Similarly, limits on lighting would harm the sign's ability to perform all of these functions and, hence, these restrictions would negatively impact sales. We also believe that companies facing restrictions will be more aware of this potential impact. Thus:

Proposition 5: Companies will report that banning the use of illuminated on-premise signage would reduce their sales.

Methodology

After the researchers developed a survey and sampling plan, a large, independent marketing research firm carried out mailing. The sample was drawn from the customer lists of two of the largest US sign companies, generally addressed to the owner of the business or the top marketing executive in the company. The national coverage of these companies ensures the sample's national representation of on-premise sign users. A total of 1053 records were available. After eliminating duplicates, a total of 750 companies were randomly selected to receive the mailing.

Respondents were sent a packet containing a cover letter, the survey itself, and a postage paid return envelope. A $10 incentive was also included. Three weeks after the initial mailing, reminder postcards were sent to those who had not yet responded. Surveys returned as 'undeliverable' were also excluded from this reminder mailing. The survey contained a number of questions focused on how businesses make use of signs. We also asked these executives about existing restrictions on signage as well their perceptions of regulations. Finally, we asked respondents about the competitive environment in which they operate and various firm demographics. Key survey questions are shown in the Appendix.

In total, 333 surveys were returned, with 48 surveys being undeliverable (35 of these were returned due to 'no mail receptacle' which typically means that the business receives its mail at a PO box independent of a store address), for a response rate of 47.4%. Of the 333 returned surveys, 8 did not contain enough information to be useable, leaving 325 usable returns.

Results and discussion

Profile of respondents and their use of signage

The respondents represent companies that have been in business for a wide range of years (see Table 1). As shown in Table 2, most are small businesses. Table 3 shows that a wide variety of types of businesses were included.

Seventy-three percent of the businesses had 10 or fewer employees, and 86% of the sample had 25 or fewer employees. This reflects that a large majority of US businesses are small business (Office of Advocacy of U.S. Small Business Administration 2007; U.S. Small Business Administration 2009).

Respondents report having an average of 1.71 illuminated on-premise signs at their place of business. The mean number of hours the business is open per day is 10.8 hours.

Table 1. Number of years in business.

Years in business	Percentage of sample
0–5 years	33%
6–25 years	32%
More than 25 years	32%

Table 2.   Number of employees.

Number of employees	Percentage of sample
10 or fewer	74%
11–25	13%
26–50	3%
51–100	2%
101–250	1%
250 or more	7%

The average number of hours per day the sign is illuminated is 13.9 hours, more than 3 hours longer. A large majority of the businesses (81%) report keeping the sign illuminated after business hours, and 30% of the companies report leaving their sign on all the time. Sixty percent indicate they turn their illuminated sign on during the day. An overwhelming proportion (91%) report they have images, such as a logo, drawing, or other artwork, on their lighted on-premise sign. In terms of types of restrictions they faced on their illuminated signs, 3% of respondents reported restrictions on hours of illumination, while 8% indicated they faced restrictions on allowable brightness level and 24% reported restrictions on the type of illuminated sign permitted.

Communicating location

Proposition 1 suggested that respondents would agree that lighted on-premise signs play a key role in communicating the location of the businesses. As shown in Table 4, results support this proposition, with the mean response being 6.17 as measured on a 7-point Likert type scale (anchored by 1 = strongly disagree and 7 = strongly agree). Similarly, when asked specifically about the performance of illuminated signage during night hours the mean was 6.19.

Table 3.   Type of business.

Type of business	Percentage of sample
Restaurant (table or fast food)	18.9%
Retail (general/grocery/apparel)	17.9%
Insurance	14.2%
Automotive or auto repair	14.2%
Consumer services	8.0%
Non-profit	4.2%
Hotel/motel	2.6%
Business services	2.2%
Gas station/mini-mart	1.6%
Entertainment	1.3%
Consulting	1.3%
Real estate	1.0%
Other	8.9%

Table 4.   Marketing functions performed by illuminated, on-premise signs.

Marketing function	Overall agreement	Restricted businesses	Unrestricted businesses	Difference between groups
Communicates business location	6.17	6.45	5.91	$p < .01$
Reinforces advertising	5.97	6.16	5.92	$p < .10$
Brands the location	6.27	6.55	6.25	$p < .05$
Enhances the store image	6.27	6.48	6.29	$p < .10$

Note: Measurements taken on using a 1−7 scale with '1' as strongly disagree and '7' as strongly agree.

Regarding Hypothesis 1, those facing restrictions were significantly more likely to believe in the importance of the locational capabilities of on-premise signage than those without restrictions ($M = 6.45$ versus $M = 5.91$, $p < .01$). Interestingly, businesses with restrictions had 1.4 times more illuminated, on-premise signs than those without restrictions. It may be that in restricted environments, more signs are a way for those businesses to enhance locational capabilities. In any event, it is clear that businesses that use lighted on-premise signs believe that they play an important role in helping them communicate the location of the businesses.

Reinforcing integrated marketing communications

As shown in Table 4, respondents agree that illuminated on-premise signs help reinforce advertising as part of IMC, with the mean score being 5.90. When asked specifically about this reinforcement function during night hours, the level of agreement was even higher, at 6.06. Thus, Proposition 2 is supported. Hypothesis 2 is partially supported. Those businesses facing restrictions were marginally more likely to believe in the importance of illuminated, on-premise signage as reinforcing IMC than those without restrictions ($M = 6.16$ versus $M = 5.92, p < .10$).

Branding the site/location

Proposition 3 suggested that companies would report that illuminated on-premise signs help the business to brand the site. As shown in Tables 4 and 5, this proposition is strongly supported, with the mean for overall agreement at 6.27 and the night hours mean at 6.21. Hypothesis 3 is also supported, as there was a significant difference between those businesses that are subject to restrictions on their illuminated on-premise sign versus those that are not ($M = 6.55$ versus 6.24; $p < .05$). Thus, results support the notion that users of illuminated signs believe that they play a key role in branding the site.

Table 5.   Marketing functions performed by illuminated, on-premise signs during night hours.

Marketing function	Overall agreement
Communicates business location	6.19
Reinforces advertising	6.06
Brands the location	6.14
Enhances the store image	6.21

Note: Measurements taken on using a 1−7 scale with '1' as strongly disagree and '7' as strongly agree.

Enhances store/business image

With means of 6.27 (overall) and 6.17 for night hours, Proposition 4 is supported. This support is indicative of firms believing that illuminated on-premise signs help to enhance the image of the store or business. Hypothesis 4 is partially supported as there was a marginally significant difference between those businesses that are subject to restrictions on their illuminated on-premise sign versus those that are not related to enhancing store image ($M = 6.48$ versus 6.29; $p < .10$).

Financial impact

Results indicate that lighted on-premise signs substantially impact the financial status of many businesses. A sizeable majority of respondents (58%) indicated they would lose sales if government regulations prevented their signs from being lit at any hour. For those who reported a sales loss, the average estimate was 21%. For the overall sample, including those businesses not reporting a loss, the average estimated loss of sales exceeded 10%. Similar to the results for sales, 58% of businesses reported they would lose customers, given such a restriction, with a decline of 18% for those indicating a loss and a 9.4% decline for the overall sample.

Impact of control variables

Analyses by years of experience

As shown in Table 6, businesses at all levels of experience strongly agree that lighted on-premise signs play key marketing functions. No statistically significant differences exist for any of the five variables.

However, newer businesses that reported a loss of sales reported significantly higher losses than older businesses ($F(2,129) = 3.47, p = .05$). Businesses less than 5 years old reported an average estimated loss of 26.6% with no illuminated sign, compared to 20.4% for those in business 6–25 years, and 16.6% for businesses older than 25 years.

Analyses by size of business

Similar to years of experience, no statistically significant differences were found for questions related to the marketing functions of signs. However, businesses with 10 or fewer employees reported an average estimated loss of 22.2%, while those with 11 or more employees reported an average loss of 17.9%. These results indicate lighted, on-premise signs are more important to the smallest businesses.

Table 6. Value of on-premise signs in key marketing functions, by years in business.

Region	Attract customers	Reinforce IMC	Build brand	Enhance image	Communicate location
0–5 years	5.93	5.78	6.18	6.21	6.17
6–25 years	6.16	6.06	6.37	6.35	6.22
25 or more years	6.03	6.04	6.41	6.43	6.26
	n.s.	n.s.	n.s.	n.s.	n.s.

Note: n.s., not significant.

Conclusion and suggestions for future research

This study shows that regardless of size and number of years in business, businesses of all types believe that lighted, on-premise signs play important marketing functions for the firm. Our results also suggest that most businesses believe it is important to keep signage lit after business hours as the signs still perform key marketing functions even after the business is closed. Importantly, most companies who use on-premise signs appear to believe that restrictions on illumination will substantially harm the financial strength of their business. The fact that most users of lighted on-premise signs report that they would lose significant sales if they were restricted is something that should be weighed by local officials and policy-makers in passing sign codes. This impact is even more pronounced for smaller and younger businesses. From a policy perspective, the finding that smaller businesses face a larger percentage sales loss if illuminated on-premise signs are subject to strict regulation, as many communities value providing conditions under which small businesses can survive and succeed. While this study does not focus on the concept of 'light pollution,' when faced with the argument that illuminated signs represent a form of pollution, policy-makers should again consider the value illuminated signs provide to business in terms of the marketing roles they play.

Future research should consider messaging on illuminated, on-premise signs. Respondents in our study noted that there are restrictions on 'scrolling' or 'flashing' messages on signs. Thus, they are unable to promote quick sales, discounts, or other promotions that might draw customers to their location. A deeper understanding of the direct impact on businesses of these restrictions would help policy-makers in decision-making. Importantly, it may also assist business owners in marketing planning. Finally, it is important to directly assess customer perceptions of on-premise signage and how restrictions impact behavior. Doing so would inform key stakeholders in decision-making and may change marketing planning.

Moving forward, it is important that policy-makers and businesses work together to develop viable, long-term solutions for illuminated, on-premise signage. Consumers demand more from businesses and the use of customer-facing technology such as signage is only increasing. Small businesses in particular are a significant growth engine around the world and their long-term health is tied to an ability to draw customers. As shown in this study, on-premise signage is a key aspect of marketing and should be evaluated in a context that promotes a fair and equitable relationship with local and national governments.

Acknowledgements

The authors would like to thank the Signage Foundation for providing funding for data collection in this study.

Disclosure statement

No potential conflict of interest was reported by the authors.

References

Ahluwalia, R., R.E. Burnkrant, and H.R. Unnava. 2000. Consumer response to negative publicity: The moderating role of commitment. *Journal of Marketing Research* 37, no. 2: 203–14.

Baek, T.H., S. Yoon, and S. Kim. 2015. When environmental messages should be assertive: Examining the moderating role of effort investment. *International Journal of Advertising* 34, no. 1: 135–57.

Berman, B., and J. Evans. 2007. *Retail management*. 10th ed. New York: MacMillan.

Chang, H., L. Zhang, and G.X. Xie. 2015. Message framing in green advertising: The effect of construal level and consumer environmental concern. *International Journal of Advertising* 34, no. 1: 158–76.

Duncan, T.R. 2005. IMC in industry: More talk than walk. *Journal of Advertising* 34, no. 4: 5–6.

Dunne, P., and R.F. Lusch. 1993. *Retailing.* 6th ed. Cincinnati, OH: Southwestern Publishing.

European Commission. 2104. *A partial and fragile recovery.* Annual report on European SMEs 2013/2015.http://ec.europa.eu/enterprise/policies/sme/facts-figures-analysis/performance-review/files/supporting-documents/2014/annual-report-smes-2014_en.pdf (accessed April 12, 2015).

Flagstaff Dark Skies. 2014. Light pollution: The problem. http://www.flagstaffdarkskies.org/dark-sky-solutions/dark-sky-solutions-2/light-pollution-the-problem/ (accessed June 1, 2014).

Fredrix, Emily. 2010. Gap gets rid of new logo. http://www.huffingtonpost.com/2010/10/12/gap-gets-rid-of-new-logo_n_759131.html (accessed March 3, 2015).

Garvey, P. 2005. On-premise commercial sign lighting and light pollution. *Leukos* 1, no. 3: 7–18.

Golden, L.L., G. Albaum, and M. Zimmer. 1987. The numerical comparative scale: An economical format for retail image measurement. *Journal of Retailing* 63, no. 4: 393–410.

Hackley, C., and A. Kelly. 2010. Advertising and promotion: An integrated marketing communications approach. *International Journal of Advertising* 29, no. 3: 501–4.

Hartmann, P., V. Apaolaza, C. D'Souza, J.M. Barrutia, and C. Echebarria. 2014. Environmental threat appeals in green advertising: The role of fear arousal and coping efficacy. *International Journal of Advertising* 33, no. 4: 741–65.

International Dark-Sky Association. 2014. Outdoor lighting. http://www.darksky.org/component/content/article?id=51 (accessed June 1, 2014).

Garretson, J. A., and S. Burton. 2005. The Role of spokescharacters as advertisement and package cues in integrated marketing communications. *Journal of Marketing* 69, no. 4: 118–32.

Keller, K.L. 2005. Branding shortcuts. *Marketing Management* 14, no. 5: 18–23.

Kerr, G., D. Schultz, C.H. Patti, and I. Kim. 2008. An inside-out approach to integrated marketing communication: An international analysis. *International Journal of Advertising* 27, no. 4: 511–48.

Kliatchko, J.G., and D.E. Schultz. 2014. Twenty years of IMC: A study of CEO and CMO perspectives in the Asia-Pacific region. *International Journal of Advertising* 33, no. 2: 373–90.

Kopp, S.W., and J. Langenderfer. 2014. Protecting appearance and atmospherics: Trade dress as a component of retail strategy. *Journal of Public Policy and Marketing* 33, no. 1, 34–48.

Lohse, G.L. 1997. Consumer eye movement patterns on yellow pages advertising. *Journal of Advertising* 26, no. 1: 61–73.

Mizik, N. 2014. Assessing the total financial performance impact of brand equity with limited time series data. *Journal of Marketing* 51, no. 6: 691–706.

Office of Advocacy of U.S. Small Business Administration. 2007. *Private businesses, establishments, employment, annual payroll and receipts by firm size, 1988–2006.* Washington, DC: Office of Advocacy of U.S. Small Business Administration.

Pessemeir, E. 1980. Store image and positioning. *Journal of Retailing* 56 (Spring): 96–7.

Royal Astronomical Society of Canada (RASC). 2003. *Light pollution abatement site.* Calgary: Royal Astronomical Society of Canada. http://ww.rasc.ca/light/home.html

Taylor, C.R. 2010. IMC in 2010 and beyond. *International Journal of Advertising* 29, no. 2: 161–4.

Taylor, C.R., S. Claus, and T. Claus. 2005. *On-premise signs as storefront marketing devices and systems.* Washington, DC: U.S. Small Business Administration.

Taylor, C.R., M. Sarkees, and H.K. Bang. 2012. Understanding the value of on-premise signs as marketing devices to businesses for legal and public policy purposes. *Journal of Public Policy and Marketing* 31, no. 2: 185–94.

U.S. Small Business Administration. 2003. *Signage sourcebook: A signage handbook.* Washington, DC: U.S. Small Business Administration.

U.S. Small Business Administration. 2009. *The small business economy: A report to the president.* Washington, DC: Office of Advocacy of the U.S. Small Business Administration.

U.S. Small Business Administration. 2012. Small business GDP: Update 2002–2010. https://www.sba.gov/content/small-business-gdp-update-2002-2010 (accessed March 4, 2015).

Zhang, J., M. Wedel, and R. Pieters. 2009. Sales effects of attention to feature advertisements: A Bayesian mediation analysis. *Journal of Marketing Research* 46, no. 5: 669–81.

Appendix. Key survey questions

I. (Usage questions) The following questions relate to your company's use of on-premise signs. Please fill in the number which you believe is most appropriate.

    1. How many illuminated on-premise signs are at your place of business? _____# signs

    2. How many hours per day is your business open? _____ # hours open

    3. How many hours per day is your sign(s) illuminated? _____ # hours illuminated

    4. Does your business face restrictions on the hours that you can illuminate your on-premise sign?   (1) Yes   (2) No

    5. Does your business face restrictions on the brightness of your illuminated on-premise sign? (1) Yes   (2) No

    6. Does your business face restrictions on what kind of illuminated sign you are allowed to use? (1) Yes   (2) No

    7. Do you keep your illuminated sign on after business hours?   (1) Yes   (2) No

II. (Marketing functions) Please circle the number that most accurately reflects your agreement with each item below. (1 strongly disagree to 7 strongly agree)

    a. Our lighted on-premise signs help us to attract customers by communicating the location of our business.   1   2   3   4   5   6   7

    b. Our lighted on-premise sign reinforces our advertising and/or other communications we have with our customers.   1   2   3   4   5   6   7

    c. Our lighted on-premise signs help us to brand our site (gives our business an identity with customers).   1   2   3   4   5   6   7

    d. Our lighted on-premise sign helps to enhance the image of our business.
    1   2   3   4   5   6   7

III. (Government regulation)

    If government regulations prevented you from lighting your sign at any hour, what impact, if any, would that have on your company? (Please check one answer for each outcome and provide estimated percentage, if applicable.)

    Outcome:

    (1) Sales decline _____%   (2) No change   (3) Increase _____%

Impact of fear appeals on pro-environmental behavior and crucial determinants

Mei-Fang Chen

Department of Business Management, Tatung University, Taipei, Taiwan

This study examines the impact of various degrees of fear appeals of climate change on an individual's intention to engage in pro-environmental behavior, and how possible factors that influence an individual's intention to engage in pro-environmental behavior vary in different degrees of fear appeals of climate change. The results indicate that the participants who read the low-fear appeal text exhibit more evoked fearful emotion and have more intentions to engage in pro-environmental behavior than do those who read the high-fear appeal text. In addition, an individual's moral obligations play a crucial role in determining his or her intention to engage in pro-environmental behavior under both low-fear and high-fear appeal conditions. However, under high-fear appeal conditions, an individual's perception of collective efficacy plays a crucial role in determining his or her intention of engaging in pro-environmental behavior. The results of this study contribute to enhancing the intercultural validation of research on fear appeals applied to people's pro-environmental behavior in a collective Chinese cultural social context in response to global warming. In addition, the findings provide implications for applying fear appeals to encourage pro-environmental behavior.

Introduction

The effects of global climate change, such as the degradation of the environment, heat waves, flooding, and extermination of animals and plants, have been described as a severe risk to the world (Lazo, Kinnell, and Fisher 2000). A widespread recognition of anthropogenic climate change as a potential threat has developed; consequently, the psychological study of environmentalism and the concern of individuals for the preservation, restoration, and improvement of the natural environment has increased. Human lifestyles and behavior must change to achieve environmental sustainability for Earth (Oskamp 2002). The documentary film *An Inconvenient Truth* (Gore and Guggenheim 2006) depicted global warming in such a manner that it caused considerable appeal from lay people. The Copenhagen Climate Science Summit held in 2009 emphasized that societies must undergo major transformations if the citizens of the world are to have any hope of avoiding dangerous climate change.

The film *Plus or Minus Two Degrees Celsius: The Truth Formosa (Taiwan) Must Face* focuses on the effects of climate change in Taiwan and was produced by the renowned Taiwanese television host Sisy Chen. The title of the documentary refers to the goal adopted at the 2009 United Nations Climate Change Conference in Copenhagen,

Denmark, of preventing Earth's average global temperature from rising more than 2 °C because beyond this point there is a risk of 'runaway' climate change that can endanger human survival. The film has received considerable attention in Taiwan, with its premiere on 22 February 2010 attended by the heads of various government branches, top entrepreneurs, academics, celebrities, and volunteers from local environmental groups; the premiere was followed by a series of promotional activities in movie theatres, universities, and other venues. The producers of the film are encouraging everyone to download or view the documentary for free on the official website and seek to increase awareness about the urgent need to take action to halt climate change. The film arouses fear in the public by using shocking images in Taiwan. The audience felt fear based on self-interest and fear for the future.

According to Gore et al. (1998), threat is an external stimulus that creates a perception in message receivers that they are susceptible to a negative situation or outcome. Fear is a negatively valenced emotion that is usually accompanied by heightened physiological arousal. Vining and Ebreo (2002) argued that threat perception is more than just cognition; it is an emotional component of fear arousal. The relationship between fear and perceived threat is positively correlated (Witte 1992, 1998). In other words, as the level of perceived threat increases, fear arousal also increases. Witte and Allen (2000) found that the use of fear appeals can lead to attitudinal and behavioral change under specific conditions. Fear is a powerful, innate emotional response to a perceived threat or dangerous event and a strong motivator for people to change their behavior to avert a potentially negative outcome. Negative emotions can be used to induce specific moods or emotions to persuade people to change their thoughts or behaviors, particularly if certain behaviors have dangerous or adverse consequences.

Fear appeals are persuasive messages designed to scare information receivers into compliance by threatening them with negative consequences of noncompliance (Witte 1992). The study of fear appeals as a persuasive tactic to encourage target audiences to engage in healthy behavior has been ongoing for over 55 years (Boster and Mongeau 1984; Witte and Allen 2000). Fear appeal communications are commonly used in persuasive health campaigns designed to reduce undesirable social behavior such as smoking, drug use, and driving while intoxicated (Shehryar and Hunt 2005). Previous studies have indicated that fear or threat appeals in advertising campaigns can lead to changes in attitude and, subsequently, behavioral changes (Arthur and Quester 2004; Dillard and Anderson 2004; Dillard and Peck 2000; Henthorne, LaTour, and Nataraajan 1993; Kohn et al. 1982; Maddux and Rogers 1983; Schoenbachler and Whittler 1996; Tanner, Hunt, and Eppright 1991; Witte and Allen 2000). However, several studies have demonstrated weak effects of fear on attitudes, intentions, and behaviors (Boster and Mongeau 1984; Witte and Allen 2000).

Most fear appeal research can be grouped according to the following three theories: drive theory (Janis and Feshbach 1953), protection motivation theory (Rogers 1983), and the parallel process and extended parallel process models (Tanner, Hunt, and Eppright 1991; Witte 1992). Early research on fear appeals was guided by drive theory (Hovland, Janis, and Kelley 1953; Janis 1967; Janis and Feshbach 1953). Fear was considered as an acquired drive that motivated a response. The most prominent hypothesis of the drive model involves an inverted-U-shaped response pattern to increasing levels of fear. The inverted-U relationship suggests that considerably low and considerably high fear levels do not motivate audiences, but moderate fear levels do. Low levels of fear induce too little threat and thus weaken the power of persuasion to avoid harm. By contrast, high levels of fear induce a threat that is too severe, resulting in full absorption in defensive mechanisms rather than attention to or complying with a proposed solution. According to Keller (1999) and Keller and Block (1996), high-fear messages are more likely to be resisted because of motivated reasoning and message discounting. Several studies have argued that there may be an optimal level of perceived threat in fear appeals for motivating behavioral change (e.g., Jones and Owen 2006). The dominant paradigm in fear-appeal research among the aforementioned three theoretical approaches asserts that differences in the persuasiveness of the communication of fear appeals are attributable in part to differences in the level of evoked fear (Keller and Block 1996; Rogers 1985; Witte 1994). Fear appeal messages vary in both the level of evoked fear and the qualitative characteristics of the threat (Hunt and Shehryar 2011). The intensity of the appeal is also a consideration (Moore and Harris 1996). Research has shown that the success of fear appeals depends on the individual person and the amount of fear invoked.

Threat perception has been determined to be a significant determinant of an individual's pro-environmental behavior (e.g., Axelrod and Lehman 1993; Baldassare and Katz 1992; Frannson and Garling 1999; Grob 1995; Johnson and Scicchitano 2000; Vining and Ebreo 2002). Research has found that people's emotional reaction to environmental changes, particularly environmental degradation, is a strong predictor of engagement in pro-environmental behavior (Kollmuss and Agyeman 2002; Stern 2000). Recent research findings on threat appeals and coping efficacy by Hartman et al. (2014) indicated that both cognitive threat level beliefs and fear arousal from exposure to climate change related environmental threat appeals can significantly increase pro-environmental intentions. This study suggests that appropriate threat appeals can increase people's responsiveness to environmental appeals and change their behavioral intentions. Based on Hofstede's (1980) cultural dimensions, in contrast to an individualistic Western cultural context, Taiwan is characterized by a collective Chinese cultural social context. According to Bandura (2002), people from collectivistic cultures can judge themselves to be more efficacious than they actually are. The findings of Homburg and Stolberg (2006) indicate that when an environmental problem is treated as a stressor, collective efficacy, rather than self-efficacy, determines coping attempts and pro-environmental behavior. Considering that there have been only a limited number of studies on fear appeals applied to the pro-environmental behavior of East Asian participants, the main objective of this study is to examine the impact of various degrees of fear appeals of climate change on an individual's intention to engage in pro-environmental behavior and how possible factors influencing an individual's intention to engage in pro-environmental behavior vary in different degrees of fear appeals of climate change in Taiwan. The main contribution of this research is to enhance the intercultural validation of research on fear appeals applied to people's pro-environmental behavior in a collective Chinese cultural social context when addressing global warming.

Determinants of pro-environmental behavior for mitigating climate change

Moral obligations

The norm-activation model (Schwartz 1977; Schwartz and Howard 1981), originally developed to explain altruistic behavior, focuses on the role of moral obligations to act in favor of the common good but has also been applied to studying why people engage in pro-environmental actions (e.g., Bamberg and Schmidt 2003; Thøgersen 1996; Van Liere and Dunlap 1978). Pro-environmental behavior is considered to be pro-social behavior because it entails benefiting others although often no direct individual benefits are received in return by engaging in this type of behavior (e.g., De Groot and Steg 2009).

According to the norm-activation model, behavior occurs in response to personal norms that are activated when individuals are aware of adverse consequences to others or the environment, and when they think they can avert these consequences. According to the conceptualization of norm-activation theory (Schwartz 1977), personal norms are typically measured as feelings of moral obligation to undertake a pro-environmental action. Schwartz (1977) suggested that, because people differ in the relative importance they attach to particular values and general norms, the activation of personal norms generate various intensities of moral obligation in different people in the same situation. In other words, an individual's intention to engage in pro-environmental behavior to mitigate climate change is related to an individual's level of moral obligation. It has been argued that the higher the level of an individual's moral obligation, the stronger his or her intentions are to engage in pro-environmental behavior.

Hypothesis 1: An individual's level of moral obligation is positively related to his or her intention to engage in pro-environmental behavior.

Trust in organizations and mass media

The intensification of mass media coverage of environmental issues, including both the causes and consequences of global warming and climate change, has reinforced and perpetuated environmental concerns (Hannigan 2006). Mass media thus play a crucial role in activating and affecting the perception of climate change, influencing knowledge about this phenomenon, consolidating social frameworks and values, and showing various possibilities for action (Arlt, Hoppe, and Wolling 2011; Nerb and Spada 2001; Stamm, Clark, and Reynolds Eblacas 2000). The media determines the information available to the public and how people should perceive it; in other words, the media constructs and shapes people's social experience (Burgess and Gold 1985).

When faced with a bifurcated flow of information, people often choose to rely on the sources that they trust most. If the source of a message seems untrustworthy, unfair, or incompetent, people can be wary or skeptical and either disengage with or react defensively to the information. Craig and McCann (1978) found that messages identified as originating from a highly credible source (e.g., public service commission) were associated with significantly more customer requests for energy conservation information and greater actual electricity savings compared with the same messages originating from a low-credibility source (e.g., local electrical utility). Priest (2001) found that trust in institutional actors was a strong predictor of support for biotechnology. Poortinga and Pidgeon (2003) examined the dimensions of trust and their relationship to risk regulation in five policy areas including climate change. Trust can be treated as a necessary construct in understanding risk perceptions and encouraging policy support. People's assessments of the risks of global warming are related to individuals' levels of trust in the mass media and the experts and scientists familiar with the subject. It can be assumed that an individual's intention to engage in pro-environmental behavior to mitigate climate change is related to his or her level of trust in institutional actors such as relevant experts and scientists and the mass media.

Hypothesis 2: An individual's level of trust in an organization is positively related to his or her intention to engage in pro-environmental behavior.

Hypothesis 3: An individual's level of trust in mass media is positively related to his or her intention to engage in pro-environmental behavior.

Risk perception

According to O'Connor, Bord, and Fisher (1999), risk perception is reflected as (1) expectations that the problem will happen or is happening, (2) expectations that negative consequences are likely for the self and others, and (3) knowledge of the causes of the problem. Thus, according to O'Connor, Bord, and Fisher (1999), risk perception can be conceptualized as the perceived likelihood of negative consequences to a person and society from one specific environmental phenomenon such as global warming and climate change (O'Connor, Bord, and Fisher 1999). It can be assumed that when an individual perceives a high climate change risk they are likely to engage in pro-environmental behavior. Risk perception regarding climate change is associated with the willingness to perform individual actions to mitigate the effects of this phenomenon on the environment. Previous studies have verified that risk perceptions account for behavioral intentions for tackling climate change (e.g., Bord, O'Connor, and Fisher 2000; Heath and Gifford 2006; O'Connor, Bord, and Fisher 1999; O'Connor et al. 2002). O'Connor et al. (2002) indicated that people who perceive climate change as a substantial risk situation give greater support to political initiatives that entail a change in the energy model as well as certain voluntary pro-environmental behavior, including buying 'environmentally friendly' products, driving less, and choosing environmentally friendly energy providers. It can be assumed that when an individual perceives more climate change risk, he or she is more likely to engage in pro-environmental behavior.

Hypothesis 4: An individual's level of risk perception of climate change is positively related to his or her intention to engage in pro-environmental behavior.

Self-efficacy and collective efficacy

The concept of self-efficacy, as introduced by Bandura (1977, 3), is construed as 'beliefs in one's capacity to organize and execute the courses of action required to produce given attainments'. Bandura advocated the self-efficacy construct for use in frameworks for analyzing fearful and avoidant behavior. The concept was derived from Hovland's theory of fear appeals, in which it was described as the 'belief in the effectiveness of coping responses' (Hovland, Janis, and Kelley 1953; Rogers 1975). Efficacy beliefs are crucial in the development of human competence because they regulate a person's thoughts, feelings, and source of motivation and actions (Bandura 1995). Bandura (1982) affirmed that self-efficacy is a major predictor of behavior that would persist in adverse times. Previous environmental studies have found that people with high levels of self-efficacy beliefs (Bandura 1986, 1995, 1997) in relation to environmentally responsible behavior are more inclined to behave in an environmentally responsible manner (e.g., Axelrod and Lehman 1993; Manzo and Weinstein 1987; Taylor and Todd 1995).

In a meta-analysis of fear appeal literature, Witte and Allen (2000) determined that perceived efficacy plays a role in predicting behavior in addition to fear and/or perceived threat. 'Fear appeals motive, attitude, intention, and behavior changes—especially fear appeals accompanied by high-efficacy messages' (Witte and Allen 2000, 605). Strong fear appeals and high-efficacy messages can produce the greatest behavioral change, whereas strong fear appeals with low-efficacy messages can produce the greatest levels of defensive responses. This means that fear appeals should be used cautiously, because they may backfire if target audiences do not believe they are able to effectively avert a threat (Witte and Allen 2000).

The concept of collective efficacy is also a crucial determinant in the study of environmental behavior because people are social beings and rely on each other to identify solutions to problems to improve their quality of life (Bandura 1986). 'Perceived collective efficacy' as defined by Bandura (1997, 477) refers to 'a group's shared belief in its conjoint capabilities to organize and execute the courses of action required to produce given levels of attainments'. People's shared belief in their collective power to produce desired results is critical in solving collective problems such as climate change. Etkin and Ho (2007, 623) argued that it is not a rational decision for most individuals to take actions to reduce risk from climate change in the absence of collective action, and collective action is extraordinarily difficult to achieve. Only when people believe that collective efforts can solve the climate change problem are their intentions to engage in pro-environmental behavior activated. Thus, it is believed that an individual's intention to engage in pro-environmental behavior to mitigate climate change is related to an individual's levels of self-efficacy and collective efficacy beliefs when confronted with a global problem such as climate change.

Hypothesis 5: An individual's level of self-efficacy towards climate change is positively related to his or her intention to engage in pro-environmental behavior.

Hypothesis 6: An individual's level of collective efficacy towards climate change is positively related to his or her intention to engage in pro-environmental behavior.

Method

Data collection and sample

Participants were recruited from a university located in Taipei, Taiwan. Undergraduate students volunteered to participate in this self-reported survey, with the importance of their cooperation stated in the opening note of the questionnaire. The instructions emphasized that 'there are no right or wrong answers; only your personal opinions matter' to minimize possible response bias. The participant's knowledge and awareness of global warming was investigated at the beginning of the questionnaire. In addition to the participant's demographic variables, the survey included measures of the levels of an individual's moral obligations, trust in organizations, trust in mass media, risk perception, self-efficacy, collective efficacy, and his or her intention to engage in pro-environmental behavior.

Research design and fear-appeal stimuli

Recruited participants were assigned to one of the following narrative scripts: low-fear appeal, moderate-fear appeal, and high-fear appeal. Under the low-fear appeal condition, recruited participants ($n = 72$) were presented with the narrative script by van Zomeren, Spears, and Leach (2010) about the climate crisis, which was originally provided as reading material under the no-fear condition in van Zomeren, Spears, and Leach's study (2010). Because truths can produce fear, the documentary film *An Inconvenient Truth* (Gore and Guggenheim 2006) caused considerable appeal from lay people. Thus, van Zomeren's narrative script was treated as a low-fear appeal condition in this study. In the moderate-fear appeal condition, the recruited participants ($n = 71$) were given additional text with the relevant analytical results of the *Plus or Minus Two Degrees Celsius: the Truth Formosa (Taiwan) Must Face* report to stimulate relevant local feelings. In the high-fear appeal condition, in addition to the combination of the narrative script by van

Zomeren, Spears, and Leach (2010) and the Taiwanese context, the recruited participants ($n = 74$) were shown a picture of a polar bear that was starved to death and explanatory notes as the fear appeal stimuli. A full description of the reading materials of the fear-appeal stimuli is provided in Appendix 1.

Measures

This study included four questions for determining the participants' knowledge and awareness of global warming: (1) Have you ever heard of climate change? (2) Have you ever heard of the documentary film *An Inconvenient Truth*? (3) Have you ever heard of the documentary film *Plus or Minus Two Degrees Celsius: The Truth Formosa (Taiwan) Must Face*? (4) How much do you think you know about climate change? The measurement scales and indicators adopted for the present study to measure all the construct variables have been validated by previous studies. All scales were adapted from Brody, Grover, and Vedlitz (2012), except the scale for an individual's self-efficacy measurement (Schwarzer and Jerusalem 1999) and the collective efficacy measurement scale (Homburg and Stolberg 2006). Individuals' moral obligations were measured using a 2-item measurement scale concerning his or her moral obligations to reduce his or her impact on global warming and climate change on behalf of future generations. Individuals' trust in organizations was measured using a 3-item measurement scale concerning his or her trust in Taiwanese government agency scientific research reports, nonprofit organizations, and environmental interest groups. Individuals' trust in mass media was measured using a 3-item measurement scale concerning his or her trust in newspapers as well as TV and radio news. Individuals' risk perception of climate change was measured using a 3-item measurement scale concerning his or her perception of the possible negative effects of global warming and climate change on health, the economic situation, and the immediate environment. Individuals' intention to engage in pro-environmental behavior was measured using a 9-item measurement scale regarding his or her willingness to take actions and/or change behaviors to reduce his or her contribution to global warming and climate change. The participants were asked to state their degrees of agreement on a 7-point Likert scale ranging from 1 = 'strongly disagree' to 7 = 'strongly agree'.

Manipulation check

The survey results of the participants' knowledge and awareness of global warming before doing the evoked fearful emotion manipulation check are shown in Table 1. The results indicate that 97.24% of the participants had heard of climate change, 73.27% had heard of the documentary film *An Inconvenient Truth*, and 64.52% had heard of the documentary film *Plus or Minus Two Degrees Celsius: the Truth Formosa (Taiwan) Must Face*. A total of 72.35% of the participants thought that they understand climate change; 4.61% thought that they understand climate change very well.

Evoked fearful emotion was measured using two items: 'Is it possible that Taiwan residents become "climate refugees" in the future?' and 'I am afraid of the negative future consequences of the climate crisis'. The mean scores of the two items were computed to determine the fear-appeal manipulation. The participants reported the evoked amount of fear under low-fear, moderate-fear, and high-fear appeal conditions as follows: $M_{\text{low fear}} = 5.40$; $S.D. = 1.00$; $M_{\text{moderate fear}} = 5.05$; $S.D. = 0.95$; $M_{\text{high fear}} = 4.93$; $S.D. = 1.29$). One-way Analysis of Variance (ANOVA) tests were adopted to determine whether there were differences in the mean scores of the participants' fear emotions among

Table 1. Survey results of the participant's previous knowledge/awareness of the global warming issue.

		Low fear ($n = 72$)	Moderate fear ($n = 71$)	High fear ($n = 74$)	Total		Chi-square value for low fear vs. high fear	P-value
Have you ever heard of climate change?	Yes	70	69	72	211	97.24%	0.0008	0.9778
	No	2	2	2	6	2.76%		
Have you ever heard of the documentary film 'An Inconvenient Truth'?	Yes	44	43	72	159	73.27%	29.27	<0.0001
	No	28	28	2	58	26.73%		
Have you ever heard of the documentary film 'Plus or Minus Two Degrees Celsius: the Truth Formosa (Taiwan) Must Face'?	Yes	49	41	50	140	64.52%	0.0040	0.9497
	No	23	30	24	77	35.48%		
Do you think you know how much of climate change?	Very unaware	2	1	2	5	2.30%	3.5878	0.3095
	Do not know	12	12	21	45	20.74%		
	Understand	52	57	48	157	72.35%		
	Very understanding	6	1	3	10	4.61%		

Note: $\chi^2_{1, 0.05} = 3.841$; $\chi^2_{3, 0.05} = 7.815$.

low-fear, moderate-fear, and high-fear appeal conditions. The results indicate that there is a significant difference between the low-fear appeal condition and the high-fear appeal condition, but there is no significant difference between the low-fear appeal condition and the moderate-fear appeal condition ($F = (2, 214) = 3.60, p = .0290 < .05$). The participants' evoked fearful emotion is stimulated more in the low-fear appeal condition than in the high-fear appeal condition. The results are consistent with those of previous studies (e.g., Keller 1999; Keller and Block 1996), which indicate that high-fear messages are more likely to be resisted because of motivated reasoning and message discounting. After determining the fear-appeal manipulation, this study examined the impact of various degrees of fear appeals of climate change (i.e., low-fear appeal condition vs. high-fear appeal condition) on an individual's intention to engage in pro-environmental behavior and how the possible factors influencing an individual's intention to engage in pro-environmental behavior vary in different degrees of fear appeals of climate change.

Data analysis and results

The descriptive statistics and correlation matrix of the studied influencing factors for both low-fear and high-fear appeal conditions are summarized in Table 2. Reliability can reflect the internal consistency of the indicators measuring a given construct. As shown in Table 2, Cronbach's (1951) alpha values of the constructs studied in both low-fear and high-fear appeal narrative scripts are confirmed by the coefficient alpha values that are higher than the recommended level of 0.7 (Nunnally 1978).

One-way ANOVA tests were conducted to examine the impact of various fear appeals of climate change on an individual's intention to engage in pro-environmental behavior. The most prominent hypothesis of the drive model, the inverted-U-shaped response pattern to increasing levels of fear, indicates that considerably low and considerably high fear levels do not motivate audiences, but moderate fear levels do. The results of determining the fear-appeal manipulation indicate that there is no significant difference between the low-fear appeal condition and the moderate-fear appeal condition; however, in this empirical study, participants' evoked fearful emotion is stimulated more under the low-fear appeal condition than under the high-fear appeal condition. Thus, it is assumed that a narrative script with low-fear appeals of climate change exerts more impact on an individual's intention to engage in pro-environmental behavior because the evoked fearful emotion is higher than that of a high-fear appeal context. As expected, the ANOVA results indicate that the mean score of participant's intention to engage in pro-environmental behavior in the low-fear appeal condition ($M_{low\ fear} = 5.61$; $S.D. = 0.85$) is higher than that of the respondents under the high-fear appeal condition [$M_{high\ fear} = 5.08$; $S.D. = 1.13$; ($F = (1, 144) = 10.53, p = .0015 < .01$)]. This means that people who read the low-fear appeal text will have a higher intention to engage in pro-environmental behavior compared with people who read the high-fear appeal text.

An ordinary least squares multiple regression equation analysis was adopted to examine the possible factors that influence an individual's intention to engage in pro-environmental behavior under the low-fear appeal condition and high-fear appeal condition. The possible factors influencing an individual's intention to engage in pro-environmental behavior include an individual's moral obligations and his or her trust in organizations and mass media, risk perception, self-efficacy, and collective efficacy. Under the low-fear appeal condition, the results of the regression analysis (Table 3) indicate that when all the possible factors are considered in the regression model, 29.62% of the variance in an individual's intention to engage in pro-environmental behavior is explained. Among all

Table 2. Descriptive statistics and correlation matrix of studied constructs.

	Low-fear appeals									High-fear appeals								
	Mean	S.D.	F1	F2	F3	F4	F5	F6	F7	Mean	S.D.	F1	F2	F3	F4	F5	F6	F7
Moral obligation	5.46	1.23	**0.94**							5.25	1.33	**0.97**						
Trust in organization	4.30	1.04	0.44	**0.83**						4.19	1.41	0.55	**0.88**					
Trust in mass media	4.22	1.42	0.31	0.67	**0.97**					4.06	1.36	0.43	0.78	**0.97**				
Risk perception	5.00	1.19	0.49	0.27	0.30	**0.89**				4.83	1.13	0.43	0.42	0.36	**0.79**			
Self-efficacy	4.08	0.96	0.13	0.32	0.41	0.16	**0.92**			4.16	0.97	0.17	0.24	0.15	0.12	**0.90**		
Collective efficacy	4.83	1.16	0.43	0.41	0.34	0.28	0.43	**0.87**		4.50	1.21	0.51	0.50	0.37	0.27	0.46	**0.90**	
Pro-environmental behavior intention	5.61	0.85	0.57	0.29	0.26	0.42	0.17	0.31	**0.90**	5.08	1.13	0.63	0.46	0.28	0.36	0.30	0.64	**0.95**

Note: The Cronbach's alpha values are shown in bold in the diagonal line.

Table 3.   Regression analysis results across different degrees of fear appeals.

	Low-fear appeals			High-fear appeals		
	β	t-value	p-value	β	t-value	p-value
Moral obligation	0.46	3.58	0.0007***	0.37	3.48	0.0009***
Trust in organization	−0.01	−0.08	0.9378	0.16	1.08	0.2841
Trust in mass media	0.03	0.24	0.8135	−0.20	−1.51	0.1370
Risk Perception	0.16	1.40	0.1670	0.09	1.01	0.3183
Self-efficacy	0.06	0.54	0.5913	0.03	0.38	0.7085
Collective Efficacy	0.03	0.25	0.8025	0.40	3.72	0.0004***
R-square		35.57%			55.74%	
Adj R-square		29.62%			51.78%	

Note: ***$p < 0.001$.

possible factors influencing an individual's intention to engage in pro-environmental behavior, only the regression coefficient of an individual's moral obligations is significantly related in the expected direction ($\beta_{\text{moral obligations}} = 0.46, p = .0007 < .001$). This means that if an individual has strong moral obligations, he or she is likely to have the intention of engaging in pro-environmental behavior.

Under the high-fear appeal condition, the results of the regression analysis indicate that when all possible factors are considered in the regression model, 51.78% of the variance in an individual's intention to engage in pro-environmental behavior is explained (Table 3). Both the regression coefficients of an individual's moral obligations ($\beta_{\text{moral obligations}} = 0.37, p = .0009 < .001$) and his or her collective efficacy perception ($\beta_{\text{collective efficacy}} = 0.40, p = .0004 < .001$) are significantly related in the expected direction among all possible factors influencing an individual's intention to engage in pro-environmental behavior. This means that if an individual has strong moral obligations and a high degree of belief in collective efficacy to mitigate climate change, he or she is likely to have the intention of engaging in pro-environmental behavior.

Discussion

One-way ANOVA tests revealed that people who read the low-fear appeal text will have more intentions to engage in pro-environmental behavior compared with people who read the high-fear appeal text ($M_{\text{low fear}} = 5.61$; $S.D. = 0.85$; $M_{\text{high fear}} = 5.08$; $S.D. = 1.13$). This is because those who read the high-fear appeal text are motivated to engage in defensive mechanisms rather than in pro-environmental behavior. The results are consistent with that of Janis and Feshbach's study (1954); low- or moderate-fear appeal was the most persuasive because higher levels of fear produced defensive reactions. The use of a shocking image of a polar bear that starved to death in Norway was in the high-fear appeal condition; however, it evoked fearful emotion that was lower than the low-fear appeal condition ($M_{\text{low fear}} = 5.40$; $S.D. = 1.00$; $M_{\text{high fear}} = 4.93$; $S.D. = 1.29$). This could be because the recruited respondents in the high-fear appeal condition not only had remote geographical and psychological distance from Norway but also wondered whether such information exaggerated the extent of the problem, despite the image emphasizing climate change. Instead, neutral visual communications provide a more emotive stimulus than do text that viewers find themselves forced to engage with (Joffe 2008). Visual images can trigger negative responses of unease or fear, thereby generating defensive psychological reactions, powerlessness, or a desensitized response to the threatening and unfamiliar events (Nicholson-Cole 2005). The results are consistent with those of Kollmuss and Agyeman (2002), who hypothesized that emotional reactions may even trigger defense mechanisms such as denial (refusing to accept the reality of a situation; e.g., the belief that global warming does not exist) and apathy (feeling that there is little people can do to change the situation; Hines, Hungerford, and Tomera 1987). People may also engage in rational distancing, in which they psychologically distance themselves from environmental problems by removing any personal sense of emotion from the problem (Kollmuss and Agyeman 2002). This may also reduce people's internal motivation to engage in pro-environmental behavior. The results further prove that when fear appeals manipulate substantially, the persuasive power decreases considerably because people's defensive mechanisms will be activated (Janis and Feshbach 1954).

The results of multiple regression equation analyses on the low-fear appeal and the high-fear appeal conditions revealed that compared with people who read the low-fear appeal text, the people who read the high-fear appeal text exhibited a collective efficacy perception that contributes to individuals' intention to engage in pro-environmental behavior in addition to individuals' moral obligations. In other words, except for moral obligations and collective efficacy, other factors (i.e., trust in an organization and mass media, risk perception, and self-efficacy) are not determinants of an individual's intention to engage in pro-environmental behavior under the low-fear appeal and the high-fear appeal conditions. This means that under the high-fear appeal condition, in addition to an individual's moral obligations, when he or she exhibits a high degree of shared belief that collective power can mitigate climate change, he or she will have more intentions to engage in pro-environmental behavior. By contrast, if a person perceives that there is little he or she can do to change the situation, he or she will become apathetic and reduce their efforts to engage in pro-environmental behavior (Hines, Hungerford, and Tomera 1987). This is the reason why the mean score of the participants' intention to engage in pro-environmental behavior under the high-fear appeal condition ($M = 5.08$; $S.D. = 1.13$) is lower than that of the respondents under the low-fear appeal condition ($M = 5.61$; $S.D. = 0.85$; $F = (1, 144) = 10.53, p = .0015 < .01$).

In this study, 97.24% of the participants had heard of climate change, 73.27% had heard of the documentary film *An Inconvenient Truth*, and 64.52% had heard of the documentary film *Plus or Minus Two Degrees Celsius: the Truth Formosa (Taiwan) Must Face*. In addition, more than 70% of the participants thought that they understood climate change. Chi-square tests were used to determine whether the recruited participants in the low-fear appeal condition and high-fear appeal condition differ in their previous knowledge and awareness. The test results are shown in the last two columns of Table 2. Except for the item 'Have you ever heard of the documentary film *An Inconvenient Truth*?,' all the test results indicate that previous knowledge and awareness of the recruited participants in the low-fear appeal condition and high-fear appeal condition are not statistically significant. The aforementioned item resulted in a chi-square value of 29.27, which is significant at the 0.01 level. This means that the number of recruited respondents in the high-fear appeal condition who had heard of the documentary film *An Inconvenient Truth* was significantly larger than that in the low-fear appeal condition. According to Averbeck, Jones, and Robertson (2011), an individual's previous knowledge and awareness of the global warming concern defends him or her against fear appeals. Thus, individuals are less likely to be influenced by a fear appeal if they have prior related knowledge. This could be the reason why the participants in the low-fear appeal condition were more stimulated with fearful emotion and had a higher intention to engage in pro-environmental behavior than those in the high-fear appeal condition.

Conclusions and implications

The results of this study indicate that various degrees of fear appeals of climate change have different impacts on an individual's intention to engage in pro-environmental behavior. The participants who read the low-fear appeal text exhibited a higher level of evoked fearful emotion and a higher intention of engaging in pro-environmental behavior than did those who read the high-fear appeal text. Determining the fear-appeal manipulation enabled verifying that an individual's fearful emotion is stimulated less by high-fear appeals under a condition of considerable threat compared with under the low-fear appeal condition. The recruited respondents in the high-fear appeal condition not only had remote geographical distance from Norway but also wondered whether the shocking image of a polar bear that starved to death in Norway exaggerated the extent of the problem. The results are consistent with those of Keller (1999) and Keller and Block (1996); when fear appeals manipulate substantially, people are motivated to engage in defensive mechanisms rather than in pro-environmental behavior. In addition, the results of this study revealed that an individual's moral obligations play a crucial role in determining whether he or she has a high intention of engaging in pro-environmental behavior under both low-fear and high-fear appeal conditions. However, under the high-fear appeal condition, an individual's perception of collective efficacy also plays a crucial role in determining his or her intention to engage in pro-environmental behavior.

The findings of this study provide several practical implications for pro-environmental behavior and mitigating climate change. First, sometimes objective information on climate change can induce fear and lead to anticipated effects in encouraging people's pro-environmental behavior. In other words, sometimes an objective account is convincing. For example, the documentary *An Inconvenient Truth* (Gore and Guggenheim 2006) portrays global warming in such a manner that it causes appeal from lay people. Consequently, people learn about the adverse effects of global climate change that are occurring daily and globally from mass media. By contrast, excessively high-fear appeals or news about severe threats of climate change can have side effects in encouraging people's pro-environmental behavior. This does not mean that fear appeals do not work at all. According to previous studies, there may be an optimal level of perceived threat in fear appeals for motivating behavioral change (Jones and Owen 2006). In other words, an excessively high-fear appeal and the implication of severe threat in the communication of climate change are not appropriate in encouraging people to engage in pro-environmental behavior. In this case, an objective account of climate change can be a favorable message strategy for encouraging people to engage in pro-environmental behavior, unless a moderate fear level of the threat of climate change can be formulated.

Fear appeals are nonmonotonic, meaning that although persuasion increases when fear increases from low to moderate levels, when fear increases from moderate to high levels, persuasion actually decreases (Sternthal and Craig 1974). In other words, the level of persuasion does not increase in proportion to the strength of the fear appeal that is used. Weak fear appeals may not attract enough attention but strong fear appeals may cause an individual's defense mechanism to block or ignore a message (Krisher, Darley, and Darley 1973). According to Janis and Feshbach's (1953) research, a moderate fear appeal would be described in a milder and more factual manner. This means that if the information sources and mass media can report the climate change problem in a factual and less personal message without exaggerated negative consequences, then such a fear appeal message may encourage people to engage in pro-environmental behaviors. Previous studies have indicated that fear alone is not enough to motivate behavioral change because there is no recommended action or a recommended action that is easily performed; this may result in the opposite effect (e.g., Keller 1999, Witte and Allen 2000). Low-fear appeal or moderate-fear appeal with feasible recommended actions could be promoted to encourage people to engage in pro-environmental behaviors.

Second, people's moral obligations to the environment should be enhanced to encourage pro-environmental behavior or prevent them from engaging in behavior that damages the environment. Although an individual's availability of energy, time, skills, social resources, and other resources may limit him or her to engage in pro-environmental behavior, individuals who perceive a *moral obligation* to 'save the planet' are considerably likely to be proactive in addressing environmental problems and behave in a pro-environmental manner. This empirical study showed that, although the climate change literacy rate was high, which may have caused the participants to defend himself or herself against fear appeals, environmental education programs targeting pro-environmental behavior such as recycling, energy saving, carbon reduction, and sustainable consumption could be successful if they addressed people's moral obligations in the context of an environmental crisis.

Third, an individual's perceived collective efficacy should be enhanced, especially when he or she is under the high-fear appeal condition. The effects of global environmental change are potentially severe and a threat to the environment and future generations. People's individual ability and the effectiveness of their actions to address this global problem (i.e., self-efficacy) are limited unless they are combined in joint efforts for collective public change. According to Hofstede (1980), collectivists refer to 'groups bind and mutually obligate individuals'. In collectivist cultures, people are tightly integrated and belong to one or more close 'in-groups'. According to Bandura (2002), people from collectivist cultures can judge themselves to be more efficacious than they actually are. The literature suggests that most Western countries rate high on individualism, whereas Asian countries are associated with high collectivism (Sivadas, Bruvold, and Nelson 2008). Rooted in profound Chinese thought and understanding, Chinese culture has a long tradition of collective identity; Taiwan is no exception. Therefore, determining how people's collective efficacy beliefs are activated is crucial for enabling the government to encourage citizens to engage in pro-environmental behavior in the collective Chinese cultural context in Taiwan. A commitment to collective efforts should be fostered by persuading people that their actions can influence their surroundings. Consequently, people would be more willing to engage in pro-environmental behavior.

The empirical findings obtained through the fear-appeal narrative designs in this study not only enhance the intercultural validation of research on fear appeals applied to people's pro-environmental behavior in a collective Chinese cultural social setting and the context of global warming but should also be helpful for both government policy makers and marketers to propose effective fear appeals in social marketing to motivate citizens to engage in pro-social behavior, including pro-environmental behavior. The main limitation of this study is that the questionnaires relied on self-reporting on pro-environmental behavioral intention without objectively assessing pro-environmental behavior. Although behavioral intention models have received strong support in numerous behavioral studies (Ajzen 2001; Eagly and Chaiken 1993), actual behavior is not always adequately predicted by attitudes and stated behavioral intentions (Belk 1985). The second limitation of this study is that the moderate-fear appeal manipulation was not successful in the study. The third limitation of this study is the small sample size. The findings should be generalized cautiously.

Recent studies examined the semantic features and implications of green message such as precision level in environmental advertising claims (Xie and Kronrod 2012), positive/negative or gain/loss framing effects for environmental sustainability messages (Chang, Zhang, and Xie 2015; Newman et al. 2012), and the effects of assertive language ('must', 'should', and 'ought') in environmental messages (Baek, Yoon, and Kim 2015). In addition to different presentation formats regarding semantic features and implications, recent studies also examined different audience predispositions, including an individual's effort investment for environmental pledges (Yoon, Kim, and Baek In Press.) and an individual's construal level and environmental concern (Chang, Zhang, and Xie 2015). These research findings are very helpful to formulate more persuasiveness messages for promoting pro-environmental behaviors. Future studies might explore the complex interaction effects between different semantic presentation formats and different audience predispositions to have fruitful insights.

Acknowledgements

This work was supported by a grant from the National Science Council, Republic of China (NSC100-2410-H-036-001-MY3).

Disclosure statement

No potential conflict of interest was reported by the author.

References

Ajzen, I. 2001. Nature and operation of attitudes. *Annual Review of Psychology* 52, no. 1: 27–58.

Arlt, D., I. Hoppe, and J. Wolling. 2011. Climate change and media usage: Effects on problem awareness and behavioural intentions. *International Communication Gazette* 73, no. 1–2: 45–63.

Arthur, D., and P. Quester. 2004. Who's afraid of that ad? Applying segmentation to the Protection Motivation Model. *Psychology & Marketing* 21, no. 9: 671–96.

Averbeck, J.M., A. Jones, and K. Robertson. 2011. Prior knowledge and health messages: An examination of affect as heuristics and information as systematic processing for fear appeals. *Southern Communication Journal* 76, no. 1: 35–54.

Axelrod, L.J., and D.R. Lehman. 1993. Responding to environmental concerns: What factors guide individual action? *Journal of Environmental Psychology* 13, no. 2: 149–59.

Baek, T.H., S. Yoon, and S. Kim. 2015. When environmental messages should be assertive: Examining the moderating role of effort investment. *International Journal of Advertising* 34, no. 1: 135–57.

Baldassare, M., and C. Katz. 1992. The personal threat of environmental problems as predictor of environmental practices. *Environment and Behavior* 24, no. 5: 602–16.

Bamberg, S., and P. Schmidt. 2003. Incentives, morality, or habit? Predicting students' car use for university routes with the models of Ajzen, Schwartz, and Triandis. *Environment and Behavior* 35, no. 2: 264–85.

Bandura, A. 1977. Self-efficacy: Toward a unifying theory of behavioral change. *Psychological Review* 84, no. 2: 191–215.

Bandura, A. 1982. Self-efficacy mechanism in human agency. *American Psychologist* 37, no. 2: 122–47.

Bandura, A. 1986. *Social foundations of thought and action: A social cognitive theory*. Englewood Cliffs, NJ: Prentice Hall.

Bandura, A. 1995. Exercise of personal and collective efficacy in changing societies. In *Self-efficacy in changing societies*, ed. A. Bandura, 1–45. Cambridge: Cambridge University Press.

Bandura, A. 1997. *Self-efficacy: The exercise of control*. New York, NY: W. H. Freeman and Company.

Bandura, A. 2002. Social cognitive theory in cultural context. *Applied Psychology* 51: 269–90.

Belk, R.W. 1985. Issues in the intention–behavior discrepancy. *Research in Consumer Behavior* 1: 1–34.

Bord, R.J., R.E. O'Connor, and A. Fisher. 2000. In what sense does the public need to understand global climate change? *Public Understanding of Science* 9, no. 3: 205–18.

Boster, F., and P. Mongeau. 1984. Fear-arousing persuasive messages. In *Communication yearbook*, ed. R.N. Bostrom and B.H. Westley, Newbury Park, CA: Sage.

Brody, S., H. Grover, and A. Vedlitz. 2012. Examining the willingness of Americans to alter behaviour to mitigate climate change. *Climate Policy* 12, no. 1: 1–22.

Burgess, J., and J. Gold. 1985. Introduction: Place, the media and popular culture. In *Geography, the Media and Popular Culture*, ed. J. Burgess and J. Gold, 1–33. Sydney: Croom Helm.

Chang, H., L. Zhang, and G.X. Xie. 2015. Message framing in green advertising: The effect of construal level and consumer environmental concern. *International Journal of Advertising* 34, no. 1: 158–76.

Craig, C.S., and J.M. McCann. 1978. Assessing communication effects of energy conservation. *Journal of Consumer Research* 5, no. 2: 82–88.

Cronbach, L.J. 1951. Coefficient alpha and the internal structure of tests. *Psychometrika* 16: 297–334.

De Groot, J.I.M., and L. Steg. 2009. Morality and prosocial behavior: The role of awareness, responsibility and norms in the norm activation model. *Journal of Social Psychology* 149: 425–49.

Dillard, J.P., and J.W. Anderson. 2004. The role of fear in persuasion. *Psychology & Marketing* 21, no. 11: 909–26.

Dillard, J.P., and E. Peck. 2000. Affect and persuasion: Emotional responses to public service announcements. *Communication Research* 27, no. 4: 461–95.

Eagly, A.H., and S. Chaiken. 1993. *The psychology of attitudes*. Fort Worth, TX: Harcourt Brace Jovanovich.

Etkin, D., and E. Ho. 2007. Climate change: Perceptions and discourses of risk. *Journal of Risk Research* 10, no. 5: 623–41.

Fransson, N., and T. Gärling. 1999. Environmental concern: Conceptual definitions, measurement methods, and research findings. *Journal of Environmental Psychology* 19, no. 4: 369–82.

Gore, P., S. Madhavan, D. Curry, G. McClurg, M. Castiglia, S.A. Rosenbluth, and R.A. Smego. 1998. Persuasive messages. *Marketing Health Services* 18, no. 4: 32–43.

Gore, A., and D. Guggenheim. 2006. *An inconvenient truth*. California Hollywood, USA: Paramount Pictures.

Grob, A. 1995. A structural model of environmental attitudes and behavior. *Journal of Environmental Psychology* 15, no. 3: 209–20.

Hannigan, J. 2006. *Environmental sociology*. New York, NY: Routledge.

Hartman, P., V. Apaloaza, C. D'Souza, J.M. Barrutia, and C. Echebarria. 2014. Environmental threat appeals in green advertising: The role of fear arousal and coping efficacy. *International Journal of Advertising* 33, no. 4: 741–65.

Heath, Y., and R. Gifford. 2006. Free-market ideology and environmental degradation: The case of belief in global climate change. *Environment and Behavior* 38, no. 1: 48–71.

Henthorne, T.L., M.S. LaTour, and R. Nataraajan. 1993. Fear appeals in print advertising: An analysis of arousal and ad response. *Journal of Advertising* 22, no. 2: 59–68.

Hines, J.M., H.R. Hungerford, and A.N. Tomera. 1987. Analysis and synthesis of research on responsible environmental behavior: A meta-analysis. *Journal of Environmental Education* 18, no. 2: 1–8.

Hofstede, G. 1980. *Culture's consequences: International differences in work-related values.* Beverly Hill, CA: Sage Publications.

Homburg, A., and A. Stolberg. 2006. Explaining pro-environmental behavior with a cognitive theory of stress. *Journal of Environmental Psychology* 26, no. 1: 1–14.

Hovland, C.I., I.L. Janis, and H.H. Kelley. 1953. *Communication and persuasion.* New Haven, CT: Yale University Press.

Hunt, D.M., and O. Shehryar. 2011. Integrating terror management theory into fear appeal research. *Social and Personality Psychology Compass* 5, no. 6: 372–82.

Janis, I.L. 1967. Effects of fear arousal on attitude change: Recent developments in theory and experimental research. Vol. 3, of *Advances in experimental social psychology*, ed. L. Berkowitz, 166–225. New York, NY: Academic Press.

Janis, I.L., and S. Feshbach. 1953. Effects of fear-arousing communications. *Journal of Abnormal and Social Psychology* 48, no. 1: 78–92.

Janis, I.L., and S. Feshbach. 1954. Differences associated with responsiveness to fear-arousing communications. *Journal of Personality* 23, no. 2: 154–66.

Joffe, H. 2008.. The power of visual material: Persuasion, emotion and identification. *Diogenes* 55, no. 1: 84–93.

Johnson, R.J., and M.J. Scicchitano. 2000. Uncertainty, risk, trust, and information: Public perceptions of environmental issues and willingness to take action. *Policy Studies Journal* 28: 633–47.

Jones, S.C., and N. Owen. 2006. Using fear appeals to promote cancer screening – Are we scaring the wrong people? *International Journal of Nonprofit & Voluntary Sector Marketing* 11, no. 2: 93–103.

Keller, P.A. 1999. Converting the unconverted: The effect of inclination and opportunity to discount health-related fear appeals. *Journal of Applied Psychology* 84, no. 3: 403–15.

Keller, P.A., and L.G. Block. 1996. Increasing the persuasiveness of fear appeals: The effect of arousal and elaboration. *Journal of Consumer Research* 22, no. 4: 448–59.

Kohn, P.M., M.S. Goodstadt, G.M. Cook, M. Sheppard, and G. Chan. 1982. Ineffectiveness of threat appeals about drinking and driving. *Accident Analysis and Prevention* 14, no. 6: 457–64.

Kollmuss, A., and J. Agyeman. 2002. Mind the gap: Why do people act environmentally and what are the barriers to pro-environmental behavior? *Environmental Education Research* 8, no. 3: 239–60.

Krisher, H.P., S.A. Darley, and J.M. Darley. 1973. Fear-provoking recommendations, intentions to take preventive actions, and actual preventive actions. *Journal of Personality and Social Psychology* 26, no. 2: 301–08.

Lazo, J.K., J.C. Kinnell, and A. Fisher. 2000. Expert and layperson perceptions of ecosystem risk. *Risk Analysis* 20, no. 2: 179–93.

Maddux, J.E., and R.W. Rogers. 1983. Protection motivation and self-efficacy: A revised theory of fear appeals and attitude change. *Journal of Experimental Social Psychology* 19, no. 5: 469–79.

Manzo, L.C., and M.D. Weinstein. 1987. Behavioral commitment to environmental protection: A study of active and nonactive members of the Sierra Club. *Environment and Behavior* 19, no. 6: 673–94.

Moore, D.J., and W.D. Harris. 1996. Affect intensity and the consumer's attitude toward high impact emotional advertising appeals. *Journal of Advertising* 25, no. 2: 37–50.

Nerb, J., and H. Spada. 2001. Evaluation of environmental problems: A coherence model of cognition and emotion. *Cognition and Emotion* 15, no. 4: 521–51.

Newman, C.L., E. Howlett, S. Burton, J.C. Kozup, and A. Heintz Tangari. 2012. The influence of consumer concern about global climate change on framing effects for environmental sustainability messages. *International Journal of Advertising* 31, no. 3: 511–27.

Nicholson-Cole, S.A. 2005. Representing climate change futures: A critique on the use of images for visual communication. *Computers, Environment and Urban Systems* 29: 255–73.

Nunnally, J.C. 1978. *Psychometric theory.* 2nd ed. New York: McGraw-Hill.

O'Connor, R.E., R.J. Bord, and A. Fisher. 1999. Risk perception, general environmental beliefs, and willingness to address climate change. *Risk Analysis* 19, no. 3: 461–71.

O'Connor, R., R. Bord, B. Yarnal, and N. Wiefek. 2002. Who wants to reduce greenhouse gas emissions? *Social Science Quarterly* 83, no. 1: 1–17.

Oskamp, S. 2002. Environmentally responsible behavior: Teaching and promoting it effectively. *Analyses of Social Issues and Public Policy* 2, no. 1: 173–82.

Poortinga, W., and N.F. Pidgeon. 2003. Exploring the dimensionality of trust in risk regulation. *Risk Analysis* 23, no. 5: 961–72.

Priest, S.H. 2001. Misplaced faith: Communication variables as predictors of encouragement for biotechnology development. *Science Communication* 23, no. 2: 97–110.

Rogers, R.W. 1975. A protection motivation theory of fear appeals and attitude change. *The Journal of Psychology* 91, no. 1: 93–114.

Rogers, R.W. 1983. Cognitive and psychological processes in fear appeals and attitude change: A revised theory of protection motivation. In *Social psychophysiology: a sourcebook*, ed. J. Cacioppo and R. Petty, 153–76. New York: Guilford.

Rogers, R.W. 1985. Attitude change and information integration in fear appeals. *Psychological Reports* 56, no. 1: 179–82.

Schoenbachler, D.D., and T.E. Whittler. 1996. Adolescent processing of social and physical threat communications. *Journal of Advertising* 25, no. 4: 37–55.

Schwartz, S.H. 1977. Normative influences on altruism. Vol. 10 of *Advances in experimental social psychology*, ed. L. Berkowitz, 221–279. New York: Academic Press.

Schwartz, S.H., and J.A. Howard. 1981. A normative decision-making model of altruism. In *Altruism and helping behaviour: Social, personality, and development perspectives*, ed. J.P. Rushton and R.M. Sorrentino, 189–211. Hillsdale, NJ: Lawrence Erlbaum.

Schwarzer, R., and M. Jerusalem, eds.1999. *Skalen zur erfassung von lehrer-und schülermerkmalen* [Scales for the Assessment of Students' Personal and Environmental Characteristics]. Berlin: Freie Universitat Berlin.

Shehryar, O., and D.M. Hunt. 2005. A terror management perspective on the persuasiveness of fear appeals. *Journal of Consumer Psychology* 15, no. 4: 275–87.

Sivadas, E., N.T. Bruvold, and M.R. Nelson. 2008. A reduced version of the horizontal and vertical individualism and collectivism scale: A four-country assessment. *Journal of Business Research* 61, no. 3: 201–10.

Stamm, K.R., F. Clark, and P. Reynolds Eblacas. 2000. Mass communication and public understanding of environmental problems: The case of global warming. *Public Understanding of Science* 9, no. 3: 219–37.

Stern, P.C. 2000. Toward a coherent theory of environmentally significant behavior. *Journal of Social Issues* 56, no. 3: 407–24.

Sternthal, B., and C.S. Craig. 1974. Fear appeals: Revisited and revised. *Journal of Consumer Research* 1, no. 3: 22–34.

Taylor, S., and P. Todd. 1995. An integrated model of waste management behavior: A test of household recycling and composting intentions. *Environment and Behavior* 27, no. 5: 603–30.

Tanner, J.F., J.B. Hunt, and D.R. Eppright. 1991. The protection motivation model: A normative model of fear appeals. *Journal of Marketing* 55, no. 3: 36–45.

Thøgersen, J. 1996. Recycling and morality: A critical review of the literature. *Environment and Behavior* 28, no. 4: 536–58.

Van Liere, K.D., and R.E. Dunlap. 1978. Moral norms and environmental behavior: An application of Schwartz's norm-activation model to yard burning. *Journal of Applied Social Psychology* 8, no. 2: 174–88.

van Zomeren, M., R. Spears, and C.W. Leach. 2010. Experimental evidence for a dual pathway model analysis of coping with the climate crisis. *Journal of Environmental Psychology* 30, no. 4: 339–46.

Vining, J., and A. Ebreo. 2002. Emerging theoretical and methodological perspectives on conservation behavior. In *Handbook of environmental psychology*, ed. R.B. Bechtel and A. Churchman, 541–58. New York: Wiley.

Witte, K. 1992. Putting the fear back into fear appeals: The extended parallel process model. *Communication Monographs* 59, no. 4: 329–49.

Witte, K. 1998. Fear as motivator, fear as inhibitor: Using the EPPM to explain fear appeal successes and failures. In *The handbook of communication and emotion*, ed. P.A. Andersen and L.K. Guerrero, 423–50. New York: Academic.

Witte, K. 1994. Fear control and danger control: A test of the extended parallel process model (EPPM). *Communication Monographs* 61, no. 2: 113–32.

Witte, K., and M. Allen. 2000. A meta-analysis of fear appeals: Implications for the effective public health campaigns. *Health Education and Behavior* 27, no. 5: 591–615.

Xie, G.X., and A. Kronrod. 2012. Is the devil in the details? The signaling effect of numerical precision in environmental advertising claims. *Journal of Advertising* 41, no. 4: 103–17.

Yoon, S., Y. Kim, and T.H. Baek. In Press. Effort investment in persuasiveness: A comparative study of environmental advertising in the United States and Korea. *International Journal of Advertising*. doi: 10.1080/02650487.2015.1061963

Appendix 1

A.1 Low-fear appeal condition

In recent decades, the amount of carbon dioxide (CO_2) in the atmosphere has increased exponentially. The main cause of this is the use of fossil fuels for transport (e.g., driving motorized vehicles), electricity, the heating of houses, and industrial uses. The increase of CO_2 in the atmosphere has resulted in an increase of the average temperature on Earth and led to climate change. Over the past 100 years, the average temperature on Earth has increased by 0.6 °C.

A.2 Moderate-fear appeal condition

As global warming is becoming more intense and extreme weather phenomena such as torrential rainstorms and strong winds are becoming more frequent, the four-season climate of Taiwan will transform into a climate featuring a long summer and a long winter, and typhoons will become more intense. There will be more extreme rainfall, with heavy rains followed by a drought and heat waves followed by cold winters. Taiwan's 'Plus or Minus two Degrees Celsius League' analysts stated that if the Arctic ice melts, the sea level will rise by 6 m and Taiwan will lose 11% of land. This means that when the Maldives become one of the world's first islands to be submerged, the land in Taiwan with an elevation below 100 m will become uninhabitable; the East Stone Harbor, Linbian, the East Port, and Mailiao will be submerged by floods. If the sea level continues to rise, the Yilan Plain, Taipei Basin, and Kaohsiung City will be inundated; local residents will have to flee and become 'climate refugees' and victims of climate change. The United Nations Intergovernmental Panel on Climate Change warned that if people do not make an effort to address the climate crisis, the negative consequences of global warming will be difficult to prevent or restrain. This means that human behavior and activities in the coming years will determine the world that future generations live in.

A.3 High-fear appeal condition

A picture of a polar bear that starved to death and the following explanatory note were provided: 'News reports stated that scientists have found polar bears that had starved to death in Norway and attributed the death to accelerating climate change; as the Arctic ice melts, polar bears, unable to hunt seals, are doomed'. The picture was obtained from the following website:
  http://www.theguardian.com/environment/2013/aug/06/starved-polar-bear-record-sea-ice-melt.

Effort investment in persuasiveness: a comparative study of environmental advertising in the United States and Korea

Sukki Yoon[a], Yeonshin Kim[b] and Tae Hyun Baek[c]

[a]Department of Marketing, Bryant University, Smithfield, USA; [b]Department of Business Administration, Myongji University, Seoul, South Korea; [c]Department of Integrated Strategic Communication, University of Kentucky, Lexington, USA

The authors of this article compare American and Korean reactions to the persuasiveness of environmental advertising campaigns that are preceded by environmental pledges. Findings indicate that environmental advertising effectiveness depends on how much effort recipients put into making environmental pledges prior to viewing the advertisements. Study 1 demonstrates that when environmental pledges requesting more effort precede ad messages, Americans are more persuaded but Koreans are less persuaded. Study 2 extends the findings and rules out an alternative explanation − mere-effort effect − by showing that the results are replicated only with an issue-relevant pledge, but not with an issue-irrelevant pledge.

> The greater the effort, the greater the glory.
> Pierre Corneille
> Effort is not effort until it begins to hurt.
> Ortega y Ortega

Introduction

Although consumers worldwide value eco-friendly behaviors such as recycling and energy conservation, they may perceive the challenges of daily eco-friendly activities quite differently, depending on their sociocultural backgrounds. As a result, they may respond quite differently to pro-environmental messages.

Consider Sarah, an American consumer who lives in Boston. She keeps two trash bins for sorting her trash throughout the week: one for recyclable materials and another for regular trash. Every Wednesday, she places the bins outside for city pickup. Although she occasionally throws recyclables into the regular trash, she usually tries to carefully follow guidelines for placing recyclables into the recycle bin. Rather than being guided by governmental regulations, she is primarily motivated by her good will. That is, she *autonomously* chooses to follow eco-friendly behavior.

On the other hand, Eunju lives in Seoul. She also sorts recyclables from the regular trash throughout the week. Unlike Sarah however, every Wednesday Eunju and neighbors from the same town take their recyclable trash to the public recycle center and sort it into bins designated for cans, bottles, plastics, and paper. She cautiously abides by the rules because her actions are salient in the public eye; the neighbors would frown on her if they saw her putting trash into a wrong bin. She sometimes feels tired and would like to throw recyclable waste into the regular trash bin, but that option is too costly because the Korean volume-based waste collection fee system mandates that all citizens must use specially designed plastic bags for regular trash. A 20-liter bag costs about $1.00, equivalent to $2.50 for a standard 13-gallon bag used in US households. Thus, it would be too expensive for Eunju to 'waste' precious purchased space if she put recyclables into a bag allocated for regular trash only. Ultimately, sociocultural pressures primarily drive her pro-environmental behavior. That is, her choice to be eco-friendly is primarily externally *imposed*.

Now imagine that Sarah and Eunju are flipping through magazines and see a two-page ad advocating recycling, printed front-to-back. The front page for both ads displays a recycling pledge: 'I will recycle my plastics, paper, and metal cans,' with a line below for the consumer to sign the promise. However, the two ads are subtly different: Sarah views an ad asking her to *transcribe* the pledge verbatim in a blank space appearing before the signature line. Eunju views an ad asking her to *read* the ad carefully before signing. The flip side of both ad versions features an ad showcasing the benefits of recycling. Which ad would be more effective? Would Sarah respond differently if she encountered the reading version rather than the transcription version? How would Eunju respond if she encountered the transcription version rather than the reading version? We argue that they would regard the messages differently. Sarah's autonomous and Eunju's imposed-choice sociocultural backgrounds and the effort they must make regarding the pledge would evoke different attitudes. We address these questions in the current article.

These are important questions, because message recipients may respond differently to persuasive messages depending on the amount of effort they expend in processing the message (Modig, Dahlén, and Colliander 2014). In particular, effort investment, which refers to the inconvenience or difficulty people experience when they expend time, energy, and resources in pursuing goals (Baek, Yoon, and Kim 2015; Kim and Labroo 2011; Yoon, Choi, and Song 2011), is related to goal value and motivation (Zhang et al. 2011), goal achievement and reward (Kivets, Urminsky, and Zheng 2006), quality judgment (Kruger et al. 2004), issue valence and issue capability (Mittal, Ross, and Tsiros 2002), and job involvement and task performance (Pierro, Kruglanski, and Higgins 2006). No prior study, however, to our best knowledge, has examined effort investment in cross-cultural contexts. We aim to fill this gap here.

Noting the importance of effort investment in environmental persuasion, we test effort investment and sociocultural background as they jointly affect advertising effectiveness. We propose that sociocultural differences cause people to feel more or less autonomous. As a result, eco-friendly requests requiring them to invest effort in pro-environmental behaviors may evoke different reactions. We investigate the idea in two experimental studies using two pro-environmental advertisements: for recycling (Study 1) and for energy saving (Study 2). Our research contributes to the growing literature on environmental persuasion by identifying culture as moderating how effort investment strengthens or weakens advertisements promoting sustainable behaviors.

Theoretical background

Asking consumers to sign environmental pledges has been found effective for increasing compliance with environmental persuasion (Baek, Yoon, and Kim 2015; Wang and

Katzev 1990), so the better social marketers and policymakers understand psychological aspects of green behaviors, the more effectively they can enforce laws and regulations and implement environmental campaigns. Unfortunately, although most consumers see themselves to be indigenous environmentalists and consistently support environmental protection, their environmental concerns do not always translate into environmentally responsible behaviors (e.g., recycling and energy conservation; Baek, Yoon, and Kim 2015; Baca-Motes et al. 2013; Kollmus and Agyeman 2002; McKay-Nesbitt and Yoon 2015; Shrum, McCarthy, and Lowrey 1995; White and Simpson 2013; Zinkhan and Carlson 1995). Considerable efforts have gone into promoting recycling programs in many countries, but people often fail to comply (Schultz, Oskamp, and Mainieri 1995; White, MacDonnell, and Dahl 2011). For instance, approximately 76% of US consumers discard most recyclable materials after using them only once (Environmental Protection Agency 2014), while only about 49% of Korean municipal wastes are recycled (United Nations Statistics Division 2011).

Particularly, building on Zhang et al. (2011), and Baek, Yoon, and Kim (2015), we argue that persuasiveness of environmental advertising campaigns varies depending on the sociocultural backgrounds of the message receivers and the effort they invest in a task related to the advocated behavior, such as making an environmental pledge, before they process the advertising messages. When consumers perceive that they are freely choosing to comply with the environmentally friendly behavior advocated in the ad, they will perceive that the effort reflects their values and personal goals. Thus, they should be more receptive to the environmental advertising when they expend more effort in making an environmental pledge before they are exposed to the ad.

Recall the introductory vignette: if Sarah, who has an autonomous sociocultural background, encountered an ad encouraging recycling, her pro-recycling attitude would increase depending on how much effort she put into making the pledge preceding the ad. On the other hand, Eunju, who lives under sociocultural norms obliging citizens to recycle collectively, might have decreased attitude toward recycling behavior if she puts significant effort into making the pledge. Feeling that compliance would restrict her autonomy in pursuing her goals, she might respond reactively and might devalue the advocated behavior to reaffirm her sense of autonomy. Because greater effort investment generates greater reactance, more effort investment could therefore backfire.

To test this idea, we experimentally controlled for the amount of effort two carefully selected populations would invest in pledging to recycle and conserve energy – the United States and Korea – where perceptions of recycling and energy conservation differ widely. Next we review prior research that led to our prediction that American and Korean consumers will receive environmental advertising differently depending on the amount of effort they invest. We then present Study 1 in which we manipulate the amount of effort that American and Korean participants invest in making the pledge. In Study 2, we replicate and extend the findings to a different context – energy conservation. Finally, we conclude with a discussion of the implications for public policy and marketing.

USA – Korea differences in the perception of environmental protection practice

Individuals from cultures that stress independence, such as North Americans and Western Europeans, are considered to be more personally agentic; those from cultures stressing interdependence such as Latin Americans and Eastern Asians, are considered to be more collectively agentic, resulting in culturally contrasting differences in cognition and human motivation (Cui et al. 2012; Kim, Han, and Yoon 2010; Markus and Kitayama

1991; Yoon 2013). Relatedly, those who are personally agentic perceive that agency emanates from the self. In turn, they are more intrinsically motivated to pursue actions they perceive as self-initiated. Those who are collectively agentic perceive agency to lie within the collective and, in turn, are more likely to pursue actions they perceive as collectively originated (Hernandez and Iyengar 2001). Following this line of thought, we question whether such East-West cultural differences might trigger people in each culture to perceive pro-environmental persuasion differently.

The US approach to environmental protection is closely tied to its individualistic cultural norms – the acknowledgement of independent human agency. Reflecting its individualistic belief system, the American way of changing public behavior about environmental protection is to convince individuals to make informed, free, autonomous, eco-friendly choices. Accordingly, public discourse about environmental protection in the United States focuses on environmental consumerism – environmental friendliness in purchasing, consuming, and disposing of goods. To this end, many public and private environmental organizations have waged campaigns to encourage individual households to be eco-friendly. For example, Keep America Beautiful sponsored a public service announcement (PSA) that featured a crying Indian; Greenpeace called for individuals to 'Stop the Catastrophe,' and Denver Water campaigned for individuals to 'Use Only What You Need' (Kronrod, Grinstein, and Wathieu 2012). As a result, public concern about environmental issues in the United States has increased over the last several decades (Chang 2012; Kollmus and Agyeman 2002; Taylor 2014). The essential driving force behind the bottom–up environmental movement in the United States is the increased public awareness of environmental issues, which in turn prompts individual consumers to voluntarily participate in pro-environmental behaviors. In sum, it is important for American consumers to *choose to* behave in environmentally friendly ways.

In contrast, the Korean approach to environmental protection appears to be top-down, rooted in collectivistic cultural norms; that is, collective responsibility to act in the interests of society. Reflecting the collectivistic belief system, the Korean government and citizens impose collective pressures to induce individual members of the society to adopt eco-friendly behaviors. For example, the volume-based fee system, introduced in 1995, is a key tenet of Korea's recycling policy (Hong 1999; Rhee 1999). The system requires that individual households pay for the waste they generate (Kim 2002; Hong 1999; Rhee 1999), a pay-as-you-throw system that mandates economic penalties in the effort to decrease unrecyclable waste (Kim 2002). Individuals are also fined for improperly disposing of unrecyclable materials and food wastes (Lee 2012). Nongovernmental citizen watch-dog activities abound as well; many neighborhoods install security cameras to ensure that residents follow correct procedures (Lee 2012). Matters are more stringent regarding energy conservation. The South Korean government commonly enforces measures to reduce electricity usage. For example, during the summer of 2013, all public offices were required to maintain indoor temperatures of 28 °C (83 °F) or above, and all commercial buildings were required to maintain temperatures of 26 °C (79 °F) or above (Phneah 2013). The energy saving measures also strictly banned businesses from leaving their doors open to attract customers off the street. Violations drew maximum fines of three million won (US$2,664). In sum, Korean consumers are required to be environmentally friendly.

US choice-driven recycling policies versus Korean obligation-driven recycling polices reflect each nation's differing cultural values. In America, individual choice to recycle apparently encourages and increases recycling, but in Korea, obligation to society may be most persuasive. The individualism–collectivism framework (Triandis 1995) indicates that Western-oriented individualists, such as Americans, are motivated by their own preferences, needs, and rights, and thus give priority to personal rather than to group goals. On the other hand, Eastern-oriented collectivists, such as Koreans, view themselves as closely linked individuals who are primarily parts of whole families, networks of cow-orkers, tribes, or nations, so they are mainly motivated by socially imposed norms and duties. Americans tend to value their freedom to choose, but East Asians do not necessar-ily prefer choice (Iyengar and Lepper 1999). For example, Americans have been shown to favor products they choose (Brehm 1956; Steele, Spencer, and Lynch 1993), but East Asians do not prefer options they select over other possibilities (Hoshino-Browne et al. 2005; Kitayama et al. 2004).

The role of effort investment in autonomous versus imposed choice

Do these cross-national differences in environmental protection perceptions – American autonomy versus Korean imposed choice – affect consumers when they must expend effort in processing advertisements for recycling and energy conservation?

A major premise of this research is that initial effort investment may intensify motiva-tions to comply with subsequent requests (Baek, Yoon, and Kim 2015). Regulatory engagement theory (Higgins 2006) provides a theoretical foundation for the efficacy of effort investment. The theory suggests that engagement strength affects whether people will perceive that their efforts will bring desirable or undesirable outcomes. That is, stron-ger engagement is likely to intensify motivational and evaluative responses, which will then determine whether individuals see positive value and attractiveness in the focal goal (Zhang et al. 2011). In the present context, if people invest more effort in completing the initial eco-friendly task (i.e., writing vs. reading pledges), they will be more strongly committed to the subsequent task (i.e., processing an environmental message) because they have invested effort, which then makes pro-environmental goals seem more attrac-tive. As a result, they will favorably evaluate the goal (Kim and Labroo 2011).

Along the same lines, Zhang et al.'s (2011) findings offer valuable insights in this regard. Although those authors did not directly examine culture, they indeed found evi-dence that consumers' initial effort investment in pursuing a goal may increase or decrease the value of the goal, depending on whether they perceive they are pursuing the goal by autonomous choice or by imposed obligation. In particular, when consumers per-ceived that they adopted the goal autonomously, they experienced their effort investment as value enhancing. Goals became truly valued only when individuals felt that they had unrestricted choice to pursue them; thus individuals interpreted their actions as reflecting their value and commitment to the goal and their effort investment intensified the initial positive value. In contrast, when consumers perceived that they were restricted in adopt-ing the goal, they experienced psychological reactance instead and lacked goal commit-ment even though the goals were of positive initial value. Considering that autonomous goal condition and imposed goal condition in Zhang et al.'s (2011) findings conceptually correspond, respectively, to the US population and the Korean population in our research, we hypothesize:

H1: Americans who invest a high level of effort in making an environmental pledge pre-ceding the ad will show *more* favorable attitudes (H1a) and behavioral intentions (H1b) regarding environmentally friendly behavior than will Americans who invest a low level of effort.

H2: Koreans who invest a high level of effort in making an environmental pledge pre-ceding the ad will show *less* favorable attitudes (H2a) and behavioral intentions (H2b) regarding environmentally friendly behavior than will Koreans who invest a low level of effort.

Pretest

The main purpose of the pretest was to verify our baseline assumption – that Americans perceive that they autonomously choose their recycling and energy-saving behaviors, while Koreans perceive that external impositions demand their recycling and energy-saving behaviors.

Participating in this study were 31 undergraduate students from a northeastern US university and 37 Korean undergraduate students from a university located in Seoul, Korea. Participants completed two sets of questions for recycling and energy saving, respectively, that begin with, 'I (or my household) recycle/save energy because...' anchored with 'I have to (1)/I want to (7)'; and 'It's the law (1)/It's my choice (7).' As expected, compared with Korean participants, American participants indicated that they recycle and save energy because they want to rather than have to (recycling: $M_{US} = 4.84$ vs. $M_{Kor} = 2.78$; $t = 4.68$, $p < .01$, energy saving: $M_{US} = 5.65$ vs. $M_{Kor} = 4.08$; $t = 4.18$, $p < .01$). Similarly, compared with Korean participants, American participants indicated that their choice rather than law directed their recycling and energy saving (recycling: $M_{US} = 4.94$, $M_{Kor} = 3.68$; $t = 3.02$, $p < .01$, energy saving: $M_{US} = 5.71$ vs. $M_{Kor} = 4.54$; $t = 3.15$, $p < .01$). Therefore, the pretest results were consistent with our conceptualization.

Study 1

In Study 1, in the context of recycling, we tested our hypotheses (H1a and H2a), using a 2 (nationality: Americans versus Koreans) X 2 (effort investment: high versus low) between-subjects design.

Method

We recruited 136 US undergraduate participants from a northeastern US university and 179 Korean participants from a university located in Seoul, Korea. Participants were randomly assigned to one of the two experimental conditions (i.e., high vs. low effort investment). The first effort investment induction task required that participants make a recycling pledge before they viewed an advertisement for recycling. After viewing the ad, they filled out a questionnaire that included measures of attitudes toward recycling.

In the high-effort investment condition, participants were instructed to *transcribe* the recycle pledge (e.g., 'I will recycle my plastics, paper, and metal cans,' 'I will use recycled-content products,' 'I will avoid the use of disposable products whenever possible,' and 'I will tell people about how important it is to recycle'), and signed their name at the bottom of the page. In contrast, participants in the low-effort investment condition were instructed to *read* the recycling program pledge and sign their names below the pledge (Baek, Yoon, and Kim 2015; Zhang et al. 2011, experiment 2). A pilot test verified the manipulation of effort investment; participants indicated how much effort they invested in signing (i.e., after *transcribing* or *reading*) the pledge to support recycling ($1 = not\ at\ all$; $7 = very\ much$). As expected, participants in the high effort investment condition – those who *transcribed* and signed – felt that they made more effort in pledging to support recycling than did those in the low-effort investment condition – those who *read* and signed – ($M_{high\text{-}effort} = 4.47$, $M_{low\text{-}effort} = 2.97$; $t = 7.01$, $p < .01$).

After signing the pledge, participants viewed the target ad which includes headline copy, an image of a recycling bin, and a paragraph describing recycling benefits. The ad headline reads, 'Recycle what you can – Recycling not only saves the environment, but also reduces landfill waste.'

Adopted from Blankenship and Wegener (2008), attitudes toward recycling were measured using seven-point semantic differential items anchored with 'bad/good,' 'foolish/wise,' 'negative/positive,' 'unfavorable/favorable,' 'unnecessary/necessary,' 'harmful/beneficial,' and 'undesirable/desirable' (alpha = .97). For the Korean partici-pants, the English questionnaire and stimuli were translated into Korean by a bilingual translator, back-translated into English by a second bilingual translator, and adjusted by a third bilingual translator.

Results

To test H1a and H2a, the attitude measure (alpha = .94) was submitted to a 2 (nationality: Americans versus Koreans) x 2 (effort investment: high versus low) factorial ANOVA. The nationality x effort investment two-way interaction effect emerged ($F(1, 311) = 9.66, p < .01$).

As shown in Figure 1, contrasts revealed that American participants showed more positive attitude toward recycling behavior ($F(1, 134) = 2.26, p < .05$), when they invested high effort ($M_{\text{high-effort}} = 5.72$) than low effort ($M_{\text{low-effort}} = 5.29$), but the oppo-site pattern emerged for Korean participants; that is, Korean participants showed less pos-itive attitude toward recycling behavior ($F(1, 311) = 10.21, p < .01$), when the invested high effort ($M_{\text{high-effort}} = 5.73$) than low effort ($M_{\text{low-effort}} = 6.09$). In addition, a main effect occurred for Nation indicating that Korean ($M_{\text{Kor}} = 5.87$) participants overall showed more positive attitude toward recycling behavior than did American participants ($M_{\text{US}} = 5.52; F(1, 311) = 10.06, p < .01$).

Discussion

Study 1 results demonstrate that Americans are more persuaded but Koreans are less per-suaded by ad messages following environmental pledges that request more effort.

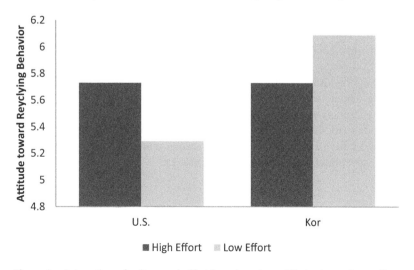

Figure 1.   Interaction of culture and effort investment on attitudes toward recycling.

However, Study 1 is open to an alternative explanation: perhaps the mere effort, not necessarily the effort relevant to the central environmental issue, caused the observed differences. Study 2 is designed to rule out this alternative explanation.

Study 2

Study 2 had two objectives. First, we aimed to conceptually replicate the findings from Study 1, using a different environmental message, energy conservation, with a different dependent variable, behavioral intention (H2a and H2b). More important, we sought to rule out a plausible alternative explanation for Study 1: the participants might have showed differences simply because they had to expend effort in making the pledge. Would the same data pattern emerge even when the pledge is irrelevant to the subsequent ad message? To test this idea, we used a 2 (nationality: Americans versus Koreans) X 2 (effort type: issue-relevant effort versus issue-irrelevant effort) between-subjects design.

Method

Participating in this study were 43 undergraduate students from a northeastern US university and 67 Korean undergraduate students from a university located in Seoul, Korea. Participants were randomly assigned to one of the two experimental conditions (i.e., issue-relevant effort versus issue-irrelevant effort). The other procedures were identical to those of Study 1 except that we changed the pledge and stimulus ad to refer to energy saving. With an image of hands holding an energy-efficient light bulb, the ad copy reads, 'Save energy – you must reduce overall energy consumption at home, school, and work').

Rather than manipulate the amount of effort invested in the pre-ad exposure pledge, we manipulated the type of effort invested; that is, all participants were asked to transcribe and sign either an energy saving pledge (relevant) or the US Pledge of Allegiance (irrelevant). In the issue-relevant effort condition, participants transcribed a pledge similar to the recycling pledge used in Study 1; for example, 'I will turn off unnecessary lights and appliances, including my computer. I will replace incandescent light bulbs with compact light bulbs. I will run the dishwasher only when full.' In the issue-irrelevant effort condition, participants transcribed the Pledge of Allegiance: 'I pledge allegiance to the flag of the United States of America and to the Republic for which it stands, one nation, under God, indivisible, with liberty and justice for all.' The same amount of effort was invested in the two conditions ($M_{relevant} = 4.04$ vs. $M_{irrelevant} = 4.02$; $t\ (108) = 0.05$, $p =$ n.s.).

In addition, this time we measured behavioral intention rather than attitude with the statement: 'I intend to conserve more energy in the next few weeks' ($1 = $ *strongly disagree*; $7 = $ *strongly agree*).

As in Study 1, for the Korean version of the questionnaire and stimuli, a bilingual translator translated it from English into Korean; a second bilingual translator back-translated it into English, and a third bilingual translator adjusted it.

Results

To test the hypotheses, the behavioral intention measure was submitted to a 2 (nationality: Americans versus Koreans) x 2 (effort investment type: relevant versus irrelevant) factorial ANOVA. The nationality x effort investment two-way interaction effect emerged ($F(1, 106) = 10.86, p < .01$).

As shown in Figure 2, contrasts revealed that American participants showed higher behavioral intention toward energy saving ($F(1, 41) = 8.38, p < .05$) when they transcribed the energy saving pledge (i.e., when their effort was issue-relevant; $M_{\text{issue-relevant}} = 5.45$) than when they transcribed the Pledge of Allegiance (i.e., when their effort was issue-irrelevant; $M_{\text{issue-irrelevant}} = 4.57$). But Koreans showed the opposite pattern; that is, they showed lower behavioral intention toward energy saving ($F(1, 65) = 6.22, p < .05$) when they invested effort into transcribing the relevant energy saving pledge ($M_{\text{issue-relevant}} = 4.59$) than when they transcribed the irrelevant Pledge of Allegiance ($M_{\text{issue-irrelevant}} = 5.42$). In addition, Nation or Effort Investment had no main effect (all p's $= n.s.$).

Discussion

The results from Study 2 extend the findings from Study 1 in several ways. First, Study 2 conceptually replicates the Study 1 findings in the context of energy saving. Second, the effect emerges on a different variable: behavioral intention. Third, Study 2 rules out an alternative explanation – whether it was merely the effort that produced the effects observed in Study 1.

General discussion

Our objective in this research is to understand differences between American and Korean consumers in their reactions to persuasive environmental advertising requiring them to invest efforts in recycling. In Study 1, we observe that Americans have more favorable attitudes toward recycling in reaction to advertising requiring them to expend high effort. In contrast, Koreans react with less-favorable attitudes. Accordingly, Study 1 demonstrates that environmental advertising persuasion depends on two key factors: (1) the amount of effort required and (2) sociocultural background. Study 2 shows the findings to be robust across contexts; that is, the same pattern emerges for an energy conservation campaign. Furthermore, Study 2 tests and rules out an important alternative hypothesis: whether it was merely the effort, regardless of the pledge content, that produced the

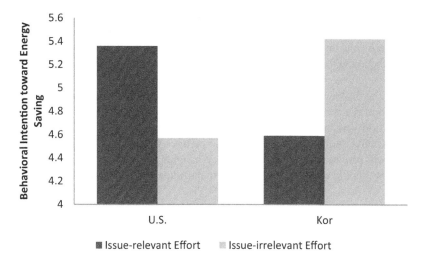

Figure 2. Interaction of culture and effort investments on behavioral intentions toward energy saving.

interaction observed in Study 1. Study 2 results indicate that an issue-relevant effort, but not an issue-irrelevant pledge, increased ad effectiveness among Americans and decreased ad effectiveness among Koreans.

Our findings have several theoretical and managerial implications. From a theoretical standpoint, the research takes the important step of analyzing the interplay of effort investment and compliance with green requests. Although previous research has identified that effort investment impacts have some boundary conditions (e.g., Baek, Yoon, and Kim 2015; Zhang et al. 2011), our study is the first to consider how effort investment effects vary depending on message recipients' national culture. The findings thus broaden our understanding of how effort investment interplays with sociocultural environments.

Some psychological variables – such as counterfactual thinking – may play a role in effort perceptions (e.g., Yoon and Vargas 2010, 2011). When individuals think counterfactually, they first consider alternative outcomes (e.g., Eunju in the introductory scenario imagines, 'I might have ended up paying more for the trash bag'). They then assess how they might have achieved the counterfactual outcome rather than the factual outcome (e.g., 'had I put recyclables into a bag allocated for regular trash'). In such causal attribution thinking processes, individuals mentally alter the perceived antecedents to undo the factual outcome and achieve the counterfactual outcome. Consumers engaging in similar counterfactuals might arrive at different emotional outcomes, depending on where they live. For example, consumers (e.g., Koreans) from a strongly regulated nation may counterfactually and guiltily attribute their actions to personal inadequacy (e.g., 'if I were honest'), whereas consumers (e.g., Americans) from a culture that emphasizes internal choice to recycle might use behavior-focused shameful counterfactuals (e.g., 'if I had recycled correctly'). Interestingly, research has found that guilt is more powerful than shame for generating positive change, so future research might examine whether Koreans and Americans actually derive different counterfactuals, which in turn may cause varying behavioral changes.

The current research has straightforward implications for global marketers. That is, our findings provide insights for green marketers dealing with global consumers (Maslowska, Smit, and van den Putte 2013). By considering the sociocultural background of target audiences, marketers may be able to craft culturally customized environmental messages using contextual cues that increase or decrease the effort message recipients must expend. In particular, when targeting Americans, it would be worthwhile to incorporate promotional tactics that encourage consumers to expend additional effort (e.g., commenting or transcribing). However, when targeting Korean audiences such effort-generating tactics should be scaled down.

In addition, this research uses stimuli that closely resemble real-world environmental ad applications in a controlled setting with minimal confounding noise. Our stimuli differ from real-world versions only in that we randomize manipulations of effort investment. As environmental campaigns commonly use pledges to reinforce issue importance, our proposed work provides green marketers key insights into when they should encourage and when they should discourage recipients to participate in processing the ad message.

Limitation

In both studies, the stimulus ad did not include the pledge – the effort investment manipulation. Instead, participants completed the pledge task separately and then watched the ad. This design allowed us to isolate the effects of the pledge from the advertising message. However, real-world ad campaigns that encompass pledges may not resemble the pledge–message sequence we employed. Future research that incorporates the pledge into an actual advertising message with heightened realism might increase ecological validity of the design.

Another caveat is that, in both Studies 1 and 2, we did not use a single experiment to consider both dependent variables – attitude and behavioral intention. Rather, we separately examined attitudes toward the recycling in Study 1 and behavioral intentions toward energy saving in Study 2. A study design that covers both variables in a single study, perhaps within a different context, will shed light on the interplay between effort investment and culture. Future research might address that question.

In addition, we did not control for possible confounding factors. Some psychological and situational variables might come into play and influence the effort–culture interaction. For example, mindfulness (e.g., Langer 1989) might reduce or eliminate the interaction effect by increasing one's attention to the emotions and thoughts occurring during the information processing. Also, in the pilot study we conducted for the manipulation check, and we only used American participants; collecting data from Korean participants would have fully completed the picture.

Disclosure statement

No potential conflict of interest was reported by the authors.

Funding

This work was supported by the National Research Foundation of Korea Grant funded by the Korean Government [grant number NRF-2013S1A2A1A01033553].

References

Baca-Motes, K., A. Brown, A. Gneezy, E.A. Keenan, and L.D. Nelson. 2013. Commitment and Behavior Change: Evidence from the Field. *Journal of Consumer Research* 39, no. 5: 1070–84.

Baek, T., S. Yoon, and Y. Kim. 2015. When assertive language enhances environmental advertising persuasion: the moderating role of effort investment. *International Journal of Advertising* 34, no. 1: 135–57.

Blankenship, K.L., and D.T. Wegener. 2008. Opening the mind to close it: considering a message in light of important values increases message processing and later resistance to change. *Journal of Personality and Social Psychology* 94, no. 2: 196–213.

Brehm, J.W. 1956. Postdecision changes in the desirability of alternatives. *Journal of Abnormal and Social Psychology* 52, no. 3: 384–9.

Chang, C. 2012. Are guilt appeals a panacea in green advertising. *International Journal of Advertising* 31, no. 4: 741–71.

Cui, G., X. Yang, H. Wang, and H. Liu. 2012. Culturally incongruent messages in international advertising. *International Journal of Advertising* 31, no. 2: 355–76.

Environmental Protection Agency. 2014. Municipal solid waste generation, recycling, and disposal in the United States: facts and figures for 2012. http://www.epa.gov/osw/nonhaz/municipal/pubs/2012_msw_fs.pdf (accessed February 18, 2015).

Hernandez, M., and S.S. Iyengar. 2001. What drives whom? A cultural perspective on human agency. *Social Cognition* 19, no. 3: 269–94.

Higgins, E.T. 2006. Value from hedonic experience and engagement. *Psychological Review* 113, no. 3: 439–60.

Hong, S. 1999. The effects of unit pricing system upon household solid waste management: the Korean experience. *Journal of Environmental Management* 57, no. 1: 1–10.

Hoshino-Browne, E., A.S. Zanna, S.J. Spencer, M.P. Zanna, S. Kitayama, and S. Lackenbauer. 2005. On the cultural guises of cognitive dissonance: The case of Easterns and Westerners. *Journal of Personality and Social Psychology* 89, no. 3: 294–310.

Iyengar, S.S., and M.R. Lepper. 1999. Rethinking the value of choice: A cultural perspective on intrinsic motivation. *Journal of Personality and Social Psychology* 76, no. 3: 349−66.

Kim, I. 2002. Korea's policy instruments for waste minimization. *Journal of Material Cycles and Waste Management* 4, no. 1: 12−22.

Kim, B., S. Han, and S. Yoon. 2010. Advertising creativity in Korea: scale development and validation. All authors contributed equally. *Journal of Advertising* 50, no. 2: 93−108.

Kim, S., and A.A. Labroo. 2011. From inherent value to incentive value: when and why pointless effort enhances consumer preference. *Journal of Consumer Research* 38, no. 4: 712−42.

Kitayama, S., A.C. Snibbe, H.R. Markus, and T. Szuki. 2004. Is there any 'free' choice? Cognitive dissonance in two cultures. *Psychological Science* 15, no. 8: 224−53.

Kivets, R., O. Urminsky, and Y. Zheng. 2006. The goal-gradient hypothesis resurrected: Purchase acceleration, illusionary goal progress, and customer retention. *Journal of Marketing Research* 43, no. 1: 39−58.

Kollmus, A., and J. Agyeman. 2002. Mind the gap: why do people act environmentally and what are the barriers to pro-Environmental behavior. *Environmental Education Research* 8, no. 3: 239−60.

Kronrod, A., A. Grinstein, and L. Wathieu. 2012. Go green! Should environmental messages be so assertive? *Journal of Marketing* 76, no. 1: 95−102.

Kruger, J., D. Wirtz, L. Van Boven, and T.W. Altermatt. 2004. The effort heuristic. *Journal of Experimental Social Psychology* 40, no. 1: 91−8.

Langer, E.J. 1989. *Mindfulness.* Merloyd Lawrence.

Lee, G. 2012. *Recycling today.* http://www.recyclingtoday.com/rtge1112-municipal-recycling-seoul.aspx#.UR0TGgE7dSI.email (accessed February 18, 2013).

Markus, H.R., and S. Kitayama. 1991. Culture and the self: implications for cognition, emotion, and motivation. *Psychological Review* 98, no. 2: 224−53.

Maslowska, E., E.G. Smit, and B. van den Putte. 2013. Assessing the cross-cultural applicability of tailored advertising. *International Journal of Advertising* 32, no. 4: 487−511.

McKay-Nesbitt, J., and S. Yoon. 2015. Social marketing communication messages: How congruence between source and content influences physical activity attitudes. *Journal of Social Marketing* 5, no. 1: 40−55.

Mittal, V., W.T. Ross, and M. Tsiros. 2002. The role of issue valence and issue capability in determining effort investment. *Journal of Marketing Research* 39, no. 4: 455−68.

Modig, E., M. Dahlén, and J. Colliander. 2014. Consumer-perceived signals of 'creative' versus 'efficient' advertising. *International Journal of Advertising* 33, no. 1: 137−54.

Phneah, E. 2013. South Korea implements energy saving measures. *ZD Net.* Available online at: http://www.zdnet.com/south-korea-implements-energy-saving-measures-7000016928/ (accessed 11 November 11 2013).

Pierro, A., A.W. Kruglanski, and T.E. Higgins. 2006. Progress takes work: effects of the locomotion dimension on job involvement, effort investment and task performance in organizations. *Journal of Applied Social Psychology* 36, no. 7: 1723−43.

Rhee, J. 1999. Economic incentives and optimal waste management: Korean Eexperiences in Uunit pricing for garbage collection. *Environmental Economics and Policy Studies* 2, no. 1: 113−28.

Schultz, P.W., S. Oskamp, and T. Mainieri. 1995. Who recycles and when? A review of personal and situational factors. *Journal of Environmental Psychology* 15, no. 2: 105−21.

Shrum, L.J., J.A. McCarthy, and T.M. Lowrey. 1995. Buyer characteristics the green consumer and their implications for advertising strategy. *Journal of Advertising* 24, no. 2: 71−82.

Steele, C.M., S.J. Spencer, and M. Lynch. 1993. Self-image resilience and dissonance: The role of affirmational resources. *Journal of Personality and Social Psychology* 64, no. 6: 885−96.

Taylor, C.R. 2014. Corporate social responsibility and advertising. *International Journal of Advertising* 33, no. 1: 11−5.

Triandis, H.C. 1995. *Individualism and collectivism. New directions in social psychology.* Boulder: Westview Press.

United Nations Statistics Division. 2011. Environmental indicators: waste − municipal waste treatment. http://unstats.un.org/unsd/environment/wastetreatment.htm (accessed February 18, 2013).

Wang, T.H., and R.D. Katzev. 1990. Group commitment and resource conservation: two field experiments on promoting Rrecycling. *Journal of Applied Social Psychology* 24, no. 4: 265−75.

White, K., R. MacDonnell, and D.W. Dahl. 2011. It's the mind-set that matters: the role of construal level and message framing in influencing consumer efficacy and conservation behaviors. *Journal of Marketing Research* 48, no. 3: 472−85.

White, K., and B. Simpson. 2013. When do (and don't) normative appeals influence sustainable consumer behaviors?" *Journal of Marketing* 77, no. 2: 78−95.

Yoon, S. 2013. Do negative consumption experiences hurt manufacturers or retailers? The influence of reasoning style on consumer blame attributions and purchase intention. *Psychology & Marketing* 37, no. 7: 555−65.

Yoon, S., Y. Choi, and S. Song. 2011. When intrusive can be likable: Product placement effects on multitasking consumers. *Journal of Advertising* 40, no. 2: 63−75.

Yoon, S., and P.T. Vargas. 2010. Feeling happier when paying more: dysfunctional counterfactual thinking in consumer affect. *Psychology & Marketing* 27, no. 12: 1075−100.

Yoon, S., and P.T. Vargas. 2011. 'No more' leads to 'want more,' but 'no less' leads to 'want less': counterfactual thinking when faced with point-of-purchase discounts. *Journal of Consumer Behavior* 10, no. 2: 93−101.

Zhang, Y., J. Xu, Z. Jiang, and S. Huang. 2011. Been there, done that: the impact of effort investment on goal value and consumer motivation. *Journal of Consumer Research* 38, no. 1: 78−93.

Zinkhan, G.M., and L. Carlson. 1995. Green advertising and reluctant consumer. *Journal of Advertising* 24, no. 2: 1−6.

The effect of non-stereotypical gender role advertising on consumer evaluation

Kyounghee Chu, Doo-Hee Lee and Ji Yoon Kim

Business School, Korea University, Seoul, Korea

Non-stereotypical gender role (NSGR) representations have been increasing gradually over time in advertising, where male celebrities endorse traditionally or stereotypically female-oriented products and vice versa. This research proposes that the overall effect of NSGR advertising on consumer evaluation is composed of two opposing effects. This study investigates the conditions in which either the positive or the negative effects are likely to prevail. Specifically, this study identifies dual mediation, a positive effect via novelty perception and a negative effect via cognitive resistance. We conduct five experiments that indicate that the sign of the overall effect of NSGR advertising depends on the self-construal and the need-for-uniqueness. The positive effect via novelty perception exists only for consumers with independent self-construal and a high need-for-uniqueness. The negative effect via cognitive resistance only appears when consumers have interdependent self-construal and a low need-for-uniqueness. This research establishes an important link between gender-incongruity and personal traits, subsequently demonstrating when marketers should use the NSGR advertising.

Introduction

A phenomenon where male celebrities endorse traditionally or stereotypically feminine-oriented products and vice versa has emerged in advertising (Kim 2009; Son 2013). For example, Seung Ki Lee, a celebrity in Korea, featured in an advertisement for rice cookers in January 2014. Further, Kim Hee-Ae, a female celebrity in Korea, featured in an advertisement for motor engine oil. Regular male models sometimes appear in advertisements for stereotypically feminine-oriented products, such as rice cookers and vacuum cleaners (Kim 2009; Son 2013). This cross-gender phenomenon of male models endorsing traditionally feminine-oriented products implies a social change in gender role stereotypes, which has historically proven challenging. Perspectives on a woman's role have changed significantly worldwide because of women's increased entry into society, and cross-gender ads have begun to reflect social changes in ads in response to changes in women's social status (Paek, Nelson, and Vilela 2011). Such cross-gender phenomena have emerged around the globe and are emerging more gradually in Asian countries compared to Western countries(Lien, Chou, and Chang 2012; Paek, Nelson, and Vilela 2011).

Traditional match-up is assumed considering the endorser's attributes and the attributes of the product (Till and Busler 2000). Advertisers often create a gender image for a brand by featuring the targeted gender in an advertising as the 'typical' user to position and reposition products. Stereotypes become essential signaling through which advertisers can communicate a product category to the target market (Lindner 2004). Because advertising is one of the most influential tools in disseminating stereotypical ideas that create perceptions, gender role stereotypes in advertising influence and reinforce the stereotypical values of society (Eisend, Plagemann, and Sollwedel 2014). Therefore, a non-stereotypical gender role (NSGR) phenomenon in advertising could influence people's perceptions and include target customers that marketers have rarely considered (Eisend, Plagemann, and Sollwedel 2014).

Despite the real impact of NSGR advertising, previous research focuses on the positive effect of a match between a model and the product's image (Caballero and Solomon 1984; Friedman and Friedman 1979). The academic research on the positive effect of mismatch is limited (Debevec and Iyer 1986; Lien, Chou, and Chang 2012). Moreover, prior research shows mixed results. Research has followed that explains and tests the 'match-up' hypothesis or the congruency between the product's gender image and the spokesperson (Caballero and Solomon 1984; Friedman and Friedman 1979; Whipple and Courtney 1985). In the match-up hypothesis, the gender image of the product and the message delivered by the spokesperson should converge in an effective advertising (Lien, Chou, and Chang 2012). On the other hand, some studies investigate the mismatch hypothesis whereby the incongruence between the product's gender image and the spokesperson results in a superior product and advertising evaluation (Debevecand Iyer 1986; Gentry and Haley 1984; Lien, Chou, and Chang 2012). For example, Lynch and Schuler (1994) suggest that a mismatch between products and spokespersons might attract greater attention to the message. Debevec and Iyer (1986) show that breaking male stereotypes in radio advertising by depicting men using female-oriented products results in superior consumer evaluation.

Therefore, we consider the combination of the mixed results of previous research and investigate the conditions in which gender-incongruity is effective. We further explore the underlying mechanisms of this process. Specifically, this study adopts a dual mediation framework to identify the underlying mechanism of consumer interpretations of NSGR advertising.

Theoretical background and hypotheses development

Stereotyping and stereotypical gender role portrayals in advertising

A stereotype is a representation of a cultural group that emphasizes a trait or set of traits that may not be an accurate representation of the group (Storms 1979). Gender stereotypes include beliefs that certain attributes differentiate gender (Ashmore and del Boca 1981). Stereotypes reflect perceivers' observations of individuals in daily life, and stereotypes serve as a cognitive shortcut for efficient communication and comprehension. Research on gender role stereotyping is increasingly studied and is considered a significant subject in social psychology because it affects society by shaping and mirroring typical beliefs and values in daily life (Knoll, Eisend, and Steinhagen 2011).

Advertising messages are created through the portrayal of idealized, stereotypical individuals. Simplistic images ignore 'the complexities of modern lives,' stereotypes thus become essential signaling through which advertisers can communicate a product category and for whom the product is intended (Lindner 2004). Stereotypes are results shaped by dominant advertising ideologies. The way women are portrayed in advertisements has long been a source of concern and the focus of study among scholars of social science and communication (Lindner 2004). Historically, advertising has portrayed gender as distinct and predictable. Women are depicted as nurturing and empathetic but softer and more dependent, and advertising targeted at women implies that a product will reduce stress and result in a more manageable life. A gender representation study of 1300 prime-time commercials find that although women purchase the majority of goods and services, they are undervalued as primary characters in prime-time commercials except for those advertising health and beauty products.

Previous research suggests that products with a feminine image include dishwashing liquid, wine, and hairspray, whereas masculine-perceived products include lawnmowers, paint, and beer (Iyer and Debevec 1986; Lien, Chou, and Chang 2012). However, as women's social status has evolved, increasing research has studied the diversity of the portrayal of women's roles in media and advertising. Debevec and Iyer (1986) find that male spokespersons in radio advertising generate more positive attitudes and purchase intentions for feminine products than their female counterparts. Therefore, incongruence represents a conflict between the preconceptions of a traditional product's user (feminine or masculine) and a spokesperson's gender (female or male).

Literature on processing stereotype-congruent and stereotype-incongruent information

Incongruity refers to "the extent that structural correspondence is achieved between the entire configuration of attribute relations associated with an object, such as a product, and the configuration specified by the schema" (Meyers-Levy and Tybout 1989, p. 40). In consumer persuasion contexts, advertising often uses incongruent or inconsistent elements (Meyers-Levy and Tybout 1989). Mandler (1982) suggests that the increased arousal and cognitive effort that accompanies increases in incongruity between a schema and an object influences the extremity of evaluation. Whether an evaluation is relatively more favorable or unfavorable is a function of how easily the processor can satisfactorily resolve the incongruity. Mandler (1982) also suggests that resolving moderate incongruity leads to a positive state, such as curiosity or interest, whereas failing to resolve extreme incongruity leads to a negative state, such as anxiety or discomfort. Non-conventional ads, such as NSGR advertising, are viewed with curiosity because they are atypical, and viewers can resolve moderate incongruity[1] (male spokespersons using female-gendered products such as home appliances).

Meyers-Levy and Tybout (1989) define moderate versus extreme product incongruity in terms of levels within the product category hierarchy; moderate incongruity can be resolved at the next level within the hierarchy, while resolution of extreme incongruity necessitates moving through multiple levels. Based on Meyers-Levy and Tybout's (1989) definition, Jhang, Grant, and Campbell (2012) define the level of incongruity in terms of the association types the consumer must consider to resolve the incongruity and understand a benefit of a product. Building on the prior research, we define the level of incongruity in terms of the complexity of the associative links the consumer must assess to resolve gender-incongruity and understand a featured advertising spokesperson of the opposite gender of the product category's gender image. For example, when customers face female-oriented product ads featuring male models, consumers attempt to create an associative link between the models and the products. This process is called elaboration (Noseworthy, Cotte, and Lee 2011). In the process of elaboration, consumers may conclude that the juicer, an example of a female-oriented product, is convenient even for males who do not know how to make juice. Similarly, if consumers find a solution by making associative links from the process of elaboration, the incongruity level might be considered moderate. On the other hand, when individuals face exclusively female product advertising featuring male models, they also create associative linkages between the models and the products (Noseworthy, Cotte, and Lee 2011). However, in cases of 'gender-exclusive' products, an individual might fail to understand, despite attempts at elaboration, the reason why such a product features a male model. Therefore, if an individual fails to make an associative linkage despite the process of elaboration, the incongruity level might be considered extreme.

NSGR advertising may stimulate greater attention and interest among audiences than traditional stereotypical gender role (SGR) advertising because its differentiation (Debevec and Iyer 1986; Lien, Chou, and Chang 2012) leads to perceived novelty and positive attitudes (Eisend, Plagemann, and Sollwedel 2014; Debevec and Iyer 1986; Lien, Chou, and Chang 2012). However, as schema-inconsistent advertising, it may also cause psychological discomfort among audiences leading to cognitive resistance and counterarguments. Therefore, NSGR advertising may represent a double-edged sword if it evokes a negative cognitive response, such as resistance or discomfort, although it is interesting to consumers familiar with typical advertising.

Recently, research on cross-gender brand extensions – masculine or feminine brands that target the opposite gender – has increased (Jung and Lee 2006;Yeo, Yoon, and Song 2010; Ulrich 2013). Jung and Lee (2006) show the positive effect of mismatch between the gender of a parent brand and the extension in additional cross-gender brands. Ulrich (2013) investigates the effect of gender role attitudes on the evaluation of cross-gender brand extension. The author shows that the attitudes of consumers who uphold more traditional gender roles are less favorable than the attitudes of consumers who uphold more liberal gender roles suggesting a reluctance to accept the extension of cross-gender brands.

Perceptions of novelty and cognitive resistance as dual mediating variables

The perceived novelty of an advertisement is defined as the degree to which a consumer perceives an advertisement to be a new and exciting alternative to existing advertising (Eisend 2007). Novelty enhances Gestalt-like global perception, whereas familiarity reinforces detail-oriented local perception. Novelty increases high-level construal relative to familiarity. Novelty is critical to the effectiveness of advertising (Mandler 1982). Advertisements with novel cues can draw attention and elicit consumer creativity and positive responses occur if consumers perceive novelty from the advertisement (Fiske 1980). Mandler (1982) and Fiske (1980) maintain that novel stimuli, because of its unexpected nature, will produce a stronger response than familiar stimuli. The study suggests that NSGR advertising can create a favorable response from some consumers compared to conventional advertising because of the novelty of stimuli.

Further, cognitive resistance to advertising provides an additional insight to the underlying process of NSGR advertising because cognitive responses are often used to provide insights on the process mechanism (Eisend 2007). Some audiences have a sense of resistance when exposed to NSGR advertising and change in gender roles, which is rooted in differences and inconsistency in their perceptions of existing schema on SGRs. Literature on cognitive psychology indicates that consumers have an intrinsic desire for psychological equilibrium (Osgood and Tannenbaum 1955). Therefore, consumers are inclined to resist change and inconsistency in their existing schema. Resistance is a normal response of customers experiencing novel stimuli (Ram 1987). Therefore, this suggests that consumers may experience cognitive resistance to the advertising when confronted with novel NSGR advertising evoking negative consequences for marketers.

Self-construal level and need for uniqueness as moderating variables

Self-construal (SC)

SC level reflects the extent to which individuals view themselves as an individuated entity or in relation to others (Zhang and Shrum 2009).People with independent SC regard themselves as distinct from others. They emphasize the value of uniqueness and individual achievement. Contrastingly, people with an interdependent SC consider themselves as a part of a group and value group connectedness, harmony, and safety (Zhang and Shrum 2009).

Empirical research analyzes the significant role of SC in consumer information processing (Stayman, Alden, and Smith 1992). The research shows that SC levels affect consumer response to the same advertisement differently by influencing consumer information processing (An 2012). Independent SCs focus primarily on the primary advertising context. These consumers are concerned with the object itself and are influenced by the target characteristics when processing information. On the other hand, interdependent SCs consider the relationship between themselves and the subject in combination. Consumers focus on the contextual information surrounding the target and the attributes of the object.

Incongruity between a product cue and a spokesperson could lead to increased elaboration. The effect of NSGR advertising is evident when consumers experience psychological arousal and pleasure from interpreting and solving the incongruity and ambiguities of the advertising content. The antecedent of interpreting the incongruity and ambiguities of NSGR advertising is elaboration effort. The important factors for elaboration effort are the person-specific variables. Some consumers have the motivation to elaborate on the incongruity to resolve it, while others do not. This individual difference in elaboration tendency leads to a different attitude towards advertising (Mandler 1982; Noseworthy, Cotte, and Lee 2011). Therefore, some consumers who are motivated to elaborate on incongruity may resolve that incongruity. A positive experience, that is, psychological arousal, pleasure, and joy caused by incongruity resolution can lead to positive attitudes toward the advertising (Peracchio and Meyers-Levy 1994; Stayman, Alden and Smith 1992). However, some consumers who are not motivated to elaborate on incongruity may not find resolution. As a result, a negative experience of unsolved incongruity can lead to negative attitudes toward the advertising (Mandler 1982; Noseworthy, Cotte, and Lee 2011).

Prior empirical research shows the different characteristics (elaboration level and type) of SC in consumer incongruent information processing. Independents increase elaboration in response to incongruity to resolve incongruity, whereas interdependents demonstrate no increase in elaboration when exposed to incongruent information (Meyers-Levy, Louie, and Curren 1994). In addition, Lee, Aaker, and Gardner (2000) also find that independents have a greater tendency towards promotion-focus, while interdependents have a tendency towards prevention-focus. Zhu and Meyers-Levy (2005) show that promotion-focused individuals, because of their emphasis on relational elaboration and its powers of integration, better comprehend and respond more favorably to ambiguous advertising. Yet, prevention-focused individuals respond more favorably to unambiguous advertising because of their prevailing use of item-specific elaboration and its focus on the particulars of data.

To apply these findings in the current research context, independents have a greater tendency for promotion focus (Lee, Aaker, and Gardner 2000) and are motivated to integrate the advertising items through relational elaboration. As a result, the gender-incongruity between the products and the models in the advertising are better understood and resolved through relational elaboration and the integration process, and the resulting positive experiences (joy and pleasure) through the resolution process can lead to positive attitudes towards advertising. Interdependents, however, because of item-specific elaboration and its focus on the particulars of data, have a weak motivation to resolve the gender incongruity between the products and the models. Interdependents are less likely to experience psychological arousal and pleasure caused by the process of resolving the advertising ambiguity and seem to experience psychological discomfort from failing to resolve the ambiguity. These experiences cause cognitive resistance to NSGR advertising, a negative impression of it, and consumers form less favorable attitudes than when exposed to general ads. Based on this reasoning, we propose the following hypotheses.

H1: SC will moderate the relationship between the advertisement type and attitude towards the advertisement.

H1a: Consumers with independent SC will have a more favorable attitude towards the NSGR advertising than the SGR advertising.

H1b: Consumers with interdependent SC will have a more favorable attitude towards the SGR advertising than the NSGR advertising.

H2: The relationship between the advertising type and the attitude towards advertisement is mediated by perceived novelty for consumers with independent SC, whereas the relationship is mediated by cognitive resistance to advertising for consumers with interdependent SC.

Need for uniqueness (NFU)

In addition to individual factors, people draw intrinsic satisfaction from the perception that they are special, unique, and separate from 'the masses', which is referred to as the 'need for uniqueness' (Snyder and Fromkin 1977).Snyder and Fromkin (1977) examine the differences between high and low NFU individuals. They suggest that high NFUs are particularly sensitive to the extent to which they are perceived as similar to others and are most likely to exhibit behaviors that establish a sense of being special, such as acquiring scarce or new products. Thus, consumers with a high NFU desire the possession and experience of unique things, which differentiates them from others (Simonson and Nowlis 2000; Tian, Bearden, and Hunter 2001). These consumers focus on dissimilarity (differentiation) rather than the similarity of objects (Ruvio 2008). This construct is theorized as a multidimensional construct of creative choice counterconformity, unpopular choice counterconformity, and avoidance of similarity (Simonson and Nowlis 2000; Tian, Bearden, and Hunter 2001).

Previous research on uniqueness motivation suggests that a high level of similarity is perceived as unpleasant (Snyder and Fromkin 1977). By forming creative, dissimilar, and unconformable behaviors, consumers with uniqueness motivation can obtain a positive social evaluation as a unique individual (Snyder and Fromkin 1977; Simonson and Nowlis 2000). Consumers in search of differentiation from others avoid consuming commonly used products and prefer differentiated products or objects. Therefore, to appeal to customer desire to be different from others, marketers have developed advertising that employs uniqueness and novelty appeals to break the rules of the reference group (Simonson and Nowlis 2000).

In the information processing context, NFU manifests in the tendency to recall and remember the stimuli that are different from others (Simonson and Nowlis 2000), suggesting that exposure to incongruent stereotypical information can enhance the enjoyment of information processing experiences among those with a high level of this need, whereas consumers with a low NFU do not place value on incongruent information (Snyder and Fromkin 1977). Simonson and Nowlis (2000) find that high NFUs are less responsive to common marketing tactics, such as traditional promotional events and advertising puffery. Therefore, high NFUs seek new and potentially discrepant information, whereas low NFUs are uninterested in seeking new stimuli that contain unmatched information and prefer the norm.

These characteristics suggest that high NFUs have a more favorable attitude towards the NSGR advertising than general advertising, because they are likely to focus on the novel cues of the NSGR advertising. When high NFUs face novel stimuli in NSRG advertising, they experience curiosity and interest simultaneously (Simonson and Nowlis 2000). This positive experience (curiosity and interest) motivates consumers to elaborate on the stimuli and increases the tendency to resolve the new stimuli (Meyers-Levy and Tybout 1989). Therefore, consumers resolve the gender incongruity between the products and the models through the relational elaboration, and the positive experiences in terms of psychological arousal and pleasure caused by this entire process can lead to positive attitudes toward advertising. Consumers place a value on the novelty, recognize the novel advertising as interesting, and accept NSGR advertising more easily. In contrast, low NFUs are less sensitive to unique or novel advertising stimuli and might experience discomfort or counterarguments in response to the NSGR advertising. This negative experience reduces the likelihood that they will be motivated to elaborate on the stimuli (Meyers-Levy and Tybout 1989) and increases the difficulty of resolving gender incongruity. Therefore, low NFUs are relatively less favorable to novel stimuli and are likely to have cognitive resistance toward the incongruent newness. This results in a negative impression of the NSGR advertising by consumers and less favorable attitudes than when exposed to general advertisements. Therefore, we propose the following hypotheses.

H3: NFU will moderate the relationship between the advertisement type and attitude towards the advertisement.

H3a: Consumers with a high NFU will have a more favorable attitude towards the NSGR advertising than the SGR advertising.

H3b: Consumers with a low NFU will have a more favorable attitude towards the SGR advertising than the NSGR advertising.

H4: The relationship between the advertisement type and attitudes toward the advertisement is mediated by perceived novelty for consumers with a high NFU, whereas it is mediated by cognitive resistance to advertising for consumers with a low NFU.

The effect of gender role stereotypes

Gender role stereotypes are beliefs that some attributes, such as role behaviors, distinguish genders (Debevec and Iyer 1986). Gender role stereotypes, once established, are typically difficult to change (Ulrich 2013).Gender role stereotypes affect consumer behaviors and have a strong effect on the evaluation and use of products or brands (Paek,

Nelson, and Vilela 2011): consumers with a high tendency to stereotype gender roles prefer brands congruent to the traditional gender and reject brands targeting the opposite gender, in contrast to consumers with a low tendency to stereotype gender roles (Ulrich 2013).Therefore, we predict that consumers with a high tendency to stereotype gender roles may respond unfavorably to NSGR advertising because they are reluctant to accept incongruity between a spokesperson's gender and the gender image of the product. Hence, consumers with a high tendency to stereotype gender roles are expected to have less favorable attitude towards NSGR advertising. We suggest the following hypothesis.

H5: Consumers with a high tendency to stereotype gender roles will react less favorably to NSGR advertising than consumers with a low tendency to stereotype gender roles.

Advertising's social role in altering pre-existing perceptions of gender role stereotypes

Advertisers use gender role portrayals as a tactic to communicate a product and brand image. Gender role stereotyping has been a focus of advertising literature since the 1950s (Eisend, Plagemann, and Sollwedel 2014). Gender role stereotypes in advertising influence and reinforce stereotypical values in society (Eisend, Plagemann, and Sollwedel 2014) and influence the effectiveness of advertising campaigns (Ferguson, Kreshel, and Tinkham 1990) because stereotypes become essential signaling through which advertisers can communicate a product category to the target market (Lindner 2004). There are various stereotypes in advertising, such as gender roles, racial, ethnic, and age-related stereotypes (Moriarty, Mitchell, and Wells 2012). Considering that advertising in society reflects 'the way people think, what moves them, how they relate to each other, how they live, eat, relax, and enjoy themselves' (de Mooij 1998, 43), it is likely that a society's stage of gender role change or related factors may be related to the representations and values that advertising reflect in that society (de Mooij 1998; Frith and Mueller 2003; Furnham and Mak 1999). Social learning theory (Bandura 1977) has garnered empirical evidence on media portrayals and their effect on individuals' consciousness. Social scientific studies indicate that gender role portrayal in advertising, as an agent of socialization, exerts considerable influence on the thought patterns of society (Dyer 1982).

Advertising is one of the most influential tools in spreading stereotypical ideas that create perceptions. McCracken (1988) points to the role of advertising in the social construction of reality and whether and how it can enhance or change meaning in the lives of consumers. As society evolves, advertising also reflects the change in society. Recent society shows the growing change in the gender role and its change is often described in the NSGR advertising. Garcia-Marques and Mackie (1999) suggest that incongruent information leads to more comprehensive retrieval and generation of exemplars because the incongruent information somehow influences the perceptions of the group to produce a valuable learning experience (Shank 1986). Previous research on incongruent stereotypical information in social psychology focuses on the impact that stereotype-incongruent information has on the perceptions of the stereotyped group's central dispositions or typical characteristics (Garcia-Marques and Mackie 1999). NSGR representations in advertising that are inconsistent with previous schema can change the perceptions towards gender role stereotypes. From this perspective, the authors conjecture that the NSGR advertising can alter the perception of gender role stereotypes. Therefore, we propose the following hypothesis.

H6: NSGR advertising changes consumers' perceptions of gender role stereotypes. Specifically, consumers' pre-existing gender role stereotypes will be less evident after exposure to NSGR advertising.

Research methodology and results

Overview of five studies

We conducted five studies. Study 1 demonstrated the predicted differences of SC and the dual mechanisms of novelty perceptions and cognitive resistance (H1, H2). Study 2 tested the predicted differences of NFU and the dual mechanisms of novelty perceptions and cognitive resistance. Study 3further replicated H1 to H4 for male-oriented product. In Study 4, we tested whether consumers with a high tendency to stereotype gender roles react less favorably to NSGR advertising than consumers with a low tendency (H5). Finally, Study 5 tested whether NSGR advertising reduces consumer's gender role stereotypes (H6). Study 1, Study 2, and Study 5 used female-oriented products (rice cookers, vacuum cleaners, frying pans) as product stimuli. Study 3 and Study 4 used male-oriented products (car repair service, toolboxes). We adopted a moderate gender-incongruity level in choosing stimuli products and excluded gender-exclusive products (brassieres and lipsticks). All studies and pretests used convenience sample who are 20–40s Korean consumers and all respondents were paid $1 for participation.

Study 1

Method

Design and participants.   This was designed as between-subjects of 2(ad type: NSGR versus SGR) ×2 (SC: independent versus interdependent), in which SC was measured. We create a measure of each participant's dominant SC, which was determined by subtracting scores on the interdependent SC subscale from scores on the interdependent SC subscale. Scores higher than zero reflect relatively greater independent SC than interdependent SC (Lalwani and Shavitt 2009). The convenience sample comprised 98 Korean consumers (20–40s, 49% males) in MBA and lifelong education center in Seoul, Korea during the fall semester 2013. Respondents were randomly assigned to each condition and collected using a face-to-face survey. The age and occupation of the respondents was diverse [20s (39%), 30s (31%), and 40s (30%); office workers (72%), students (21%), others (7%)].

Pretest and stimulus development.   Three pretests were conducted to select a product, spokespersons, and photo stimuli for the purpose of the study.

The first pretest: The purpose of the first pretest (total $n = 28$) was to select a product. First, we conducted telephone interviews with 10 consumers. Interviewees were asked to indicate the products that had female-gendered images. We identified10 female-oriented products: kitchen appliances (rice cookers, cooking utensils), cleaning supplies (vacuum cleaners), nail products, etc. Next, we conducted a short face-to-face survey ($n = 18$) to explore the gendered image of 10 products by just measuring four items (e.g., 'generally, women use this product more than men' and 'this product has a female-gendered image') adapted from Debevec and Iyer (1986) and Fugate and Phillips (2010). A rice cooker was chosen (feminine-gendered image: $M = 5.2$).

The second pretest: The purpose of the second pretest ($n = 24$) was to select a celebrity actor and actress who were appropriate for the product category and familiar with consumers, who had not previously represented the stimulus product and who possessed similar moderate likeability/familiarity and masculine/feminine images. We asked respondents to recall the celebrities, and subjects were asked to indicate their agreement with statements, such as, 'I like the celebrity,' and 'I am familiar with the celebrity,' 'The celebrity is masculine/feminine.' using a seven-point scale. Based on the results, we selected Jinhee Ji ($M = 4.7/5.2$ and $M = 5.0/3.3$ for likeability/familiarity and masculine/feminine images, respectively) as the male spokesperson and Hojung Yu ($M = 4.6/5.0$ and $M = 2.9/5.4$ for likeability/familiarity and masculine/feminine images, respectively) as the female spokesperson.

The third pretest: For the third pretest ($n = 31$), respondents were asked to evaluate the attractiveness of color photos of two spokespersons on a seven-point semantic differential scale. We obtained photos ensuring that the two spokespersons did not have different degrees of attractiveness (t-test, $p > .1$). The ad copy and illustrations referred to practical rice cooker ads. To prevent preexisting attitudes or effects of product and brand familiarity that might confound the experimental results, the product photos were selected from a Japanese company unknown to Koreans (manipulation check of product familiarity: $M = 2.4$), and we did not provide the brand name to exclude its effect.

Procedures and measures. After seeing the color print ads in questionnaire including a spokesperson, product images, head copy, core attributes of the product on an individual basis (see Supplemental data for ad stimulus), the participants were asked for their ad attitudes, cognitive resistance, perceived novelty, attitude toward the spokesperson, SC, the product-gendered image (feminine, masculine), product involvement, mood, and demographic variables. The participants were then thanked and dismissed. SC ($\alpha = 0.85$) measures were adopted from Triandis and Gelfand (1998). Perceived novelty ($\alpha = 0.81$) measures (familiar/unusual, regular/irregular, old/new) were adopted from Holbrook (1981). Cognitive resistance ($\alpha = 0.79$) were adopted from Wright (1973) (e.g., the rguments concerning the product contained in the ads were convincing). Ad attitude ($\alpha = 0.91$) measures were adopted from MacKenzie et al. (1986). The female-gendered image of rice cookers was measured by four items ($\alpha = 0.82$) like the first pretest. The other variables were adopted from the literature: purchase intention (Kabadayi and Lerman 2011), product involvement (Zaichkowsky 1985); mood (Batra and Stayman 1990). We considered attitude toward a spokesperson as a covariate, and the respondent's sex as a blocking variable based on previous research (Baker and Churchill 1977; Debevec and Iyer 1986). Attitude toward the spokesperson ($\alpha = 0.92$) was measured by two items (e.g., like/dislike).

Data analysis. We used PASW 18 and Hayes' (2013) PROCESS. PROCESS is a macro program developed to analyze the integrated model which consists of moderation and mediation or combination of them (Hayes 2013). To validate the interaction effect of ad type and SC, ANCOVA and planned contrast are used, and then we verify how the effect of ad type on ad attitude is moderated by SC, that is, the mediated moderation through PROCESS. In the mediated moderation model, the interaction effect of the independent variable (IV) and moderator on the dependent variable (DV) is transmitted through the mediator. A prerequisite of mediated moderation is the occurrence of overall moderation between IV and DV (Baron and Kenny 1986). The effect of the IV on the DV must depend on the moderator. Mediated moderation can be used to explain the causal relationship between four variables (IV, DV, mediator, and moderator).

Results

Manipulation check

We conducted a manipulation check for ad type (NSGR ad vs. SGR ad) with three 7-point scales (e.g., this product generally uses a female model as advertising model). Results

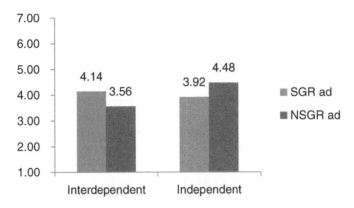

Figure 1.   Interaction effect of ad type and self-construal on ad attitude (Study 1).

showed that an incongruity score between a product's gender image and a spokesperson's sex is significantly higher in the NSGR ad than the SGR ad ($M = 5.14$ vs. 2.57, $p < .01$). Therefore, manipulation was successful.

Testing for the moderating effect of SC

To verify our H1, we first conducted the ANCOVA analysis including an attitude toward the spokesperson as a covariate and an individual's sex as a blocking variable. Next, we conducted planned contrast. This indicated that independent SCs had a more favorable attitude toward the NSGR ad ($M = 4.48$) than the SGR ad ($M = 3.92$) ($F(1, 93) = 3.713$, $p = .057$, $\eta^2 = .033$). Planned contrast indicated that interdependent SCs had a more favorable attitude toward the SGR ad ($M = 4.14$) than the NSGR ad ($M = 3.56$) ($F(1, 93) = 3.981$, $p = .049$, $\eta^2 = .036$). These results supported H1a and H1b (see Table 1, Table 2, and Figure 1).

Table 1.   Cell mean and size by each condition (Study 1).

	Independent	Interdependent
NSGR ad	4.48 ($n = 27$)	3.56 ($n = 22$)
SGR ad	3.92 ($n = 25$)	4.14 ($n = 24$)

DV: Ad attitude.

Table 2.   ANCOVA results.(Study 1).

Source	SS	DF	MS	F-value	p-value
Constants	92.405	1	92.405	97.287	.000
Attitude toward a spokesperson	5.364	1	5.364	5.648	.020
Ad type*	.174	1	.174	.183	.669
Self-construal level	2.199	1	2.199	2.316	.131
Ad type × self-construal level	8.135	1	8.135	8.565	.004
Error	88.333	93	.950		

DV: ad attitude, ad type: contrast coding ($-1 =$ SGR ad, $1 =$ NSGR ad), self-construal level: contrast coding ($-1 =$ interdependent ad, $1 =$ independent)

Testing for mediated moderation

To test H2, mediated moderation model (see Figure 2), we followed the procedure to analyze conditional indirect effects developed by Preacher et al. (2007). Specifically, we conducted bootstrap mediated moderation analyses with ad type (IV), ad attitude (DV), dual mediation (perceived novelty and resistance) as mediators, and SC as a moderator. A growing literature advocates the use of bootstrapping for assessing indirect effects. Moderated mediation models try to explain both when and how a given effect occurs (Preacher et al. 2007). Formally, "mediated moderation occurs when the strength of indirect effect depends on the level of some variable, or when mediation relationships are contingent on the level of a moderator" (Preacher et al. 2007, p. 193).

First, there was the significant effect of ad type on perceived novelty and cognitive resistance ($t = 4.75, p < .01, t = 3.26, p < .01$). Whereas perceived novelty positively influences attitude toward ad ($t = 2.41, p < .05$), cognitive resistance negatively influences attitude toward ad ($t = -2.14, p < .05$). There was also the significant interaction effect of ad type and SC on perceived novelty ($t = 3.04, p < .01$), implying that the relationship between ad type and perceived novelty is moderated by SC. There was the significant interaction effect of ad type and SC on cognitive resistance ($t = -2.89, p < .01$), implying that the relationship between ad type and cognitive resistance is moderated by SC (see Table 3).

Second, the top of Table 4 indicates whether a conditional indirect effect by SC on ad attitude via dual mediators (perceived novelty and resistance) is significant. It is found that there is the mediated moderation effect, as the 95% bootstrap BC confidence interval (BCCI) does contain 0 (perceived novelty: {.02, .32} and resistance: {.00, .27}). The bottom of Table 4 indicates that for perceived novelty, the conditional indirect effect of ad type is significant only for independent SCs. Especially, independent SC is significantly different from 0 as the 95% BCCI {.05, .33} of a bootstrap does not contain 0. On the contrary, interdependent SC yields the 95% BCCI {−.02, .15}. It does contain 0, so the indirect effect at interdependent SC is not significantly different from 0. For cognitive resistance, the indirect effect at independent SC is not significantly different from 0 as the 95% bootstrap BCCI {−.06, .15} contains 0. Interdependent SC, however, yields the 95% bootstrap BCCI {−.27, −.01}. It does not contain 0, indicating that the indirect effect at interdependent SC is significantly different from 0. As a result, H2 is confirmed. These results show that for independent SCs, the NSGR ad produces higher perceived

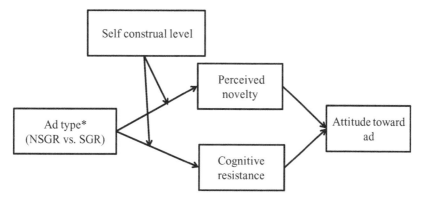

* NSGR ad: Non-stereotypical gender role advertising
SGR ad: Stereotypical gender role advertising

Figure 2. Conceptual-mediated moderation model of Study 1.

Table 3. Mediated moderation results[a] (Study 1).

DV: perceived novelty	B	SE b	t	LL CI	UL CI
Attitude toward a spokesperson	.10	.06	1.60	−.02	.24
Ad type	.40	.08	4.75**	.23	.57
Self-construal level	.65	.08	7.49**	.48	.82
Ad type × self-construal level	.26	.08	3.04**	.09	.42

DV: cognitive resistance	B	SE b	t	LL CI	UL CI
Attitude toward a spokesperson	−.05	.07	−.75	−.20	.09
Ad type	.31	.09	3.26**	.12	.51
Self-construal level	−.87	.09	−8.78**	−1.06	−.67
Ad type x Self-construal level	−.28	.10	−2.89**	−.47	−.08

DV: ad attitude	b	SE b	t	LL CI	UL CI
Attitude toward a spokesperson	.13	.07	1.73	−.01	.28
Ad type	.00	.11	.01	−.22	.23
Perceived novelty	.24	.10	2.41*	.04	.45
Cognitive resistance	−.18	.08	−2.14*	−.35	−.01

[a]bootstrapped conditional indirect effect of ad type on ad attitude via the mediator at specific values of the moderator, self- construal level.
$N = 5000$ Bootstrapping resamples; LL CI and UL CI = lower level and upper level of the bias corrected and accelerated confidence interval for $\alpha = 0.05$.
*$p < .05$, **$p < .01$.

Table 4. Conditional indirect effect by self-construal level[a] (Study 1).

DV	Mediators	Indirect effect	Boot SE	LL CI	UL CI
Ad attitude	Perceived Novelty	.12	.07	.02	.32
	Cognitive resistance	.10	.06	.00	.27

DV	Moderators	Indirect effect	Boot SE	LL CI	UL CI
Perceived novelty	Independent	.16	.07	.05	.33
	Interdependent	.03	.04	−.02	.15
Cognitive resistance	Independent	−.00	.02	−.06	.15
	Interdependent	−.10	.06	−.27	−.01

[a]bootstrapped conditional indirect effect of ad type on ad attitude via the mediator at specific values of the moderator, self- construal level.

novelty, which, in turn, leads to a more positive attitude towards ad. For interdependent SCs, NSGR ad produces higher cognitive resistance, which, in turn, leads to a less positive attitude towards ads.

Study 2

Study 2 tested hypotheses 3 and 4.

Method

Design and participants. It used a 2 (ad type: NSGR versus SGR) × 2(NFU: high vs. low) between design, in which NFU was measured. A median split was used for NFU.

The convenience sample comprised 119 Korean consumers (20–50s, 46% males) in life-long education center in Seoul, Korea during the fall semester 2013. Respondents were randomly assigned to each condition and collected using a face-to-face survey. The age and occupation of the consumers was diverse [32% (20s), 34% (30s), and 34% (40–50s); office workers (63%), students (15%), others (22%)].

Pretest and stimulus development. Two pretests were conducted to select a product and photos for the purpose of the study.

The first pretest: The purpose of the first pretest ($n = 20$) was to select a product. We conducted a short face-to-face survey on the gendered image of the products identified in the first pretest of study, measuring it using the same measures as those in Study 1. A vacuum cleaner was chosen (feminine-gendered image: $M = 4.9$). We also selected the same celebrities as Study 1.

The second pretest: Respondents ($n = 19$) were first asked to evaluate the attractiveness of color photos of the two spokespersons. We obtained photos that ensured that the two spokespersons did not have a different degree of attractiveness (*t*-test, $p > .1$). To prevent preexisting attitudes or effects of product and brand familiarity that might confound the experimental results, the product photos were selected from a German company unknown to Koreans (manipulation check of product familiarity: $M = 2.5$), and we did not provide the brand name to exclude its effect.

Procedures and measures. The study's procedures and measures were identical to Study 1. NFU was adopted from Tian, Bearden, and Hunter (2001). The internal consistency (α) of all measurement scales was above .80.

Data analysis. The study's data analysis methods were identical to Study 2 (ANCOVA, planned contrast, PROCESS).

Results

Manipulation check

We conducted a manipulation check for ad type like Study 1. Results showed that an incongruence score between a product's gender image and a spokesperson's sex is significantly higher in the NSGR ad than the SGR ad ($M = 4.85$ vs. 2.80, $p < .01$). Therefore, manipulation was successful.

Testing for moderating effect of NFU

To verify H3, we conducted the ANCOVA analysis including an attitude toward the spokesperson as a covariate and sex as a blocking variable. Then, we examined H3 by using the planned contrast. Planned contrast indicated that high NFUs had a more favorable attitude toward the NSGR ad ($M = 4.47$) than the SGR ad ($M = 3.68$) ($F(1,114) = 9.388$, $p = .003$, $\eta^2 = .063$). Next, planned contrast indicated that low NFUs had more favorable attitude toward the SGR ad ($M = 4.17$) than the NSGR ad ($M = 3.23$) ($F(1,114) = 13.819$, $p = .000$, $\eta^2 = .093$). These results supported H3a and H3b (see Table 5, Table 6, and Figure 3).

Testing for mediated moderation

To test H4, mediated moderation model (see Figure 4), we followed the same procedure as Study 1. First, there was the significant effect of ad type on perceived novelty and

Table 5.   Cell mean and size by each condition (Study 2).

	High NFU	Low NFU
NSGR ad	4.47(n = 37)	3.23(n = 29)
SGR ad	3.68 (n = 23)	4.17(n = 30)

DV: ad attitude.

Table 6.   ANCOVA results (Study 2).

Source	SS	DF	MS	F-value	p-value
Constants	74.487	1	74.487	79.290	.000
Attitude toward a spokesperson	4.415	1	4.415	4.700	.032
Ad type	.022	1	.022	.024	.878
Need-for-uniqueness	2.639	1	2.639	2.809	.096
Ad type × need-for-uniqueness	19.501	1	19.501	20.758	.000
Error	107.094	114	.939		

DV: ad attitude, ad type: contrast coding (−1 = SGR ad, 1 = NSGR ad), need-for-uniqueness: contrast coding (−1 = low NFU, 1 = high NFU).

cognitive resistance ($t = 4.47, p < .01, t = 6.18, p < .01$). Whereas perceived novelty positively influences ad attitude ($t = 5.41, p < .01$), cognitive resistance negatively influences it ($t = -2.51, p < .05$). There was also the significant interaction effect of ad type and NFU on perceived novelty ($t = 3.21, p < .01$), implying that the relationship between ad type and perceived novelty is moderated by NFU. There was the significant interaction effect of ad type and NFU on cognitive resistance ($t = -6.25, p < .01$), implying that the relationship between ad type and cognitive resistance is moderated by NFU (see Table 7).

Second, the top of Table 8 indicates that there is the mediated moderation effect, as the 95% BCCI does contain 0 (perceived novelty: {.08, .54} and cognitive resistance: {.01, .45}). The bottom of Table 8 indicates that for perceived novelty, the conditional indirect effect of ad type is significant only for high NFUs. High NFU is significantly different from 0 as the 95% BCCI {.15, .55} of a bootstrap does not contain 0. On the

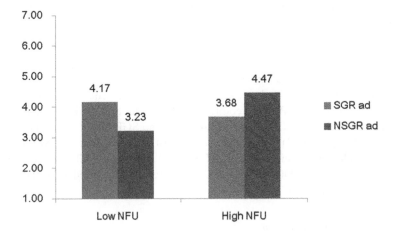

Figure 3.   Interaction effect of ad type and need for uniqueness on ad attitude (Study 2).

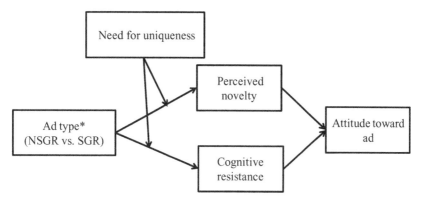

*NSGR ad: Non-stereotypical gender role advertising
SGR ad: Stereotypical gender role advertising

Figure 4.   Conceptual-mediated moderation model of Study 2.

contrary, low NFU yields the 95% BCCI {−.06, .18}. It does contain 0, so the indirect effect at low NFU is not significantly different from 0. For cognitive resistance, the indirect effect at high NFU is not significantly different from 0 as the 95% bootstrap BCCI {−.04, .04} contains 0. Low NFU, however, yields the 95% bootstrap BCCI {−.43, −.01}. It does not contain 0, indicating that the indirect effect at low NFU is significantly different from 0. H4 is confirmed.

Therefore, the results show that for high NFUs, the NSGR advertising produces higher perceived novelty, which, in turn, leads to a more positive attitude towards ads.

Table 7.   Mediated moderation results[a] (Study 2).

DV: perceived novelty	b	SE b	t	LL CI	UL CI
Attitude toward a spokesperson	.16	.06	2.46*	.03	.30
Ad type	.41	.09	4.47**	.23	.60
Need-for-uniqueness	.35	.09	3.80**	.17	.54
Ad type × need-for-uniqueness	.29	.09	3.21**	.11	.48
DV: cognitive resistance	b	SE b	t	LL CI	UL CI
Attitude toward a spokesperson	−.01	.06	−.27	−.13	.10
Ad type	.51	.08	6.18**	.35	.68
Need-for-uniqueness	−.39	.08	−4.63**	−.56	−.22
Ad type × need-for-uniqueness	−.52	.08	−6.25**	−.69	−.35
DV: ad attitude	b	SE b	t	LL CI	UL CI
Attitude toward a spokesperson	.06	.06	1.12	−.05	.18
Ad type	−.10	.10	−1.02	−.30	.09
Perceived novelty	.44	.08	5.41**	.28	.60
Cognitive resistance	−.20	.08	−2.51*	−.36	−.04

[a]bootstrapped conditional indirect effect of ad type on ad attitude via the mediator at specific values of the moderator, need-for-uniqueness
*$p < .05$, **$p < .01$

Table 8.   Conditional indirect effect by need-for-uniqueness[a] (Study 2).

DV	Mediators	Indirect effect	Boot SE	LL CI	UL CI
Ad attitude	Perceived novelty	.26	.11	.08	.54
	Cognitive resistance	.21	.10	.01	.45
DV	Moderators	Indirect effect	Boot SE	LL CI	UL CI
Perceived Novelty	High NFU	.31	.09	.15	.55
	Low NFU	.05	.06	−.06	.18
Cognitive resistance	High NFU	.00	.02	−.04	.04
	Low NFU	−.21	.10	−.43	−.01

[a]bootstrapped conditional indirect effect of ad type on ad attitude via the mediator at specific values of the moderator, need-for-uniqueness.

For low NFUs, NSGR advertising produces higher resistance, which, in turn, leads to a less positive attitude towards ads.

Study 3

Study 3replicated hypotheses 1−4 for male-oriented products.

Method

Design and participants.   This used a 2 (ad type: NSGR vs. SGR) × 2 (SC: independent vs. interdependent) × 2(NFU: high vs. low) between-subject design. SC and NFU's measurements were the same as those used in Study 1 and Study 2. The convenience sample comprised 130 Korean students (20−40s, 54% males) under undergraduate and graduate course in universities in Seoul, Korea during the spring semester 2015. The age was diverse [44% (20s), 30% (30s), and 26% (40s)].

Pretest and stimulus development.   Three pretests were conducted to select a product, regular models, and photo stimuli for the purpose of the study. The procedures and measures were the same as those in Study 1 except a focus group discussion (FGD).

The first pretest: The purpose of the first pretest (total $n = 22$) was to select a product. First, we conducted FGD ($n = 8$). Participants were asked to indicate the products they perceived had a male-gendered image. We identified male-oriented products: toolboxes, car repair service, sports goods, etc. Next, we conducted a short face-to-face survey (n = 14) on the gendered image of products using the same measures as Study 1. Finally, a toolbox was chosen (male-gendered image: M = 5.7).

The second pretest: The purpose of the second pretest ($n = 20$) was to select the regular models who had similar moderate likeability using the same measures as those in Study 1.We selected two regular models with similar likeability ($M = 4.0$ vs. $M=4.1$, respectively).

The third pretest: Respondents ($n = 20$) were asked to evaluate the attractiveness of color photos of two regular models using the same measures as those used in Study 1. We obtained photos to ensure that the two photos did not have a different degree of attractiveness (*t*-test, $p > .05$). The ad copy and illustrations referred to practical toolbox ads. To prevent preexisting attitudes or the effects of familiarity with the products and brand that might confound the experimental results, the product's photos were selected from a German company unknown to Koreans (manipulation check of product familiarity: $M = 2.8$), and we did not provide the brand name to exclude its effect.

Procedures and measures. This study's procedures and measures were the same as Study 1 and Study 2(see the Supplemental data for ad stimuli). The internal consistency (α) of all measurement scales was above .80.

Data analysis

The study's data analysis methods were identical to Study 1 and Study 2(ANCOVA, planned contrast, PROCESS).

Results

Manipulation check

We conducted a manipulation check for ad type (NSGR ad vs. SGR ad). Results showed that an incongruence score between a product's gender image and a model's sex is significantly higher in NSGR ad than SGR ad ($M= 5.54$ vs. 2.23, $p < .001$). Manipulation was successful.

Testing for the moderating effect of SC

Planned contrast indicates that independent SC had a more favorable attitude toward the NSGR ad ($M = 4.50$) than the SGR ad ($M = 3.88$) ($F(1, 125) = 5.562, p = .02, \eta^2 = .037$). Next, planned contrast indicated that interdependent SC had a more favorable attitude toward the SGR ad ($M = 4.32$) than the NSGR ad ($M = 3.45$) ($F(1, 125) = 11.071, p = .001, \eta^2 = .073$). These results supported H1a and H1b (see Table 9 and Figure 5).

Testing for mediated moderation: SC

To revalidate H2, we conducted mediated moderation analyses with dual mediators. First, there was the significant effect of ad type on perceived novelty and cognitive resistance ($t = 4.21, p < .01, t = 3.06, p < .01$). Whereas perceived novelty positively influences attitude toward ad ($t = 3.73, p < .01$), cognitive resistance negatively influences attitude toward ad ($t = -2.22, p < .05$). There was also the significant interaction effect of ad type and SC on perceived novelty ($t = 2.38, p < .01$), implying that the relationship between ad type and perceived novelty is moderated by SC. There was the significant interaction effect of ad type and SC on cognitive resistance ($t = -2.23, p < .05$), implying that the relationship between ad type and cognitive resistance is moderated by SC (see Table 10).

Table 9. Cell mean and size by each condition (Study 3).

	Independent	Interdependent
NSGR ad	4.50 ($n = 42$)	3.45 ($n = 29$)
SGR ad	3.88 ($n = 25$)	4.32 ($n = 34$)

DV: ad attitude

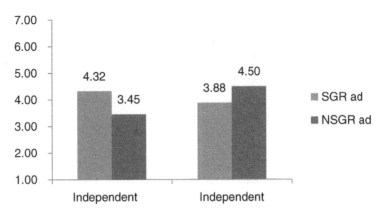

Figure 5.   Interaction effect of ad type and self-construal on ad attitude (Study 3).

Second, the top of Table 11 indicates whether a conditional indirect effect by SC on ad attitude via dual mediators is significant. It is found that there is the mediated moderation effect, as the 95% bootstrap BCCI does contain 0 (perceived novelty: {.01, .31} and cognitive resistance: {.00, .20}). The bottom of Table 11 indicates that for perceived novelty, the conditional indirect effect of ad type is significant only for independent SCs. Especially, independent SC is significantly different from 0 as the 95% BCCI {.08, .35} of a bootstrap does not contain 0. On the contrary, interdependent SC yields the 95% BCCI {−.01, .14}. It does contain 0, so the indirect effect at interdependent SC is not significantly different from 0. For cognitive resistance to ad, the indirect effect at

Table 10.   Mediated moderation results[a] (Study 3).

DV: perceived novelty	b	SE b	t	LL CI	UL CI
Attitude toward a spokesperson	.06	.10	.65	−.13	.27
Ad type	.36	.08	4.21**	.19	.53
Self-construal level	.43	.08	5.10**	.26	.60
Ad type × self-construal level	.20	.08	2.38*	.03	.37
DV: cognitive resistance	b	SE b	t	LL CI	UL CI
Attitude toward a spokesperson	−.14	.11	−1.30	−.36	.07
Ad type	.28	.09	3.06**	.10	.46
Self-construal level	−.35	.09	−3.90**	−.53	−.17
Ad type × self-construal level	−.20	.09	−2.23*	−.38	−.02
DV: ad attitude	b	SE b	t	LL CI	UL CI
Attitude toward a spokesperson	.19	.11	1.73	−.02	.41
Ad type	−.09	.10	−.95	−.30	.10
Perceived novelty	.34	.09	3.73**	.16	.52
Cognitive resistance	−.19	.08	−2.22*	−.37	−.02

[a]bootstrapped conditional indirect effect of ad type on ad attitude via the mediator at specific values of the moderator, self- construal level
*$p < .05$,**$p < .01$.

Table 11. Conditional indirect effect by self-construal level[a] (Study 3).

DV	Mediators	Indirect effect	Boot SE	LL CI	UL CI
Ad attitude	Perceived novelty	.13	.07	.01	.31
	Cognitive resistance	.08	.05	.00	.20
DV	Moderators	Indirect effect	Boot SE	LL CI	UL CI
Perceived novelty	Independent	.19	.06	.08	.35
	Interdependent	.05	.04	−.01	.14
Cognitive resistance	Independent	−.01	.03	−.10	.03
	Interdependent	−.09	.04	−.21	−.02

[a]bootstrapped conditional indirect effect of ad type on ad attitude via the mediator at specific values of the moderator, self- construal level.

independent SC is not significantly different from 0 as the 95% bootstrap BCCI {−.10, .03} contains 0. Interdependent SC, however, yields the 95% bootstrap BCCI {−.21, −.02}. It does not contain 0, indicating that the indirect effect at interdependent SC is significantly different from 0. H2 is reconfirmed.

Testing for moderating effect of NFU

We reexamined H3 in male-oriented product through the planned contrast. Planned contrast indicated that high NFUs had a more favorable attitude toward the NSGR ad ($M = 4.51$) than the SGR ad ($M = 4.07$) ($F(1,125) = 2.816, p = .09, \eta^2 = .02$). Next, planned contrast indicated that low NFUs had more favorable attitude toward the SGR ad ($M = 4.24$) than the NSGR ad ($M = 3.71$) ($F(1,125) = 3.410, p = .06, \eta^2 = .024$). These results supported H3a and H3b (see Table 12 and Figure 6).

Testing for mediated moderation: NFU

To retest H4 in male-oriented product, we conducted bootstrap mediated moderation analyses. First, there was the significant effect of ad type on perceived novelty and cognitive resistance ($t = 5.01, p < .01, t = 2.05, p < .05$). Whereas perceived novelty positively influences attitude toward ad ($t = 3.73, p < .01$), cognitive resistance negatively influences attitude toward ad ($t = -2.22, p < .05$). There was also the significant interaction effect of ad type and NFU on perceived novelty ($t = 3.21, p < .01$), implying that the relationship between ad type and perceived novelty is moderated by NFU. There was the significant interaction effect of ad type and NFU on cognitive resistance ($t = -4.18, p < .01$), implying that the relationship between ad type and cognitive resistance is moderated by NFU (see Table 13).

Table 12. Cell mean and size by each condition (Study 3).

	High NFU	Low NFU
NSGR ad	4.51 ($n = 32$)	3.71 ($n = 39$)
SGR ad	4.07 ($n = 37$)	4.24 ($n = 22$)

DV: ad attitude.

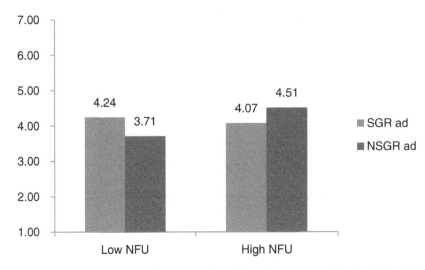

Figure 6.   Interaction effect of ad type and need-for-uniqueness on ad attitude (Study 3).

Second, the top of Table 14 indicates whether a conditional indirect effect by NFU on ad attitude via dual mediators is significant. It is found that there is the mediated moderation effect, as the 95% bootstrap BCCI does contain 0 (perceived novelty: {.06, .41} and cognitive resistance: {.03, .30}). The bottom of Table 14 indicates that for perceived novelty, the conditional indirect effect of ad type is significant only for high NFUs. High NFU is significantly different from 0 as the 95% BCCI {.12, .44} of a bootstrap does not contain 0. On the contrary, low NFU yields the 95% BCCI {−.01, .16}. It does contain 0,

Table 13.   Mediated moderation results[a] (Study 3).

DV: perceived novelty	b	SE b	t	LL CI	UL CI
Attitude toward a spokesperson	.13	.10	1.24	−.08	.35
Ad type	.45	.09	5.01**	.27	.63
Need-for-uniqueness	.17	.09	1.95	−.00	.35
Ad type × need-for-uniqueness	.29	.09	3.21**	.11	.46
DV: cognitive resistance	b	SE b	t	LL CI	UL CI
Attitude toward a spokesperson	−.19	.10	−1.83	−.39	.01
Ad type	.17	.08	2.05*	.00	.35
Need-for-uniqueness	−.35	.08	−4.08**	−.52	−.18
Ad type × need-for-uniqueness	−.36	.08	−4.18**	−.53	−.19
DV: ad attitude	b	SE b	t	LL CI	UL CI
Attitude toward a spokesperson	−.19	.11	−1.83	−.39	.01
Ad type	−.09	.10	−.95	−.30	.10
Perceived novelty	.34	.09	3.73**	.16	.52
Cognitive resistance	−.19	.08	−2.22*	−.37	−.02

[a]bootstrapped conditional indirect effect of ad type on ad attitude via the mediator at specific values of the moderator, need-for-uniqueness
*p < .05,**p < .01.

Table 14. Conditional indirect effect by need-for-uniqueness[a] (Study 3).

DV	Mediators	Indirect effect	Boot SE	LL CI	UL CI
Ad attitude	Perceived novelty	.19	.08	.06	.41
	Cognitive resistance	.14	.06	.03	.30

DV	Moderators	Indirect effect	Boot SE	LL CI	UL CI
Perceived novelty	High NFU	.25	.08	.12	.44
	Low NFU	.05	.04	−.01	.16
Cognitive resistance	High NFU	.03	.03	−.01	.12
	Low NFU	−.10	.04	−.22	−.02

[a]bootstrapped conditional indirect effect of ad type on ad attitude via the mediator at specific values of the moderator, need-for-uniqueness.

so the indirect effect at low NFU is not significantly different from 0. For cognitive resistance to ad, the indirect effect at high NFU is not significantly different from 0 as the 95% bootstrap BCCI {−.01, .12} contains 0. Low NFU, however, yields the 95% bootstrap BCCI {−.22, −.02}. It does not contain 0, indicating that the indirect effect at low NFU is significantly different from 0. H4 is reconfirmed.

Study 4

Method

Design and participants. We used a 2 (ad type: NSGR vs. SGR) × 2(gender role stereotypes: high vs. low) between-subject design, in which gender role stereotypes were measured. A median split was used. The convenience sample comprised 100 Korean consumers (20−40s, 54% males) in lifelong education center in Seoul, Korea during the spring semester 2015. Respondents were randomly assigned to each condition and collected using a face-to-face survey. The age and occupation of the respondents was diverse [20s (38%), 30s (42%), and 40s (20%); office workers (39%), students (31%), others (30%)].

Pretest and stimulus development. Two pretests were conducted to select a product and photos for the purpose of the study.
   The first pretest: The purpose of the first pretest ($n = 16$) was to select a product. We conducted a survey on the gendered image of identified products through FGD in Study 3 using the same measures as those in Study 1. A car repair service was chosen (male-gendered image: $M = 5.9$).
   The second pretest: The purpose of the second pretest ($n = 16$) was to select the regular models who had similar moderate likeability using the similar measures as those in Study 3.We selected two regular models with similar likeability ($M = 3.7$ versus $M = 3.8$, respectively).
   The third pretest: Respondents ($n = 14$) were asked to evaluate the attractiveness of color photos of two regular models using the same measures as those used in Study 3. We obtained photos to ensure that the two photos did not have a different degree of attractiveness (t-test, $p > .05$). The ad copy and illustrations referred to practical car repair shop ads. To prevent preexisting attitudes or the effects of familiarity with the products and

brand that might confound the experimental results, the product's photos were selected from a German company unknown to Koreans (manipulation check of product familiarity: $M = 3.0$), and we did not provide the brand name to exclude its effect.

Procedures and measures. This study's procedures and measures were the same as Study 3 (see the Supplemental data for ad stimuli). For gender role stereotypes, we adopted a more recent generalist gender attitude measure, the Gender Attitude Inventory (Ashmore et al. 1995). To categorize traditional as opposed to egalitarian consumers, we used the subscale of acceptance of traditional stereotypes which was appropriate for the subject and had been widely accepted by previous research (Lyndon et al. 2007; Robinson et al. 2004; Ulrich 2013). The internal consistency (α) of all measurement scales was above .80.

Data analysis

To validate H5, ANCOVA and planned contrast are used.

Results

Manipulation check. We conducted a manipulation check for ad type like Study 1. Results showed that an incongruence score between a product's gender image and a spokesperson's sex is significantly higher in the NSGR ad than the SGR ad ($M = 5.66$ vs. 2.19, $p < .001$). Therefore, manipulation was successful.

Testing for the relationship between gender role stereotypes and attitudes toward NSGR advertising. We posited that consumers with a high tendency to stereotype gender roles will react less favorably to NSGR advertising than consumers with a low tendency to stereotype gender roles. To verify H5, ANCOVA analysis and planned contrast were used including an attitude toward a spokesperson as a covariate and an individual's sex as a blocking variable. Planned contrast revealed that consumers with a high tendency to stereotype gender roles had a less favorable attitude toward the NSGR ad ($M = 2.51$) than the SGR ad ($M = 3.41$) ($F(1, 95) = 9.224$, $p = .003$, $\eta^2 = .08$). These results supported H5 (see Table 15, Table 16, and Figure 7).

Study 5

Method

Design and participants. We used the between-subjects design of 2 (ad type: NSGR vs. SGR). The convenience sample comprised 77 Korean consumers (20–40s, 52% males) in lifelong education center in Seoul, Korea during the spring 2014. Respondents were randomly assigned to each condition and collected using a face-to-face survey. The age

Table 15. Cell mean and size by each condition (Study 4).

	High gender role stereotypes	Low gender role stereotypes
NSGR ad	2.51 ($n = 20$)	3.66 ($n = 22$)
SGR ad	3.41 ($n = 37$)	3.14 ($n = 21$)

DV: ad attitude.

Table 16.   ANCOVA results (Study 4).

Source	SS	DF	MS	F-value	p-value
Constants	52.492	1	52.492	46.057	.000
Attitude toward a spokesperson	12.767	1	12.767	11.202	.001
Ad type	.000	1	.000	.000	.989
Gender role stereotype	3.759	1	3.759	3.298	.073
Ad type × gender role stereotype	3.817	1	3.817	3.349	.070
Error	108.274	95	1.140		

DV: ad attitude, ad type: contrast coding(-1 = SGR ad, 1 = NSGR ad), gender role stereotype: contrast coding (-1 = low group, 1 = high group).

and occupation of the respondents was diverse [20s (32%), 30s (36%), and 40s (20%); office workers (32%), students (31%), others (30%)].

Pretest and stimulus development.   Two pretests were conducted to select a product and photos for the purpose of the study.

The first pretest: The purpose of the first pretest ($n = 14$) was to select a product. We conducted a short face-to-face survey on the gendered image of the products identified in the first pretest of Study 1. A frying pan was chosen as the product category for Study 2 (feminine-gendered image: $M = 4.8$). Study 5 selected the same celebrities as Study 1.

The second pretest: To prevent preexisting attitudes or effects of product and brand familiarity that might confound the experimental results, the product photos were selected from a German company unknown to Koreans. Respondents ($n = 16$) were asked to evaluate product familiarity (manipulation check of product familiarity: $M = 2.5$). We did not provide the brand name to exclude its effect.

Procedures and measures.   The study's procedures and measures were identical to Study 1. Gender role stereotype measures were adopted from Storms (1979). Gender role stereotype (before and after exposure to the ad) was measured with a time interval (10 minutes) using filler tasks. The internal consistency (α) of all measurement scales was above .80.

Data analysis.   To validate H6, repeated ANCOVA are used.

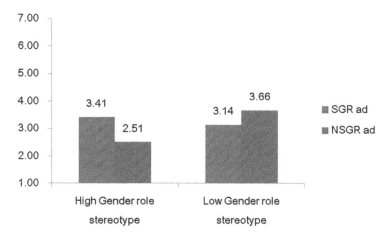

Figure 7.   Interaction effect of ad type and gender role stereotype (Study 4).

Results

Manipulation check

We conducted a manipulation check for ad type like Study 1. Results showed that an incongruence score between a product's gender image and a spokesperson's sex is significantly higher in the NSGR ad than the SGR ad ($M = 4.85$ vs. 3.01, $p < .01$). Therefore, manipulation was successful.

Testing for the effect of NSGR advertising on consumer's gender role stereotype

We posited that NSGR advertising would influence the gender role stereotypes of audience after exposure to it. To verify H6, the repeated ANCOVA was used including an attitude toward a spokesperson as a covariate and an individual's sex as a blocking variable. The results showed that consumers' gender role stereotypes was reduced after exposure to NSGR advertising ($M_{before} = 4.32$ $M_{after} = 3.68$, $F = 18.264$, $p < .001$). H6 is supported. We performed additional analysis for consumers with high tendency to stereotype gender roles, and found that gender role stereotypes decreased after exposure to it ($M_{before} = 5.58$ $M_{after} = 5.12$, $F = 6.346$, $p < .05$). This implies that the audience's gender role stereotype decreases after exposure to NSGR advertising even in people with high tendency to stereotype gender roles.

Conclusion and implications

In practice, NSGR advertising is used to achieve specific objectives: to increase public attention, interests, and sales. However, evidence of the true effect on consumer evaluation is scarce and ambiguous. This research examines the influence of NSGR advertising on consumer response depending on SC and NFU and indicates the relevance of two mechanisms; perceived novelty and cognitive resistance. We also investigate the decrease in consumer's gender role stereotyping after exposure to NSGR advertising even in consumers with a high tendency to stereotype gender roles, which implies that NSGR advertising changes consumers' stereotypes and could at least lead to minor changes in society. Hence, NSGR advertising could play a positive social role in influencing gradual societal change.

These in-depth investigations on NSGR advertising yield valuable academic implications. First, Rotfeld and Taylor (2009) and Taylor (2013) point out that many studies are conducted without exploring the underlying mechanisms and, particularly the societal effects of advertising. Therefore, in this regard, this research on NSGR advertising that changes consumer stereotypes and might encourage positive behavioral changes in society makes a contribution to the knowledge of advertising's societal effect. Further, this research contributes to the knowledge on advertising stereotypes. Advertising stereotypes take many forms including gendered, racial, ethnic, and age-related stereotypes (Moriarty et al. 2012). This study shows that stereotypes concerning gender roles can be changed through NSGR advertising. This study has significance because it highlights the significant role of advertising in shaping and changing stereotypes. Second, based on previous studies on the definitions of the product-incongruity level, a new definition of the level of gender-incongruity is suggested. Moreover, this study extends prior conceptualizations of incongruity in NSGR advertising. Third, this study extends the existing studies by combining the competing arguments of match-up and mismatch hypotheses. Specifically, this research shows that consumer evaluation is affected by dual mediators (perceived novelty and cognitive resistance) according to individual characteristics. The research results are expected to explain why mixed results are found in previous research. Fourth, Mandler (1982) argues that novel stimuli produce positive reactions. This research extends the previous research by demonstrating the effects of novelty in the NSGR advertising context.

This research also yields valuable insights for marketers. First, with the deployment of changing gender roles in advertising, marketers are challenged by a new era of social responsibility. Social responsibility is a concern in the design of advertisements (Furnham and Mak 1999) because advertising's social influence is quite influential (Chang 2012; Taylor 2013). Typically, change follows a phenomenon. If a cross-gender phenomenon in advertising can alter gender role stereotyping in society, the positive social impact of NSGR advertising would be significant. Second, many companies have tried to develop differentiated marketing, but such advertising may provoke a cognitive response such as resistance or discomfort among consumers. We recommend that marketers consider the conditions in which NSGR advertising is beneficial. To establish an effective advertising strategy, marketers should analyze the underlying mechanisms of consumer evaluation of NSGR advertising to implement effective communication strategies.

This study has some limitations. First, we focus on gender-oriented products, but future research should consider gender-exclusive products (shavers and lipstick) to further extend the effect of NSGR advertising. Moreover, future research needs to investigate the impact of the level of gender-incongruity in NSGR advertising on consumers' attitudes, depending on their psychological traits. Second, the findings are limited to eastern countries such as Korea. Cross-cultural research that compares eastern and western countries would be valuable. Third, research to investigate the effect of other moderators, which stimulate consumers' cognitive response, is required. For example, regulatory focus is closely connected with SC (Lee, Aaker, and Gardner 2000). It is predicted that promotion-focused people are more favorable for NSGR advertising, similar to consumers with independent SC, but prevention-focused people are more favorable for SGR advertising similar to consumers with interdependent SC.

Disclosure statement

No potential conflict of interest was reported by the authors.

Note

1. The current research conducted a pre-test on 20 subjects to establish the constructs on the level of gender incongruity before the experiment. The consumers perceived the male models featuring female-oriented products and vice versa as moderately incongruent, while the male models featuring female-exclusive products and vice versa were perceived as extremely incongruent.

Supplemental data

Supplemental data for this article can be accessed at http://dx.doi.org/10.1080/02650487.2015.1110942

References

An, E.M. 2012. The effect of the type of innovation product and self-construal on consumer's attitude toward innovation product. *Korean Journal of Consumer and Advertising Psychology* 13, no. 2: 121–36.

Ashmore, R.D., and F.K. del Boca. 1981. Conceptual approaches to stereotypes and stereotyping. In *Cognitive processes in stereotyping and intergroup behavior*, ed. D.L.Hamilton, 1–35. Hillsdale, NJ: Lawrence Erlbaum Associates.

Ashmore, R.D., F.K. del Boca, and S.M. Bilder. 1995. Construction and validation of the gender attitude inventory, a structured inventory to assess multiple dimensions of gender attitudes. *Sex roles* 32, no. 11–12: 753–85.

Baker, M.J., and G.A. Churchill Jr. 1977. The impact of physically attractive models on advertising evaluations. *Journal of Marketing Research* 14, no. 4: 538–55.

Bandura, A. 1977. *Social learning theory*. Englewood Cliffs, NJ: Prentice Hall.

Baron, R.M., and D.A. Kenny. 1986. The moderator-mediator variable distinction in social psychological research: Conceptual, strategic, and statistical consideration. *Journal of Personality and Social Psychology* 51: 1173–82.

Batra, R., and D.M. Stayman. 1990. The role of mood in advertising effectiveness. *Journal of Consumer Research* 17, no. 2: 203–14.

Caballero, M.J., and P.J.Solomon. 1984. Effects of model attractiveness on sales response. *Journal of Advertising* 13:17–33.

Chang, C. 2012. The effectiveness of advertising that leverages sponsorship and cause-related marketing. *International Journal of Advertising* 31, no. 2: 317–38.

Debevec, K., and E. Iyer. 1986. The influence of spokespersons in altering a product's gender image: Implications for advertising effectiveness. *Journal of Advertising* 15, no. 4: 12–20.

de Mooij, M.K. 1998. *Global marketing and advertising: Understanding cultural paradoxes*. Thousand Oaks, CA: Sage.

Dyer, G. 1982. *Advertising as Communication*. London: Methuen.

Eisend, M. 2007. Understanding two-sided persuasion: An empirical assessment of theoretical approaches. *Psychology & Marketing* 24, no. 7: 615–40.

Eisend, M., J. Plagemann, and J .Sollwedel. 2014. Gender roles and humor in advertising: The occurrence of stereotyping in humorous and nonhumorous advertising and its consequences for advertising effectiveness. *Journal of Advertising* 43, no. 3: 256–73.

Ferguson, J.H., P.J. Kreshel, and S.F. Tinkham. 1990. In the pages of Ms.: Sex role portrayals of women in advertising. *Journal of Advertising* 19, no. 1: 40–51.

Fiske, S. 1980. Attention and weight in person perception: The impact of negative and extreme behavior. *Journal of Personality and Social Psycholog y*38:889–906.

Friedman, H.H., and L. Friedman. 1979. Endorser effectiveness by product type. *Journal of Advertising Research* 19: 63–71.

Frith, K.T., and B. Mueller. 2003. *Advertising and societies: Global issues*. New York: Peter Lang.

Fugate, D. L., and J. Phillips. 2010. Product gender perceptions and antecedents of product gender congruence. *Journal of Consumer Marketing* 27, no. 3: 251–61.

Furnham, A., and T. Mak. 1999. Sex-role stereotyping in television commercials: A review and comparison of fourteen studies done on five continents over 25 years. *Sex Roles* 41, no.5–6: 413–37.

Garcia-Marques, L., and D.M. Mackie. 1999. The impact of stereotype-incongruent information on perceived group variability and stereotype change. *Journal of Personality and Social Psychology* 77, no. 5: 979–90.

Gentry, J.W., and D.A. Haley. 1984. Gender schema theory as a predictor of Ad recall, in NA. *Advances in Consumer Research* 11: 259–64.

Holbrook, M.B. 1981. Integrating compositional and decompositional analyses to represent the intervening role of perceptions in evaluative judgments. *Journal of Marketing Research* 18: 13–28.

Iyer, E., and K. Debevec. 1986. Gender stereotyping of a product: Are products like people? In *Academy of marketing science*, ed. N.K. Maholtra, and J.M. Hawes, 40–5. Atlanta: Developments in Marketing Science.

Jhang, J.H., S.J. Grant, and M.C. Campbell. 2012. Get it? Got it. Good! Enhancing new product acceptance by facilitating resolution of extreme incongruity. *Journal of Marketing Research* 49, no. 2: 247–259.

Jung, K., and W. Lee. 2006. Cross-gender brand extensions: Effects of gender of the brand, gender of consumer, and product type on evaluation of cross-gender extensions. *Advances in Consumer Research* 33:67–74.

Kabadayi, S., and D. Lerman. 2011. Made in China but sold at FAO Schwarz: Country-of-origin effect and trusting beliefs. *International Marketing Review* 28, no. 1: 102–26.

Kim, S.J. 2009. Bum Kim, Chaeyoung Han: Cross-sexual blow in advertising. *Money Today*. http://star.mt.co.kr (accessed May 6, 2009).

Knoll, S., M. Eisend, and J. Steinhagen. 2011. Gender roles in advertising. *International Journal of Advertising: The Review of Marketing Communications* 30, no. 5: 867–88.

Lalwani, A.K., and S. Shavitt. 2009. The "me" I claim to be: Cultural self-construal elicits self-presentational goal pursuit. *Journal of Personality and Social Psychology* 97, no. 1: 88–98.

Lee, A.Y., J.L. Aaker, and W.L. Gardner. 2000. The pleasures and pains of distinct self-construals: The role of interdependence in regulatory focus. *Journal of Personality and Social Psychology* 78, no. 6: 1122–33.

Lien, N.H., H.Y. Chou, and C.H. Chang. 2012. Advertising effectiveness and the match-up hypothesis: Examining spokesperson sex, attractiveness type, and product image. *Journal of Current Issues & Research in Advertising* 33, no. 2: 282–300.

Lindner, K. 2004. Images of women in general interest and fashion magazine advertisements from 1955 to 2002. *Sex Roles* 51:409–20.

Lynch, J., and D. Schuler. 1994.The matchup effect of spokesperson and product congruency: A schema theory interpretation. *Psychology & Marketing* ll, no. 5: 417–45.

Lyndon, A.E., J.W. White, and K.M. Kadlec. 2007. Manipulation and force as sexual coercion tactics: Conceptual and empirical differences. *Aggressive behavior* 33, no. 4: 291–303.

MacKenzie, S.B., R.J. Lutz, and G.E. Belch. 1986. The role of attitude toward the ad as a mediator of advertising effectiveness: A test of competing explanations. *Journal of marketing Research* 23, no. 2: 130–43.

Mandler, G. 1982. The structure of value: Accounting for taste. In *Affect and Cognition: The Seventeenth Annual Carnegie Symposium on Cognition*, ed. M.S. Clark, and S.T. Fiske, 3–36.Hillsdale, NJ: Erlbaum.

McCracken, G. 1988. *Culture and consumption*. Bloomington, IN: Indiana University Press

Meyers-Levy, J., T.A. Louie, and M.T. Curren. 1994. How does the congruity of brand names affect evaluations of brand name extensions? *Journal of Applied Psychology* 79, no. 1: 46–57.

Meyers-Levy, J., and A.M. Tybout. 1989. Schema congruity as a basis for product evaluation. *Journal of Consumer Research* 15:39–54.

Moriarty, S., N. Mitchell, and W. Wells. 2012. *Advertising & IMC: Principles and practice*. 9th ed. England: Pearson.

Noseworthy, T.J., J. Cotte, and S.H. Lee. 2011. The effects of Ad context and gender on the identification of visually incongruent products. *Journal of Consumer Research* 38, no. 2: 358–75.

Osgood, C.E., and P.H. Tannenbaum. 1955. The principle of congruity in the prediction of attitude change. *Psychological Review* 62, no. 1: 42–55.

Paek, H.J., M.R. Nelson, and A.M. Vilela. 2011. Examination of gender-role portrayals in television advertising across seven countries. *Sex Roles* 64:192–207.

Peracchio, L.A., and J. Meyers-Levy. 1994. How ambiguous cropped objects in ad photos can affect product evaluations. *Journal of Consumer Research* 21, no. 3: 190–204.

Preacher, K.J., D.D. Rucker, and A.F. Hayes. 2007. Addressing moderated mediation hypotheses: Theory, methods, and prescriptions. *Multivariate Behavioral Research* 42, no. 1: 185–227.

Ram, S. 1987. A model of innovation resistance. *Advances in Consumer Research* 14, no. 1: 208–12.

Robinson, D.T., G. Gibson-Beverly, and J.P. Schwartz. 2004. Sorority and fraternity membership and religious behavior: Relations to gender attitudes. *Sex Roles* 50: 871–7.

Rotfeld, H.J., and C.R. Taylor. 2009. The advertising regulation and self-regulation issues ripped from the headlines with (sometimes missed) opportunities for disciplined multi-disciplinary research. *Journal of Advertising* 38, no. 4: 5–14.

Ruvio, A. 2008. Unique like everybody else? The dual role of consumers' need for uniqueness. *Psychology & Marketing* 25, no. 5: 444–64.

Shank, R.C. 1986. *Explanation patterns: Understanding mechanically and creatively*. Hillsdale, NJ: Erlbaum.

Simonson, I., and S. Nowlis. 2000. The role of explanations and need for uniqueness in consumer decision making: Unconventional choices based on reasons. *Journal of Consumer Research* 27, no. 1: 49–68.

Snyder, C.R., and H.L. Fromkin. 1977. Abnormality as a positive characteristic: The development and validation of a scale measuring need for uniqueness. *Journal of Abnormal Psychology* 86, no. 5: 518–27.

Son, S.Y. 2013. Research on case study of cross-sexual advertisement. *Journal of Korean Society of Communication Design* 21:111–20.

Stayman, D.M., D.L. Alden, and K.M. Smith. 1992. Some effects on schematic processing on consumer expectations and disconfirmation judgments. *Journal of Consumer Research* 14, no. 5: 240–55.

Storms, M.D. 1979. Sex role identity and its relationships to sex role attributes and sex role stereotypes. *Journal of Personality and Social Psychology* 37, no. 10: 1779–89.

Taylor, C.R. 2013. On the economic effects of advertising-evidence that advertising information. *International Journal of Advertising* 32, no. 3: 339–42.

Tian, K.T., W.O. Bearden, and G.L. Hunter. 2001. Consumers' need for uniqueness: Scale development and validation. *Journal of Consumer Research* 28, no. 1: 50–66.

Till, B.D., and M. Busler. 2000.The match-up hypothesis: Physical attractiveness, expertise, and the role of fit on brand attitude, purchase intent and brand beliefs. *Journal of Advertising* 29, no. 3: 1–13.

Triandis, H.C., and M.J. Gelfand. 1998. Converging measurement of horizontal and vertical individualism and collectivism. *Journal of Personality and Social Psychology* 74, no. 1: 118–28.

Ulrich, I. 2013. The effect of consumer multifactorial gender and biological sex on the evaluation of cross-gender brand extensions. *Psychology and Marketing* 30, no. 9: 794–810.

Whipple, T.W., and A.E. Courtney. 1985. Female role portrayals in advertising and communication effectiveness: A review. *Journal of Advertising* 14, no. 3: 4–9.

Wright, P.L. 1973. The cognitive processes mediating acceptance of advertising. *Journal of Marketing Research* 10, no. 1: 53–62.

Yeo, J.S., T.S. Yoon, and H.W. Song. 2010. Effect of gender consistency on brand extension evaluation. *Journal of Korean Marketing Association* 25, no. 2: 1–15.

Zaichkowsky, J.L. 1985. Measuring the involvement construct. *Journal of Consumer Research* 12, no. 3: 341–52.

Zhang, Y., and L.J. Shrum. 2009. The influence of self-construal on impulsive consumption. *Journal of Consumer Research* 35, no. 5: 17–28.

Zhu, J., and J. Meyers-Levy. 2005. Exploring the cognitive mechanism that underlies regulatory focus effects. *Journal of Consumer Research* 34, no. 1: 89–96.

In distrust of merits: the negative effects of astroturfs on people's prosocial behaviors

Jungyun Kang[a], Hyungsin Kim[b], Hosang Chu[a], Charles H. Cho[c] and Hakkyun Kim[a]

[a]School of Business Sungkyunkwan University,Seoul, Republic of Korea; [b]College of Education, Ewha Womans University,Seoul, Republic of Korea; [c]ESSEC Business School, Cedex, France

Astroturf organizations are fake grassroots organizations that hide their true identity by using deceptive and fraudulent tactics as propaganda, but try to convince the public that they are authentic. In this study, we focus on the potential influences of astroturf organizations within the context of prosocial behaviors. Building on the notion that deceptive advertisements engender distrust and undermine the trustworthiness of subsequent advertising, we suggest that people who read messages from astroturf organizations will become more distrustful toward nonprofit organizations and will display lower willingness to engage in prosocial behaviors than people who read messages from grassroots organizations. Results from studies 1 and 2 indicate that messages from astroturf organizations can engender people's distrust toward nonprofit organizations, thereby lowering their willingness to engage in prosocial behaviors. In addition, the negative effect of astroturf organizations is moderated by skepticism toward advertising. Given that the insidious use of astroturf organizations is growing in popularity, we provide meaningful insights into the influence of fake grassroots organizations, with the possibility to forewarn the public about their undesirable effects on the community.

The phenomenon of global warming, also referred to as climate change, in and of itself is hardly a debate nowadays – a plethora of sound and rigorous scientific evidence has been validated by the Intergovernmental Panel on Climate Change (IPCC), which remains the most eminent and authoritative body providing scientific advice to global policymakers under the auspices of the United Nations, the World Meteorological Organization, and the United Nations Environment Program (National Oceanic and Atmospheric Administration 2014). Concretely speaking, and according to NASA scientists, the average global temperature has risen by approximately 1.4 °F (0.8 °C) since 1880. Consequently, the planet is suffering from various climate anomalies or unusual weather conditions that can be attributed to global warming (IPCC 2007).

As such, scientific evidence supports the view that the current warming trend does exist, and most lay people appear to have adopted the perspective that global warming is unquestionably real. However, when it comes to what possibly causes the global warming phenomenon, the story is not that simple. On one hand, the dominant view concerning the cause of global warming is anthropogenic, with a series of actions advocating against human-induced climate change (Cook et al. 2013; Oreskes 2004). On the other hand are climate change deniers, who support the perspective that carbon dioxide emissions from human activities do not constitute the main cause of global warming. Further, some groups of scientists argue that global warming is 'just' a natural phenomenon, trivializing the role of human beings in the progressive warming of the Earth. Such significant disparities with the respect to the main cause(s) of global warming are not merely issues for scientific debate. More importantly, such a lack of consensus regarding human-created climate change and the continuous debate around this issue have engendered skepticism concerning scientific opinion and have led to widespread indifference to global warming among the public, thereby undermining their engagement in the subject. In fact, according to a survey, 26% of respondents were found to believe that 'until we are sure that climate change is really a problem, we should not take any steps that would have economic costs' (Bouton et al. 2010, 38).

An interesting aspect of these disparities between arguments about the main cause(s) of global warming is that scientific consensus on anthropogenic global warming is at 97.1%, and the consensus is nearly unequivocal in the field of climate science, while the number of deniers is extremely small, and the sources of such views are now well known. In fact, although ample evidence should enhance conviction as to human activities as the cause, people's concerns about global warming have ironically dropped over time (Newport 2010; Cho et al. 2011). This increased uncertainty or weakened conviction among the public is due to certain types of organizations promoting a specific scientific view that refutes the perspectives of traditional scientists on human causes. These organizations have basically conducted climate change denial campaigns to undermine the public's confidence that it is human beings and activities that are warming the climate. Such organizations are known as 'astroturf' organizations. 'Astroturf' is a term used to describe a campaign by a fake grassroots organization while being covertly supported by a large corporation[1]. Effectively, fossils fuel industries subsidize astroturf organizations and use them as a means to attract the public's attention in their favor. In addition, the American Petroleum Institute, a powerful Washington-based lobbying organization for oil and gas industries, has recruited 'ordinary-looking' people to insert pro-oil and gas messages.

As noted above, astroturf organizations have directly influenced the minds of the public regarding various aspects on global warming (Cho et al. 2011). In part, due to astroturf organizations that deny human responsibility for global warming, fewer people regard global warming as a serious threat, and more people believe that scientists are unsure about global warming. Also, people are now almost evenly split in their views concerning whether human activities vs. natural causes are responsible for increases in the Earth's temperature (Newport 2010). Could there be other effects besides these explicit harms of astroturf organizations?

The current research aims at examining the influences of astroturf organizations in a broader context. Since people's perceptions of grassroots organizations can change following their exposure to the messages of astroturf organizations, we argue that there can be other negative effects of astroturf organizations beyond the specific scope that astroturf organizations target. As such, we examine whether astroturf organizations can negatively affect people's perceptions of nonprofit organizations, and whether astroturf organizations can lower people's engagement in prosocial behaviors. Building on the notion that exposure to astroturf organizations can increase skepticism or suspicion toward other benign and authentic grassroots organizations, we posit that exposure to astroturf organizations can make individuals more logically defensive and can decrease their trust toward messages from other nonprofit organizations. Specifically, we suggest that people who read messages from astroturf organizations will be more distrustful toward nonprofit organizations and will exhibit a lower willingness to engage in prosocial behaviors than those who read messages from grassroots organizations. In doing so, we advance the argument that the outcome of individuals' experience of astroturf organizations is not merely confined to a particular issue that these organizations seek to blur. Rather, the harm of an astroturf organization working on a particular agenda can be leveraged onto other areas and can erode the goodwill of other real grassroots movements and of the entire community. Therefore, this research identifies the indirect effects that astroturf organizations can have on human perceptions in society.

Conceptual background

Astroturfs vs. grassroots

Grassroots organizations are defined as 'local political organizations which seek to influence conditions not related to the working situation of the participants and which have the activity of the participants as their primary resource' (Gundelach 1979, 187). In other words, a grassroots organization is most likely to operate at the local level to protect public opinion against the political power structure. For example, Walker (2010) defined these organizations as the 'weapon of the weak.' Most grassroots organizations are supported by volunteer workers who want to achieve prosocial goals (Brainard and Brinkerhoff 2004; Gallicano 2013; Simons 1970; Smith 1999). As such, it is organized to improve the way in which a society becomes more socially and environmentally aware.

Following grassroots movements, artificially induced grassroots organizations called astroturf organizations have been created. These organizations are defined as 'fake grassroots organizations animated by a clever public relations campaign and a huge budget' (Hoggan and Littlemore 2009, 36) and hide their true identity by using rhetorical language to convince the public. It can be inferred that large corporations sponsor astroturf organizations so as to employ deceptive and fraudulent tactics for their propaganda or persuasion purposes. According to prior research, these organizations have tendency to provide selective and limited information to the targeted public to achieve a corporation's goals (Beder 1998; Hainsworth and Meng 1988; Heath and Nelson 1985; Lyon and Maxwell 2004; McNutt 2010; McNutt and Boland 2007; Mix and Waldo 2015; Stauber and Rampton 1995; Walker 2010; Cho et al. 2011). One of the most common examples of astroturf organizations are those receiving financial support from ExxonMobil Corporation and deliver information that denies anthropogenic global warming (Greenpeace USA 2007).

Astroturf organizations first gained attention at the initial stages of research on organizational and political contexts. Mattingly (2006) conducted qualitative research to determine the mechanisms linked between corporate and political environments. Evidence from interviewing public relations representatives suggests that corporate political strategy-making can be influenced by both external and internal factors. Namely, getting along with grassroots organizations can enhance the firms' integrity and social images. On the other hand, feeding information in favor of the firms by hiding the firms' names or identities (i.e., the use of astroturf organizations) could help achieve their intended goals but might put the firms in a position receiving social disapproval and scorn when the firms are discovered as being the true message creators. Therefore, astroturfing is to be avoided since the credibility of firms can be at risk when revealed. Lyon and Maxwell (2004) also suggested that astroturfing is one of the formal models of lobbying strategies, and that disclosing astroturfing payments would reduce the effectiveness of astroturfing.

McNutt and Boland (2007) demonstrated the progression of nonprofit organization advocacy by arguing that it has become more difficult to differentiate between traditional nonprofit organizations and spurious nonprofits due to the new media, which results in a distrusting society. In particular, unlike front groups who focus on policy-makers and election outcomes, astroturf organizations aim at changing public opinion. Thus, information fed by astroturf organizations lacks trustworthiness and can result in the erosion of overall trustworthiness and goodwill of the community.

Consequences of astroturfing: Public distrust and disengagement

While numerous prior studies have been conducted regarding astroturf organizations, little research has examined the effects of astroturfing from the perspectives of advertising and consumer behavior. As an exception, Cho et al. (2011) found that astroturf websites can significantly increase uncertainty about the existence of global warming and humans' role in the phenomenon. Further, their research showed that such an effect still occurs although website users do not trust the source of the websites. In other words, while browsing an astroturf organization website, they cast doubt on the website itself. However, their doubt is also directed at the human role in global warming, thus showing the power of astroturfing.

In marketing communication, sending out messages with the true identity hidden is routinely employed in front-group stealth campaigns, which can exert influence on public attitudes. As noted by Pfau, Haigh, Sims and Wigley (2007), such campaigns can succeed in influencing public opinion in the direction hoped for by corporations (i.e., message senders). However, its positive side can be counteracted by *post hoc* exposure and preemptive warnings. Thus, astroturfing can backfire when the identity of the corporations behind it is later revealed.

Such a boomerang effect is also observed in deceptive advertisements, in that message recipients may lower their level of trust toward message senders after exposure to such deceptive advertisements (Campbell and Kirmani 2000; Darke and Ritchie 2007; DeCarlo 2005; Friestad and Wright 1994; Kirmani and Campbell 2004; Kirmani and Zhu 2007; Main, Dahl, and Darke 2007; Olson and Dover 1978). In order to persuade consumers to select a certain brand over others, or to obtain favorable attention or impressions, advertisements are usually expressed in rhetorical language and with exaggeration. Although the advertisements are used as a means of persuasion tactics, if consumers become aware of the advertisements as being fraudulent or deceptive, the desired results are hardly likely to occur (Armstrong, Gurol, and Russ 1979). When the sellers' ulterior motives are salient, consumers present less favorable ratings and more negative responses (Boerman, van Reijmersdal, and Neijens 2012; Campbell and Kirmani 2000; Kirmani and Zhu 2007; DeCarlo 2005). Boerman, van Reijmersdal, and Neijens (2014) demonstrate that when duration of sponsorship disclosure is extended in noncommercial television programs, attitudes toward the brand are worsened. Similarly, Wei, Fischer, and Main (2008) also show that when persuasion knowledge is activated, consumers lower evaluations of brands embedded in radio programs.

More importantly, Darke and Ritchie (2007) found that deceptive advertisements can make consumers self-protective, such that they may tend to view marketing stimuli from an angle of distrust. As a result, consumers who have been exposed to deceptive advertising will increase their likelihood to be skeptical toward subsequent advertising, which should make persuasion more difficult even for honest and sincere sellers.

A similar process of engendering distrust is also found in interpersonal relationships. An interaction that is not in line with people's prior knowledge or expectations can make them modify their attitudes, beliefs, or behaviors (van Knippenberg et al. 1999). After repeated experience with incompatibility between what people have heard and what they see, they are likely to form distrust and suspicion (Fox 1974; Nye, Zelikow, and King 1997; Pew 1998; Sitkin and Roth 1993), given that individuals' a priori expectations, as well as their a posteriori attributions, influence their perceptions and judgments. Thus, distrust should be heightened if interpersonal influence violates individuals' expectations about others' trustworthiness (Lindskold 1978; Pilisuk and Skolnick 1968; Rotter 1980). Furthermore, when people notice situational cues or contextual information implying that others might have ulterior motives, suspicion is likely to be aroused (Fein 1996).

Drawing on these research streams regarding the process of defensive stereotyping and chain reactions after interactions with distrustful entities (e.g., astroturfs), we distinguish two types of nonprofit organizations (i.e., astroturf organizations and grassroots organizations) and predict that information from astroturf organizations affect people's trust toward overall nonprofit organizations. Specifically, it is expected that people who read messages from astroturf organizations will be more distrustful toward nonprofit organizations and will display lower willingness to engage in prosocial behaviors than those who read messages from grassroots organizations.

Study 1

The purpose of Study 1 was to test the negative effect of astroturf organizations on people's trust toward nonprofit organizations and willingness to engage in prosocial behaviors. In this study, we varied the types of nonprofit organizations working on global warming (astroturf vs. grassroots). We expect that information from astroturf organizations affects not only relevant issues or organizations but also the level of trust toward nonprofit organizations in general, which could then lower people's willingness to engage in prosocial behaviors (e.g., donations and charitable giving).

Participants and procedure

A total of 72 undergraduate students (mean age = 21.83; 52.8% male) in Canada participated in this study in exchange for course credit. We used a one-factor design with two levels of organization types (astroturf vs. grassroots). Participants were randomly assigned to one of the two conditions.

Participants were given a survey booklet, including several unrelated studies. They were first asked to read excerpts of a website (astroturf vs. grassroots). They were told that the excerpts were from the website of a nonprofit organization working on addressing issues related to global warming. In the astroturf organization condition, participants were given articles showing that global warming is a natural phenomenon; thus, no change is urgently needed (see Appendix 1). In contrast, in the grassroots organization condition, participants read articles supporting the perspective that global warming is the result of greenhouse gases (GHGs) emitted by humans; thus, people need to effectively stop emitting GHGs (see Appendix 2). Only the information content was manipulated. Other than the content of the messages, the substance of the articles such as length and structure was identical. All of the content was based on information found on real-world grassroots and astroturf websites.

After reading the article, participants responded to the questionnaires about global warming issues. Participants indicated their uncertainty levels about the causes of global warming on seven-point semantic differential scales ('The argument that humans are causing global warming appears to be'; 1 = inappropriate, incorrect, scientifically unproven, and inaccurate, 7 = appropriate, correct, scientifically proven, and accurate), adopted from Cho et al. (2011). Responses to these four items were combined into an uncertainty level about the causes of global warming index (α = .87). Then, participants then proceeded to an unrelated second study. They were told that the purpose of the second study was to investigate consumer attitudes and intentions on a variety of issues. In the second study, participants generated their trust toward nonprofit organizations on seven-point scales ('Nonprofit organizations try to better the world,' and 'I trust nonprofit organizations'; 1 = strongly disagree, 7 = strongly agree). Responses to these two items were combined into a trust toward nonprofit organizations index (r = .72, p < .05). Then, participants indicated the extent that they would be willing to engage in several prosocial behaviors on five-point scales ('I am willing to assist someone experiencing car trouble,' 'I like to give someone directions,' 'I will give money to someone who needs it or asks for it,' 'I am willing to do volunteer work for charity,' 'I will donate blood,' and 'I want to help carry another person's belongings'; 1 = does not describe me at all, 5 = describe me greatly). Responses to these six items were combined into a willingness to engage in prosocial behaviors index (α = .55). Finally, participants were debriefed and thanked.

Results

We first assessed whether the messages of nonprofit organizations (astroturf vs. grassroots) affected participants' uncertainty levels about the causes of global warming. The one-way analysis of variance (ANOVA) run on uncertainty yielded a significant effect ($F(1, 70) = 11.54, p < .01$). Participants who read the article from astroturf organizations were more likely to be uncertain about the causes of global warming relative to those who read the article from grassroots organizations ($M_{grassroots}$ = 5.32, SD = 1.12 vs. $M_{astroturf}$ = 4.43, SD = 1.12). Replicating the results of previous research (Cho et al. 2011), astroturf organizations were found to create uncertainty about the causes of global warming.

Next, an ANOVA, with trust toward nonprofit organizations as the dependent variable and the type of organization as the independent variable, yielded a significant effect ($F(1, 70) = 4.38, p < .05$). The results showed that participants who viewed the article from the astroturf organization were more likely to be distrustful of nonprofit organizations than those who viewed the article from the grassroots organization ($M_{astroturf}$ = 4.14, SD = 1.48 vs. $M_{grassroots}$ = 4.80, SD = 1.16). Thus, messages from astroturf organizations lowered people's trust toward nonprofit organizations. In addition, exposure to the article from an astroturf organization appeared to have an impact on people's willingness to engage in prosocial behaviors ($F (1, 70) = 4.77, p < .05$). Specifically, people who viewed the article from the astroturf organization indicated that they were less likely to engage in prosocial behaviors, compared to those who viewed the article from the grassroots organization ($M_{astroturf}$ = 3.11, SD = .63 vs. $M_{grassroots}$ = 3.48, SD = .77). Thus, messages from astroturf organizations may lower their willingness to engage in prosocial behaviors.

Discussion

Study 1 demonstrated that information from an astroturf organization could lower people's trust toward nonprofit organizations and their willingness to engage in prosocial behaviors. Taken as a whole, astroturf organizations may not only confuse people about a specific issue that the respective astroturf organizations aims to attack, but they can also cause severe detriment for the entire society.

Study 2

The purpose of Study 2 was to replicate the results of Study 1, and also to investigate the role of skepticism toward advertising claims. Skepticism toward advertising, defined as 'the general tendency toward disbelief of advertising claims' (Obermiller and Spangenberg 1998, 159), is a construct relevant to consumers' information integration and internalization. In other words, skepticism toward advertising regulates the level of distrust and suspicion toward advertisement as a result of learning from past encounters with advertising and people's personal experience, but it is not a stable personality factor.

Previous research suggests that the outcome of persuasion tasks are dependent upon skepticism toward advertising to some degree in that skepticism toward advertising can influence whether consumers embrace a message fully as written or said. Escalas (2007) showed when consumers were skeptical about an advertisement, analytical thoughts were activated. This analytical process reduced intentions to accept advertising claims. Since all advertisements show only the positive aspects of products, any aspect casting doubt on such products can lead to lower consumer evaluations. Prior research showed that more skeptical consumers evaluated an advertisement using altruistic (public-serving) appeals more negatively, rather than an advertisement using egoistic (firm-serving) appeals (Forehand and Grier 2003). Furthermore, skepticism toward advertising can further exacerbate the negativity of people's attitudes toward these advertisements and their associated products/brands (Obermiller, Spangenberg, and MacLachlan 2005). Chen and Leu (2011) also demonstrated that doubt about advertising claims had a negative effect on product involvement, as well as brand attitude and purchase intention.

Recent years have seen a great deal of attention paid to consumers' skepticism toward green advertisements (e.g., Bickart and Ruth 2012; Finisterra do Paço and Reis 2012; Fowler and Close 2012; Matthes and Wonneberger 2014; Sheehan and Atkinson 2012). Vermeir and Verbeke (2006) pointed out that misleading green claims are prevalent (Carlson et al. 1996; Easterling, Kenworthy, and Nemzoff 1996; Montoro-Rios et al. 2006); therefore, consumers have often been skeptical of these green advertising claims (Bickart and Ruth 2012; Sheehan and Atkinson 2012). Matthes and Wonneberger (2014) found that green advertisement skepticism is related to green consumerism (environmental concern, attitudes toward green products, and green purchase behavior), and that consumers who are more skeptical toward green advertisements perceive the efficacy of these products as low, compared to those who are less skeptical toward green advertisements. Parguel, Benoit-Moreau, and Rusell (2015) also showed that natural-evoking elements in advertisements could mislead consumers' evaluation for the company when their knowledge in environmental issues is insufficient.

Drawing on this line of research with respect to the role of consumer skepticism toward advertising, we propose that advertising skepticism can moderate the effect of messages by astroturf vs. grassroots organizations. Specifically, we hypothesize that people who are less skeptical of advertising should be influenced more by astroturf organizations compared to those who are more skeptical. Therefore, in Study 2, we measured participants' advertising skepticism and show that the effects of astroturf organizations depend on the level of people's skepticism toward advertising.

Participants and procedure

A total of 297 undergraduate students (mean age = 23.6; 56.8% male) in South Korea participated in this study, in exchange for course credit. Participants were randomly assigned to one of the two conditions (astroturf vs. grassroots).

Participants were asked to carefully read an article of a nonprofit organization working on addressing issues related to global warming. The procedures of Study 2 were similar to those of Study 1. After reading the article, participants were asked to respond to the questionnaires about the global warming issue. Then, we measured participants' uncertainty levels about the causes of global warming using the same scales as in Study 1 (α = .92). Then, participants represented their opinions and attitudes on various social issues, including trust toward nonprofit organizations. Participants generated trust toward nonprofit organization on seven-point scales, which were the same as in Study 1 (r = .48, p < .01). Next, we measured the advertisement skepticism of participants' on seven-point scales (1 = strongly disagree, 7 = strongly agree): 'These messages often exaggerate their claims,' 'These messages tell only the good things about their claims,' 'These messages are very annoying,' and 'These messages do not tell much useful information' (Alwitt and Prabhaker 1992; Gaski and Etzel 1986; Mangleburg and Bristol 1998; Rossiter 1977). Responses to these four items were combined into a skepticism toward advertising index (α = .78). Participants were also asked to indicate their involvement in global warming issue: 'I have an interest in global warming,' 'Global warming is an important issue,' 'I am concerned about global warming,' 'My life has been related to global climate change,' and 'I am knowledgeable about global warming.' Responses to these five items were combined into an involvement in global warming index (α = .83). Finally, participants were debriefed and thanked.

Results

As expected, viewing the messages from an astroturf organization had an impact on participants' uncertainty levels about the causes of global warming. The one-way ANOVA run on uncertainty yielded a significant effect ($F(1, 293) = 114.21, p < .001$). Participants who were exposed to information from an astroturf organization exhibited a higher level of uncertainty about the causes of global warming relative to those who were exposed to information from a grassroots organization ($M_{grassroots}$ = 5.06, SD = .93 vs. $M_{astroturf}$ = 3.73, SD = 1.21).

We also analyzed the effect of messages from an astroturf organization on participants' trust toward nonprofit organizations. As in Study 1, an ANOVA run on trust toward nonprofit organizations revealed a main effect of organization type ($F(1, 293) = 8.22, p < .01$). That is, participants who viewed the article from the astroturf organization were more likely to be distrustful of nonprofit organizations than those who viewed the article from the grassroots organization ($M_{astroturf}$ = 4.65, SD = .97 vs. $M_{grassroots}$ = 4.95, SD = .87). Therefore, messages from astroturf organizations were more likely to lower people's trust toward nonprofit organizations.

Next, we examined whether participant involvement in global warming moderated the influence of the astroturf organization. Scores were centered on involvement in global warming prior to being entered into the analysis in order to reduce potential problems stemming from multicollinearity (Aiken and West 1991). As a result, the interaction between type of nonprofit organization and involvement in global warming was not significant ($\beta = .09$, $t = .32$, ns).

We also assessed whether skepticism toward advertising moderated the effect of the messages from astroturf organizations on participant trust toward nonprofit organizations. We regressed trust toward nonprofit organizations on the type of organization (0 = astroturf; 1 = grassroots), the advertisement skepticism score, and their interaction. Scores were centered on advertisement skepticism such as involvement in global warming.

As predicted, the interaction between type of nonprofit organization and advertising skepticism was significant ($\beta = -.20$, $t = -2.00$, $p < .05$). To examine this interaction in more details, we tested the simple slopes (West, Aiken, and Krull 1996) on trust toward nonprofit organizations when skepticism toward advertising was centered at 1 standard deviation above and 1 standard deviation below the mean. As shown in figure 1, a spotlight analysis at one standard deviation below the mean of the skepticism score showed that participants who were exposed to information from the astroturf organization expressed greater distrust toward nonprofit organizations than those who were exposed to information from the grassroots organization ($\beta = .25$, $t = 3.13$, $p < .01$), which yielded a similar effect of astroturfing in the previous study. Thus, our foundational prediction was once again supported.

However, at one standard deviation above the mean of the skepticism score, the type of organization did not significantly influence trust toward nonprofit organizations ($\beta = .03$, $t = .32$, ns). Therefore, the lack of a significant difference among consumers skeptical of advertising indicates that people who are not easily swayed by advertising messages are not further affected by astroturf organizations with respect to whether or not to trust nonprofits. These combined results suggest that astroturfing makes the act of persuasion more infeasible by inducing trusting consumers to be doubtful and skeptical, thus creating a new type of social cost of astroturfing.

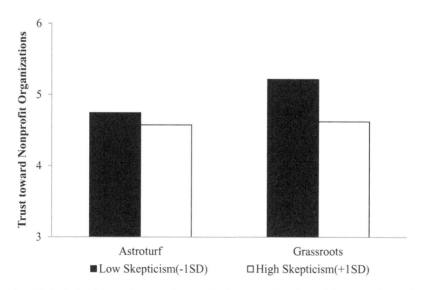

Figure 1.   Study 2: trust toward nonprofit organizations as a function of the type of organization and advertisement skepticism.

Discussion

Study 2 replicated the results of Study 1, in that information from an astroturf organization can lower people's trust toward nonprofit organizations. Study 2 also showed a moderating effect of skepticism toward advertising claims, such that the trust-lowering effect of astroturf organizations is particularly likely and serious among consumers who are not skeptical of advertising claims vs. those who are skeptical.

General discussion

The purpose of this article was to examine whether information from astroturf organizations can influence people's trust toward nonprofit organizations and their willingness to engage in prosocial behaviors. Building on the notion that deceptive advertisements may engender distrust toward subsequent advertisements, we hypothesized and found that people who view messages from astroturf organizations will become more distrustful of nonprofit organizations and will be less likely to engage in helping behaviors than those who view messages from grassroots organizations. As such, this research suggests that information from astroturf organizations can affect not only relevant issues or organizations, but also the public's perceptions as to nonprofit organizations in general, which can then lower people's willingness to engage in prosocial behaviors. Taken as a whole, astroturf organizations may not only confuse people about a specific issue that the respective astroturf organizations aim to attack, but they can also significantly weaken people's trust toward nonprofit organizations in general, which suggests a severe detriment for the entire society.

We also identified a moderating effect of skepticism toward advertising claims. Prior literature has shown that deceptive advertising could lead consumers to adopt a broad negative attitude toward future advertising (e.g., Darke and Ritchie 2007; Pollay 1986; Pollay and Mittal 1993). Extending this line of thinking in advertising, we show that people who are less skeptical of advertising tend to be more strongly influenced by messages from astroturf organizations, compared to those who are more skeptical. Thus, these results indicate that the negative effects of astroturf organizations are further exacerbated among 'innocent' people, as they engender growing distrust within a society.

Our study extends prior research in several aspects. In particular, by demonstrating that people exposed to information from astroturf organizations view others with suspicion and skepticism, the current research suggests that the effects of exposure to astroturf messages are not limited to a specific issue. Rather, these effects can be far-reaching and diverse, since such messages can evoke skepticism toward the benign intentions and programs of nonprofit organizations. Given that the insidious use of astroturf organizations is growing in popularity, this article provides meaningful insights into the influence of fake grassroots organizations and provides the opportunity to forewarn the public about their undesirable effects on the community.

Our findings suggest several directions for future research. Our research focuses on the negative effect of astroturf organizations which pretend to be grassroots organizations. According to prior research, the influence of astroturf organizations depends on the disclosure of funding sources (Cho et al. 2011). Future research could examine whether the negative effect of astroturf campaigns on people's trust toward nonprofit organizations is changed if funding sources are disclosed. Further work could also consider other moderating variables beyond consumer skepticism toward an advertisement. We predict that the influence of astroturf organizations depends on the consumers' dispositional differences. For example, given that persuasion knowledge requires cognitive capacity or resources, consumers' need for cognition or effort investment could moderate the effect of astroturf organizations (Baek, Yoon, and Kim 2015; Campbell and Kirmani 2000). Finally, we recruited only undergraduate students who were enrolled in an introductory-level business class in our studies. Although we predict they are not necessarily more knowledgeable or more involved in environmental issues than the general population, future research could employ real consumers rather than students.

Note

1. The term comes from 'AstroTurf,' which is a brand of synthetic carpeting designed to look like natural grass, but is in fact, fake grass.

Disclosure statement

No potential conflict of interest was reported by the authors.

Funding

This research was supported by a National Research Foundation of Korea Grant, funded by the Korean government [grant number NRF-2013S1A5A2A03045216].

References

Aiken, L.S., and S.G. West. 1991. *Multiple regression: Testing and interpreting interactions.* Thousand Oaks, CA: Sage.

Alwitt, L.F., and P.R. Prabhaker. 1992. Functional and belief dimensions of attitudes to television advertising: Implications for copytesting. *Journal of Advertising Research* 32, no. 5: 30–42.

Armstrong, G.M., M.N. Gurol, & F.A. Russ. 1979. Detecting and correcting deceptive advertising. *Journal of Consumer Research* 6, no. 3: 237–46.

Baek, T.H., S. Yoon, and S. Kim. 2015. When environmental messages should be assertive: Examining the moderating role of effort investment. *International Journal of Advertising* 34, no. 1: 135–57.

Beder, S. 1998. Public relations' role in manufacturing artificial grass roots coalitions. *Public Relations Quarterly* 43, no. 2: 20–3.

Bickart, B.A., and J.A. Ruth. 2012. Green eco-seals and advertising persuasion. *Journal of Advertising* 41, no. 4: 51–67.

Boerman, S.C., E.A. van Reijmersdal, and P.C. Neijens. 2012. Sponsorship disclosure: Effects of duration on persuasion knowledge and brand responses. *Journal of Communication* 62, no. 6: 1047–64.

Boerman, S.C., E.A. van Reijmersdal, and P.C. Neijens. 2014. Effects of sponsorship disclosure timing on the processing of sponsored content: A study on the effectiveness of European disclosure regulations. *Psychology and Marketing* 31, no. 3: 214–24.

Bouton, M.M., R. Bronson, G. Holyk, C. Hug, S. Kull, B.I. Page, S. Veltcheva, and T. Wright. 2010. *Constrained internationalism: Adapting to new realities.* Chicago, IL: The Chicago Council on Global Affairs.

Brainard, L.A., and J.M. Brinkerhoff. 2004. Lost in cyberspace: Shedding light on the dark matter of grassroots organizations. *Nonprofit and Volunteer Sector Quarterly* 33, no. 3: 32–53.

Campbell, M.C., and A. Kirmani. 2000. Consumers' use of persuasion knowledge: The effects of accessibility and cognitive capacity on perceptions of an influence agent'. *Journal of Consumer Research* 27, no. 1: 69–83.

Carlson, L., S.J. Grove, N. Kangun, and M.J. Polonsky. 1996. An international comparison of environmental advertising: Substantive versus associative claims. *Journal of Macromarketing* 16, no. 2: 57–68.

Chen, F., and J. Leu. 2011. Product involvement in the link between skepticism toward advertising and its effects. *Social Behavior and Personality* 39, no. 2: 153–59.

Cho, C.H., M.L. Martens, H. Kim, and M. Rodrigue. 2011. Astroturfing global warming: It isn't always greener on the other side of the fence. *Journal of Business Ethics* 104, no. 4: 571–87.

Cook, J., D. Nuccitelli, S.A. Green, M. Richardson, B. Winkler, R. Painting, R. Way, P. Jacobs, and A. Skuce. 2013. Quantifying the consensus on anthropogenic global warming in the scientific literature. *Environmental Research Letters* 8, no. 2: 1–7.

Darke, P.R., and R.B. Ritchie. 2007. The defensive consumer: Advertising deception, defensive processing, and distrust. *Journal of Marketing Research* 44, no. 1: 114–27.

DeCarlo, T.E. 2005. The effects of suspicion of ulterior motives and sales messages on salesperson evaluation. *Journal of Consumer Psychology* 15, no. 3: 238–49.

Easterling, D., A. Kenworthy, and R. Nemzoff. 1996. The greening of advertising: A twenty-five-year look at environmental advertising. *Journal of Marketing Theory and Practice* 4, no. 1: 20–34.

Escalas, J.E. 2007. Self-referencing and persuasion: Narrative transportation versus analytical elaboration. *Journal of Consumer Research* 33, no. 4: 421–9.

Fein, S. 1996. Effects of suspicion on attributional thinking and the correspondence bias. *Journal of Personality and Social Psychology* 70, no. 6: 1164–84.

Finisterra do Paço, A.M., and R. Reis. 2012. Factors affecting skepticism toward green advertising. *Journal of Advertising* 41, no. 4: 147–55.

Forehand, M.R., and S. Grier. 2003. When is honesty the best policy? The effect of stated company intent on consumer skepticism. *Journal of Consumer Psychology* 13, no. 3: 349–56.

Fowler, A.R. III, and A.G. Close. 2012. It ain't easy being green. Macro, meso, and micro green advertising agendas. *Journal of Advertising* 41, no. 4: 119–132.

Fox, A. 1974. *Beyond contract*. London: Faber Publications.

Friestad, M., and P. Wright. 1994. The persuasion knowledge model: How people cope with persuasion attempts. *Journal of Consumer Research* 21, no. 1: 1–31.

Gallicano, T.D. 2013. Internal conflict management and decision making: A qualitative study of a multitiered grassroots advocacy organization. *Journal of Public Relation Research* 25, no. 4: 368–88.

Gaski, J.F., and M.J. Etzel. 1986. The index of consumer sentiment toward marketing. *Journal of Marketing* 50, no. 3: 71–81.

Greenpeace USA. 2007. ExxonMobil's continued funding of global warming denial industry. http://www.greenpeace.org.

Gundelach, P. 1979. Grassroots organizations. *Acta Sociologica* 22, no. 2: 187–89.

Hainsworth, B., and M. Meng. 1988. How corporations define issue management. *Public Relations Review* 14, no. 4: 18–30.

Heath, R.L., and R.A. Nelson. 1985. Image and issue advertising: A corporate and public policy perspective. *Journal of Marketing* 49, no. 2: 58–68.

Hoggan, J., and R. Littlemore. 2009. *Climate cover-up: The crusade to deny global warming*. Vancouver, BC: Greystone Books.

IPCC (Intergovernmental Panel on Climate Change). 2007. *Climate change 2007: Synthesis report. Contribution of Working Groups I, II, and III to the Fourth Assessment Report of the Intergovernmental Panel on Climate Change*. Cambridge: Cambridge University Press.

Kirmani, A., and M.C. Campbell. 2004. Goal seeker and persuasion sentry: How consumer targets respond to interpersonal marketing persuasion. *Journal of Consumer Research* 31, no. 3: 573–82.

Kirmani, A., and R. Zhu. 2007. Vigilant against manipulation: The effect of regulatory focus on the use of persuasion knowledge. *Journal of Marketing Research* 44, no. 4: 688–701.

Lindskold, S. 1978. Trust development, the GRIT proposal, and the effects of conciliatory acts on conflict and cooperation. *Psychological Bulletin* 85, no. 4: 772–93.

Lyon, T.P., and J.W. Maxwell. 2004. Astroturf: Interest group lobbying and corporate strategy. *Journal of Economics and Management Strategy* 13, no. 4: 561–97.

Main, K.J., D.W. Dahl, and P.R. Darke. 2007. Deliberative and automatic bases of suspicion: Empirical evidence of the sinister attribution error. *Journal of Consumer Psychology* 17, no. 1: 59–69.

Mangleburg, T.F., and T. Bristol. 1998. Socialization and adolescents' skepticism toward advertising. *Journal of Advertising* 27, no. 3: 11–21.

Matthes, J., and A. Wonneberger. 2014. The skeptical green consumer revisited: Testing the relationship between green consumerism and skepticism toward advertising. *Journal of Advertising* 43, no. 2: 115–27.

Mattingly, J.E. 2006. Radar screens, Astroturf and dirty work: A qualitative exploration of structure and process in corporate political action. *Business and Society Review* 111, no. 2: 193–221.

McNutt, J.G. 2010. Researching advocacy groups: Internet sources for research about public interest groups and social movement organizations. *Journal of Policy Practice* 9, no. 3–4: 308–12.

McNutt, J.G., and K. Boland. 2007. Astroturf, technology and the future of community mobilization: Implications for nonprofit theory. *Journal of Sociology and Social Welfare* 34, no. 3: 165–78.

Mix, T.L., and K.G. Waldo. 2015. Know(ing) your power: Risk society, astroturf campaigns, and the battle over the red rock coal-fired plant' *The Sociological Quarterly* 56, no. 1: 125–51.

Montoro-Rios, F.J., T. Luque-Martinez, F. Fuentes-Moreno, and P. Canadas-Soriano. 2006. Improving attitudes toward brands with environmental associations: An experimental approach. *Journal of Consumer Marketing* 23, no. 1: 26–33.

National Oceanic and Atmospheric Administration. 2014. Global warming. http://www.ncdc.noaa.gov/monitoring-references/faq/global-warming.php, accessed on September 27, 2014.

Newport, F. 2010. Americans' global warming concerns continue to drop. http://www.gallup.com/poll/126560/americans-global-warming-concerns-continue-drop.aspx, accessed on March 11, 2010.

Nye, J.S., P.D. Zelikow, and D.C. King. 1997. *Why people don't trust government.* Cambridge, MA: Harvard University Press.

Obermiller, C., and E.R. Spangenberg. 1998. Development of scale to measure consumer skepticism toward advertising. *Journal of Consumer Psychology* 7, no. 2: 159–86.

Obermiller, C., E.R. Spangenberg, and D.L. MacLachlan. 2005. Ad skepticism: The consequences of disbelief. *Journal of Advertising* 34, no. 3: 7–17.

Olson J.C., and P.A. Dover. 1978. Cognitive effects of deceptive advertising. *Journal of Marketing Research* 15, no. 1: 29–38.

Oreskes, Naomi. 2004. The scientific consensus on climate change. *Science* 306, no. 5702: 1686.

Parguel, B., F. Benoit-Moreau, and C.A. Russel. 2015. Can evoking nature in advertising mislead consumers? The power of 'executional greenwashing. *International Journal of Advertising* 34, no. 1: 107–34.

Pew Research Center for the People and the Press. 1998. *Deconstructing distrust: How Americans view government.* Washington, DC: Pew Press.

Pfau, M., Haigh, M.M., Sims, J. and Wigley, S. 2007. The influence of corporate front groups stealth campaigns. *Communication Research* 34, no. 1: 73–99.

Pilisuk, M., and P. Skolnick. 1968. Inducing trust: A test of the Osgood proposal. *Journal of Personality and Social Psychology* 8, no. 2: 121–33.

Pollay, R.W. 1986. The distorted mirror: Reflections on the unintended consequences of advertising. *Journal of Marketing* 50, no. 2: 18–36.

Pollay, R.W., and B. Mittal. 1993. Here's the beef: Factors, determinants, and segments in consumer criticism of advertising. *Journal of Marketing* 57, no. 3: 99–115.

Rossiter, J.R. 1977. Reliability of a short test measuring children's attitudes toward television commercials. *Journal of Consumer Research* 3, no. 4: 179–84.

Rotter, J.B. 1980. Interpersonal trust, trustworthiness, and gullibility. *American Psychologist* 35, no. 1: 1–7.

Sheehan, K., and L. Atkinson. 2012., Special issue on green advertising: Revisiting green advertising and the reluctant consumer. *Journal of Advertising* 41, no. 4: 5–7.

Simons, H.W. 1970. Requirements, problems, and strategies: A theory of persuasion for social movements. *Quarterly Journal of Speech* 56, no. 1: 1–11.

Sitkin, S.B., and N.L. Roth. 1993. Explaining the limited effectiveness of legalistic remedies for trust/distrust. *Organization Science* 4, no. 3: 367–92.

Smith, D.H. 1999. The effective grassroots association, part one: Organizational factors that produce internal impact. *Nonprofit Management and Leadership* 9: 443–56.

Stauber, J.C., and S. Rampton. 1995. Democracy for hire: Public relations and environmental movements. *The Ecologist* 25, no. 5: 173–80.

Van Knippenberg, B., D. Van Knippenberg, E. Blaauw, and R. Vermunt. 1999. Relational considerations in the use of influence tactics. *Journal of Applied Social Psychology* 29, no. 4: 806–19.

Vermeir, I., and W. Verbeke. 2006. Sustainable food consumption: Exploring the consumer attitude–behavioral intention gap. *Journal of Agricultural and Environmental Ethics* 19, no. 2: 169–94.

Walker, E.T. 2010. Industry-driven activism. *Contexts* 9, no. 2: 44–9.

Wei, M., E. Fischer, and K.J. Main. 2008. An examination of the effects of activating persuasion knowledge on consumer response to brands engaging in covert marketing. *Journal of Public Policy and Marketing* 27, no. 1: 34–44.

West, S.G., L.S. Aiken, and J.L. Krull. 1996. Experimental personality designs: Analyzing categorical by continuous variable interactions. *Journal of Personality* 64, no. 1: 1–48.

Appendix 1. An astroturf organization

Climate Clarity is a non-profit organization run by dedicated volunteers comprised mainly of earth and atmospheric scientists, engineers, and other professionals.

We have assembled a Scientific Advisory Board of esteemed climate scientists from around the world to offer a critical mass of current science on global climate and climate change to policymakers, as well as any other interested parties. We also do extensive literature research on these scientific subjects.

Concerned about the abuse of science displayed in the politically inspired Kyoto protocol and other so-called research findings/results, we offer critical evidence that challenges the premises of people who exaggerate global warming trends. We also present alternative causes of climate change.

Appendix 2. A grassroots organization

Climate Clarity is a non-profit organization run by dedicated volunteers comprised mainly of earth and atmospheric scientists, engineers, and other professionals.

We have assembled a Scientific Advisory Board of esteemed climate scientists from around the world to offer a critical mass of current science on global climate and climate change to policy-makers, as well as any other interested parties. We also do extensive literature research on these scientific subjects.

Concerned about the ignorance of science displayed in various research findings/results, we offer evidence showing that the current cycle of global warming is changing the rhythm of the climate that all living things have come to rely on. We also present possible solutions as to how to slow this warming and how to cope with climate change.

Empowering social change through advertising co-creation: the roles of source disclosure, sympathy and personal involvement

Davide C. Orazi, Liliana L. Bove and Jing Lei

Department of Management & Marketing, The University of Melbourne, Australia

Despite the emerging trend of adopting co-creative approaches in public and non-profit advertising, research has overlooked participatory approaches in non-commercial settings. This research extends current knowledge on consumer-generated advertising to communications fostering positive social change. The results of an experimental study show that the disclosure of consumer participation in the ad creation process results in positive ad evaluations and reduces positive attitudes towards unhealthy eating. The main effect of source disclosure on ad evaluations is mediated by sympathy towards the ad creator. In addition, floodlight analyses show that the main effect of source disclosure on ad evaluations and attitudes is amplified when the audience is highly involved with the advertised issue. Implications for theory, practice and public policy are discussed.

1. Introduction

Public and non-profit organizations dealing with social and health issues are gradually adopting more participative processes of advertising creation (Dibb and Carrigan 2013). For example, the Office for Road Safety of Western Australia recently invited students to participate in a contest for the creation of the best anti drink-driving ads (Office of Road Safety WA 2012). This phenomenon is clearly inspired by consumer-generated advertising (CGA), namely communications designed by consumers with the look and feel of professionally developed commercials (Ertimur and Gilly 2012). Peaking in popularity in 2007, when several companies invited consumers to design commercials to be aired during the Super Bowl, CGA has since been integrated in the media strategy of many successful brand holdings, such as Unilever and PepsiCo (Ertimur and Gilly 2012).

To date, however, the effect of disclosing consumer participation in ad creation (i.e., source disclosure effect) remains largely unexplored for communications fostering positive social change (from this point forward, socially empowering ads or SEAs). Previous research has examined the effect of source disclosure in a commercial context, but the results are mixed and difficult to extend to a different domain (Thompson and Malaviya 2013; Lawrence, Fournier, and Brunel 2013). In addition, previous findings in CGA research are also mixed with regard to the effects of the ad creator's identity, advertising skills and ad creator's motives (Ertimur and Gilly 2012; Thompson and Malaviya 2013; Lawrence, Fournier, and Brunel 2013).

These results, albeit mixed, point towards the existence of a relationship between source disclosure and the audience's reactions, both at the evaluative and attitudinal levels. Drawing from literature on source effects (Wilson and Sherrell 1993; Kang and Herr 2006), sympathy in advertising (Escalas and Stern 2003), personal involvement (Zaichkowsky 1994) and consumer responsibilization (Shamir 2008; Giesler and Veresiu 2014), we form our predictions on how source disclosure, sympathy towards the ad creator and personal involvement with the advertised issue interact to affect the evaluations of socially empowering ads (SEAs).

Our research complements and furthers extant knowledge on CGA by isolating the source disclosure effect, the mediating role of sympathy towards the ad creator and the moderating role of personal involvement with the advertised issue in collaboratively created public communications. In doing so, we add to a growing body of literature on consumer empowerment in social and health care (Giesler and Veresiu 2014; Boivin et al. 2014). Our findings also have relevant implications for advertisers and policy makers, providing guidelines and strategies to design and implement effective co-created SEAs.

The remainder of the paper is organized as follows. First, we review the relevant literature on CGA and identify differences and similarities in the application of this strategy in the private and public sectors. Then, we develop our hypotheses on source disclosure, sympathy and personal involvement. We follow by presenting our methodology and the results of the experimental study. Implications for theory, practice and public policy are then discussed, along with limitations and avenues for future research.

2. Theoretical framework

2.1 Consumer-generated advertising

CGA refers to communications designed by consumers to resemble professionally developed commercials 'whose subject is a collectively recognized brand' (Berthon, Pitt, and Campbell 2008, 8). Literature on CGA identifies four main factors influencing the audience's ad and brand evaluations: the audience's inferences about (1) the ad creator's identity, (2) the ad creator's advertising skills, (3) the ad creator's motives and (4) the audience's brand loyalty (Ertimur and Gilly 2012; Thompson and Malaviya, 2013; Lawrence, Fournier, and Brunel 2013).

CGA studies on the effects of mere source disclosure – namely how the audience differentially evaluates the same message depending on the disclosure of different message sources – produced mixed results. First, Thompson and Malaviya (2013) found that disclosing that an ad is consumer-generated (vs. company created) triggers a process of identification which positively influences ad and brand evaluations. This positive effect is further amplified when the ad creator is perceived as similar to the audience and when the audience's brand loyalty is high. In contrast, Lawrence, Fournier, and Brunel (2013) found no significant difference between CGA and company-created ads on the extent to which the audience identifies with the ad creator.

Second, results are also mixed regarding the impact of the ad creator's perceived advertising skills on ad and brand evaluations. Thompson and Malaviya (2013) found that source disclosure also causes skepticism towards the advertising competence of the ad creator. This skepticism, in turn, leads to negative ad and brand evaluations. Conversely, Lawrence, Fournier, and Brunel (2013) found that disclosure of consumer sources helps ad evaluations by lowering the expectations of ad competence of the ad creator and by making the audience value the creativity and authenticity associated with CGA more so than the ad creator's advertising skills (Lawrence, Fournier, and Brunel 2013).

Third, although research suggests that the perceived egoistic motives for creating CGA, such as monetary rewards and self-promotion (Berthon, Pitt, and Campbell 2008), may trigger negative audience's responses (Ertimur and Gilly 2012; Lawrence, Fournier, and Brunel 2013), the existing empirical evidence does not support this contention. Lawrence, Fournier, and Brunel (2013), for example, tested the impact of economic (i.e., monetary reward) and non-economic motives (i.e., ad creator brand loyalty) on the perceived trustworthiness of the ad creator and on ad evaluations, but did not find significant results.

The above results, albeit mixed, highlight how the audience's response to CGA is influenced by inferences made about the ad creator upon source disclosure. For instance, disclosing the identity of the ad creator may lead the audience to infer about the advertising skills and motives of the message source, or to what extent the audience feels similar to the ad creator. Such inferences can be further influenced by individual factors, such as brand loyalty (see Thompson and Malaviya 2013).

2.2 The main effect of source disclosure

The CGA strategy described thus far refers mainly to the private sector, where the labels 'consumer-generated' and 'co-created' have been used almost interchangeably to define either solely consumer-generated ads or ads created with the support of the sponsoring brands (Ertimur and Gilly 2012; Thompson and Malaviya 2013). In the public and non-profit sectors, however, both practice and theory are converging towards the adoption of a fully collaborative approach. The invitation of the Office for Road Safety of Western Australia to create anti drink-driving ads (Office of Road Safety WA 2012), for instance, is a practical manifestation of the process of consumer responsibilization investigated by Giesler and Veresiu (2014). Consumer responsibilization calls for a re-definition of social issues from the perspective of an empowered, responsible consumer who becomes the central problem-solver.

While it is true that social messages can be solely generated by consumers deeply involved with a social or health issue (e.g., Mothers Against Drunk Driving), the sensitivity (Guttman and Salmon 2004) and need for informational accuracy characterizing most social issues (e.g., health literacy, Parker and Ratzan 2010) suggest that this is the exception rather than the norm. The negative consequences that may stem from lack of sensitivity or informational accuracy in communications dealing with social, health and environmental issues can be far more disastrous than some loss of brand equity due to a mocking CGA in the commercial sector (e.g., Chevrolet Cameo). Consequently, this research is confined to the application of consumer-driven content in public sector advertising that is supported by institutional or institutionally accredited organizations.

We define co-created SEA as the advertising product of the collaboration between consumers and public or non-profit organizations on issues relevant to the common good (cf. Giesler and Veresiu 2014). Because of the co-creative nature of the process, the awareness of institutional participation lends legitimacy to the contribution provided by the consumer-creators both in terms of information reliability and executional quality. This legitimization should to a large extent reduce the potential skepticism towards the advertising competence of the ad creator (Thompson and Malaviya 2013). Meanwhile, consumer participation in the creation of SEA would make the audience appreciate the ad content as it incorporates the experiences and insights of their own in-group. Therefore, we expect that disclosing consumer participation in ad creation will have a positive effect on ad evaluations and attitudes toward the advertised issue.[1] Formally stated:

H1. The disclosure of consumer participation in SEA creation has a positive effect on a) ad evaluations and b) attitudes towards the advertised issue.

2.3   The mediating effect of source identification

Research on source effects and social influence (Wilson and Sherrel 1993; Cialdini and Trost 1998) suggests that message recipients tend to be persuaded to a greater extent when they can self-reference to the message source. According to attribution theory (Kelley 1967), sources perceived as similar trigger a process of identification. Identification then guides the audience behavior as they tend to act more on messages received from someone they can self-reference to. Source effects literature (Wilson and Sherrell 1993; Kang and Herr 2006) identifies two key determinants of the identification process, the source's physical attractiveness and ideological similarity. While physical attractiveness refers to aesthetic appearance, ideological similarity refers to the audience's perceptions of 'shared interests, feelings, opinions, values or beliefs' with the message source (Kreuter and McClure 2004, 443).

In investigating the identification process, celebrity endorsement literature has typically focused on the influence of physical attractiveness on ad and brand evaluations, whereas the CGA literature has focused on ideological similarity. The very nature of celebrity endorsement as an advertising strategy implies an association between an endorsing celebrity and an endorsed brand, often facilitated by the attractiveness of the celebrity (Erdogan 1999; Amos, Holmes, and Strutton 2008). In CGA research, conversely, the message source is typically disclosed through a few lines of text providing background information about the ad creator, without relying on visual depictions (see Thompson and Malaviya 2013; Lawrence, Fournier, and Brunel 2013). Therefore, most CGA research employs ideological similarity rather than physical attractiveness to measure the process of identification with the message source. But are a few words describing consumer participation in ad creation sufficient to generate attributions of ideological similarity? Will they be strong enough to trigger the identification process?

The disclosure of consumer participation adds an additional layer of information that must be brief and impactful (cf. Thompson and Malaviya 2013) for message formats whose average gaze duration is typically short (Pieters and Wedel 2004). Given the challenges of displaying succinct content adapted to the format of the ad and brief ad exposures, source disclosure manipulations are often limited to mentioning consumer participation, without including other information necessary to form attributions of ideological similarity.

We contend that sympathy towards the ad creator better captures the identification process for co-created SEA than ideological similarity. In advertising research, sympathy defines a feeling of enhanced awareness of someone's state of mind, feelings and circumstances that does not necessarily entail emotional absorption (Escalas and Stern 2003). Sympathy is cognitive, voluntary and oriented toward an understanding of the other

---

[1]The positive effect of source disclosure on attitudes entails both the increase of positive attitudes toward a healthy or desirable behavior and, as it is the case of the current research, the decrease of positive attitudes towards an unhealthy or undesirable behavior.

person and his or her perspective and feelings (Escalas and Stern 2003). Sympathy can capture the identification process even when consumer participation is disclosed but little information on the consumer is provided – particularly information that could facilitate the formation of attributions of ideological similarity. Although the related construct of empathy is often cited in advertising, empathy describes emotional reactions congruent to another person or situation's emotional state, mainly configuring itself as absorption in the feelings of another individual (Eisenberg and Strayer 1987).

Sympathy is thus more common response to short ads since the understanding and cognitive elaboration of emotional states (i.e., sympathy) is easier to evoke than emotional absorption (i.e., empathy; Escalas and Stern 2003). We therefore utilize sympathy to capture how the audience consciously evaluates and critically assess the contribution of the ad creator, and how, in the context of social and health issues, this process generates a sense of we-ness between audience and ad-creator that culminates in more positive ad evaluations. Because sympathy has no direct effects at the attitudinal level (Escalas and Stern 2003), we do not extend the mediating role of advertising sympathy to attitudes towards the advertised issue. Formally stated:

H2. Sympathy towards the ad creator mediates the effect of source disclosure on ad evaluations.

2.4 The moderating effect of personal involvement

Different operationalizations of personal involvement exist in advertising literature, typically in reference to (1) the advertised product (i.e., product involvement), (2) the advertisement itself (i.e., advertising engagement) and (3) the purchase behavior (Zaichkowsky 1994). In addition to these interpretations, CGA research has conceptualized personal involvement as involvement with the sponsoring brand or brand loyalty (Thompson and Malaviya 2013). In commercial CGA, the operationalization of personal involvement as brand loyalty is managerially relevant since the very definition of CGA identifies the subject in a collectively recognized brand (Berthon, Pitt, and Campbell 2008).

In a SEA context aimed at fostering positive social change by influencing attitudes and behaviors, it is more relevant to consider personal involvement with the advertised cause – comparable to product involvement – rather than involvement with the public institution – comparable to brand loyalty in the private sector. In line with other advertising research investigating personal involvement with social and health issues (e.g., environmental concern; see D'Souza and Taghian 2005), we define personal involvement as the extent to which an individual considers the advertised issue to be relevant to his or her system of values, beliefs, interests and experiences.

The lion's share of research on personal involvement in advertising revolves around the elaboration likelihood model (ELM; Petty and Cacioppo 1986). The ELM contends that highly involved individuals process messages following a central route of elaboration, whereas low involved individuals process messages following a peripheral route of elaboration (Petty, Cacioppo, and Schumannn 1983). Central elaboration is characterized by systematic thinking, careful examination of the message and sensitivity to informational content. Peripheral elaboration is characterized by heuristic thinking, rapid skimming of the message and sensitivity to emotional content (Kirmani and Shiv 1998).

We expect that, for static visual ads, the effect of source disclosure on ad evaluations and attitudes towards unhealthy eating depends on the audience's level of personal involvement with healthy eating. Highly involved individuals are characterized by a baseline condition of interest and personal relevance towards the advertised issue. When confronted with a message dealing with an issue perceived as important, highly involved individual will be sensitive to informational elements and carefully scrutinize the message. The acknowledgment that the normative message backed up by an involved referent (i.e., the formerly affected consumer-creator) is expected to amplify positive inferences regarding the ad creation process while stifling potential negative inferences about motives and executional quality (see Hypothesis 1). Therefore, for highly involved individuals, a message disclosing the participation of a formerly affected consumer in ad creation will be more effective than a message disclosing a traditional, institutional source. The moderating effect of personal involvement is also expected to hold for the main effect of source disclosure on sympathy, further facilitating the process of self-referencing to the message source. The more the audience is involved with the advertised issue, the stronger the sympathy towards the ad creator will be, since the awareness of similar experiences and interests will facilitate the process of recognition and understanding of the consumer-creator's experiences, motives and feelings.

Low involved consumers, conversely, are characterized by a baseline state of disinterest and lack of personal relevance towards the advertised issue. When confronted with a message dealing with an issue perceived as not important, uninvolved individuals will quickly skim through the message in search for emotional content (Petty and Cacioppo 1986). Even if they pay attention to the message source, the meanings embedded in the disclosure of a horizontal collaboration between institutions and formerly affected consumers will not resonate. We therefore expect that, under conditions of low involvement, there will be no significant difference between the two source disclosure conditions. Formally stated, we hypothesize the following interaction effects:

H3. The impact of disclosing a co-created source on a) sympathy b) ad evaluations and c) attitudes towards the advertised issue is stronger under conditions of high personal involvement with the advertised issue.

Figure 1 summarizes the relationships hypothesized thus far in a coherent framework.

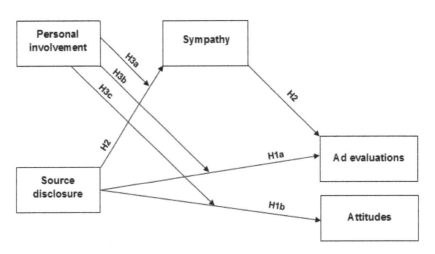

Figure 1. Hypothesized relationships.

3. Method

3.1 Research design and stimulus

This study aims to assess the main effect of source disclosure on ad evaluations and attitudes toward unhealthy eating, while elucidating (1) the mediating effect of the process of identification with the ad creator and (2) the moderating effect of personal involvement with the advertised issue. To test the associated hypotheses, an online experiment was conducted manipulating source disclosure as a categorical factor and measuring involvement with the advertised issue as a continuous moderator. Source disclosure was manipulated by varying the information provided about the message source. Involvement with the advertised issue was measured on a continuous scale and simple effects tests were performed using a floodlight analysis (Spiller et al. 2013). This resulted in a 2 (source disclosure: co-created vs. control) × 2 (involvement with the advertised issue: low vs. high) between-subjects design.

Real ads targeting unhealthy eating were employed in this study. The advertisement was originally developed by the New York City Department of Health (NYCHD). The logo of the NYCHD was removed. The same advertisement was used in both experimental conditions. In the control condition ($n = 64$), participants were informed that the ad was created by the Department of Health. In the co-created condition ($n = 63$), participants were informed that the ad was created by a formerly affected consumer in collaboration with the Department of Health (see stimuli in Appendix 1).

3.2 Participants and procedure

One-hundred-and-forty US residents were recruited from an online panel in return for a small incentive. Participants were invited to complete a short online questionnaire on the effectiveness of socially responsible ads. On the first page, participants were presented the plain language statement informing them of the goals and methods of the research, and reassuring them about the anonymity of their responses. On the second page, participants were asked to report their involvement with healthy eating, gender, ethnicity, height, weight, age, highest educational degree and frequency of fast-food consumption. On the third page, participants were randomly assigned to one of the two experimental conditions. None of the participants reported to have seen the ad previously. Ad exposure time was constrained to 30 seconds, after which the survey progressed to the next page. The time allowed to view the ad was longer than the average gaze duration of 2.8 seconds reported by Pieters and Wedel (2004). This was done to allow respondents enough time to read the information about the ad creator. The duration of ad exposure was timed ($M_{Time} = 13.67$, $SD = 7.86$) and used in subsequent control tests.

Following exposure to the experimental conditions, participants were presented with a treatment check and asked to indicate if the ad was created by the Department of Health, or by a formerly affected consumer in collaboration with the Department of Health. Of the original sample of 140 respondents, 13 were excluded from the analyses as they failed the treatment check. The final sample included 127 US residents ($M_{Age} = 39.07$; $SD = 11.97$; 55.9% male). After exposure to the experimental condition and ensuing treatment check, participants were asked to answer a battery of questions on identification with the ad creator, ad evaluations and attitudes towards unhealthy eating. The stimulus was not present when participants were asked to complete the dependent variables measures.

3.3 Measures

Established measures were used for all the variables of interest. Involvement with the advertised issue was operationalized as involvement with healthy eating and measured with a 10-item, seven-point Likert scale (Kähkönen, Tuorila, and Rita 1996). Sympathy towards the consumer-creator was measured with a five-item, seven-point Likert scale adapted from Escalas and Stern (2003). Ad evaluations were measured with a five-item, seven-point semantic differential scale (Thompson and Malaviya 2013). Attitudes towards unhealthy eating were measured with a three-item, seven-point Likert scale (Kearney, Hulshof, and Gibney 2001). Control variables included time of ad exposure and socio-demographic factors, namely height, weight, age, gender and education. Height and weight were used to compute the body mass index ((weight in Kgs/(height in meters),[2] World Health Organization 2014). Table 1 reports the scales, items, and associated internal consistency indexes.

Table 1. Scales, items and Cronbach's α.

Scale	Cronbach's α	Items
Involvement with healthy eating	$\alpha = .86$	When thinking about your own health, how concerned are you about the following issues?
		(1) Getting a lot of salt in my food
		(2) Getting a lot of fat in my food
		(3) Getting a lot of sugar in my food
		(4) Getting many calories
		(5) Food additives in my food
		(6) Risk for high blood pressure
		(7) Risk for coronary heart disease
		(8) Getting a lot of cholesterol in my food
		(9) Gaining weight
Identification with the ad creator (sympathy)	$\alpha = .74$	When thinking about the ad you have seen a moment ago, to what extent do you agree with the following statements?
		(1) I tried to understand the events as they occurred
		(2) I understood what was bothering the ad creators
		(3) I tried to understand the ad creators' motivation
		(4) I understood what the ad creators were feeling
		(5) I was able to recognize the problems that the ad creators wanted to address
Ad evaluations	$\alpha = .86$	Overall, what is your impression of this ad?
		1 = Unfavorable −7 = Favorable
		1 = Negative −7 = Positive
		1 = Dislike −7 = Like
		1 = Unconvincing −7 = Convincing
		1 = Bad −7 = Good
Attitudes towards unhealthy eating	$\alpha = .93$	Thinking about your eating habits
		(1) I make conscious effort to try and eat a healthy diet
		(2) I try to keep the amount of fat I eat to a healthy amount
		(3) I do not need to make changes to my diet as it is healthy enough

4. Results

4.1 Main effect of source disclosure

Hypothesis 1 predicts a positive effect of source disclosure on (1) ad evaluations and (2) attitudes towards the advertised issue. Independent t-tests were conducted to test H1. Source disclosure was employed as the fixed factor, and ad evaluations and attitudes toward unhealthy eating as the dependent variables. Diagnostic tests for univariate normality and homogeneity of variances return satisfactory results. The two groups do not significantly differ in terms of gender, ethnicity, body mass index, age, education, frequency of fast-food consumption and involvement with the advertised issue. The two groups significantly differ in terms of ad exposure time ($M_{Control} = 10.31$, $M_{Treatment} = 16.70$; $t(125) = -4.97$, $p < .001$). When included in a generalized linear model together with the independent variables and the other control factors, however, ad exposure time neither has significant effects on any of the dependent variables ($F(8, 115) < 1$, $p > .10$), nor does it interact with any of the independent variables. Regarding the direct effects of the other control factors on the dependent variables, body mass index ($F(8, 115) = 3.79$, $p = .054$), frequency of fast-food consumption ($F(8, 115) = 90.34$, $p < .001$) and age ($F(8, 115) = 7.20$, $p < .01$) have a significant effect on attitudes toward unhealthy eating but do not interact with the independent variables. Therefore, the analyses reported below do not include controls.

For ad evaluations, the difference between the control condition ($M = 4.46$, SD $= 1.15$) and the source disclosure condition was significant ($M = 5.26$, SD $= 1.18$; $t(125) = -3.87$, $p < .001$). These results support H1a, suggesting that the disclosure of consumer participation in ad creation returns more positive ad evaluations. For attitudes toward unhealthy eating the difference between the control condition ($M = 4.31$, SD $= 1.66$) and the source disclosure condition was marginally significant ($M = 3.73$, SD $= 1.79$; $t(125) = 1.89$, $p = .060$). These results partially support H1b, suggesting that the effect of source disclosure goes beyond ad evaluations, decreasing positive attitudes toward unhealthy eating. Table 2 reports the means and standard deviations for all the variables of interest.

4.2 Mediating effect of source identification

Hypothesis 2 predicts that the positive effect of source disclosure on ad evaluations is mediated by sympathy towards the ad creator. A mediation analysis using PRO-CESS (Preacher and Hayes 2004) was conducted to test H2. Source disclosure was employed as the independent variable, sympathy as the mediating factor and ad evaluations as the dependent variable. The standardized direct effect of source disclosure on sympathy was significant ($\beta = .19$, $p < .05$), the standardized direct effect of sympathy on ad evaluations was significant ($\beta = .18$, $p < .05$), and the standardized direct effect of source disclosure on ad evaluations was significant ($\beta = .29$, $p < .001$). The standardized indirect effect of source disclosure on ad evaluations was $\beta_{Indirect} = .034$. Test of significance of this indirect effect were conducted using bootstrapping procedures with 5000 repetitions. Unstandardized indirect effects were computed for each of 5000 bootstrapped samples, and the 95% confidence interval was computed by determining the indirect effects at the 2.5th (LLCI) and 97.5th percentiles (ULCI). The bootstrapped unstandardized indirect effect of source disclosure on ad evaluations was .08 (SE $= .06$, LLCI $= .005$; ULCI $= .245$). Since the unstandardized indirect effect falls within the 95%

Table 2. Means and standard deviations for control and treatment conditions.

Variable	Control ($n = 64$) Mean (SD)	Co-created ($n = 63$) Mean (SD)	t	Sig.
Age	37.30 (12.45)	40.87 (11.28)	−1.70	^
BMI	28.34 (9.23)	27.23 (8.07)	0.72	n.s.
Frequency	3.64 (2.05)	3.38 (2.08)	0.71	n.s.
Ad exposure time	10.31 (6.72)	16.70 (7.72)	−4.97	***
Involvement	4.23 (1.25)	4.41 (1.21)	−0.82	n.s.
Identification	5.86 (0.75)	6.14 (0.74)	−2.01	*
Ad evaluations	4.46 (1.15)	5.26 (1.18)	−3.87	***
Attitudes	4.31 (1.66)	3.73 (1.79)	1.90	^
Gender	% (N)	% (N)	−1.51	n.s.
Male	62.5% (40)	49.2% (31)		
Female	37.5% (24)	50.8% (32)		
Ethnicity			0.62	n.s.
Caucasian	82.8% (53)	85.7% (54)		
Afro-american	0.0% (0)	3.2% (2)		
Hispanic	7.8% (5)	3.2% (2)		
Asian	9.4% (6)	7.9% (5)		
Education			1.30	n.s.
High school	37.5% (24)	50.8% (32)		
College	50.0% (32)	39.7% (25)		
Masters	10.9% (7)	7.9% (5)		
PhD	1.6% (1)	1.6% (1)		

$^{***}p < .001$; $^{*}p < .05$; $^{\wedge}p < .10$; n.s. = non-significant.

confidence intervals, which do not contain zero, we can conclude that identification significantly mediates the relationship between source disclosure and attitudes towards unhealthy eating as a complementary mediation (i.e., the mediated and direct effect both exist and point in the same direction; Zhao, Lynch, and Chen 2010). These results support H2.

The same procedure was used to ensure that, as suggested by Escalas and Stern (2003), the mediating effect of sympathy did not hold at the attitudinal level. Source disclosure was employed as the independent variable, sympathy as the mediating factor and attitudes towards unhealthy eating as the dependent variable. The standardized direct effect of source disclosure on sympathy was significant ($\beta = .19$, $p < .05$), the standardized direct effect of sympathy on attitudes toward unhealthy eating was not significant ($\beta = .04$, $p > .10$), and the standardized direct effect of source disclosure on attitudes toward unhealthy eating was significant ($\beta = −.18$, $p < .05$). Test of significance of the standardized indirect effect of source disclosure on attitudes toward unhealthy eating returned non-significant results (SE $= .07$, LLCI $= −.083$; ULCI $= .210$). Since the unstandardized indirect effect contained zero, sympathy does not mediate the relationship between source disclosure and attitudes towards unhealthy eating, configuring the resulting model as a direct-only non-mediation (Zhao, Lynch, and Chen 2010).

4.3 Moderating effect of personal involvement

Hypothesis 3 predicts that the positive effect of source disclosure on (1) sympathy, (2) ad evaluations and (3) attitudes towards the advertised issue is moderated by personal involvement. With regard to H3a, a linear regression on sympathy with source disclosure (0 = control; 1 = source disclosure), involvement with healthy eating ($M = 4.32$, SD = 1.23), and the two-way interaction as predictors indicated no significant source disclosure by involvement interaction ($\beta = .03$, $t = 0.29$, $p > .10$). Therefore, H3a is rejected.

With regard to H3b, a linear regression on ad evaluations with source disclosure (0 = control; 1 = source disclosure), involvement with healthy eating ($M = 4.32$, SD = 1.23), and the two-way interaction as predictors indicated a significant source disclosure by involvement interaction ($\beta = .23$, $t = 2.05$, $p < .05$). Table 3 presents the regression models for (1) the direct effects only and (2) the interaction effect.

A floodlight analysis was conducted to decompose this interaction, using the Johnson–Neyman technique to identify the ranges of involvement with healthy eating for which the simple effect of source disclosure was significant (Spiller et al. 2013). The Johnson–Neyman point was located at $JN_{Involvement} = 3.48$. The analysis revealed a significant positive effect of source disclosure on ad evaluations for any model where involvement was greater than 3.48 ($B_{JN} = 0.47$, SE = .24, $p = .05$), but not for any model where involvement was lower than 3.48. $B_{JN} = 0.47$ indicates the group difference (unstandardized effect) in terms of ad evaluations between the control and the source disclosure conditions when X (i.e., involvement) equals the Johnson–Neyman point (Figure 2). These results suggest that the positive main effect of source disclosure on ad evaluations is enhanced (vs. no effect) under conditions of high (vs. low) involvement with healthy eating. These findings fully support H3b.

With regard to H3c, the same linear regression analysis was performed on attitudes towards unhealthy eating, finding a significant source disclosure by involvement interaction ($\beta = -.31$, $t = -2.66$, $p < .01$). Table 4 presents the regression models for (1) the direct effects only and (2) the interaction effect.

Table 3. Hierarchical regression models on ad evaluations.

| | Dependent variable: ad evaluations | | | | | | | |
| | Model 1 | | | | Model 2 | | | |
	B	β	t	Sig.	B	β	t	Sig.
Main effects								
Source disclosure	.758	.310	3.76	**	.757	.309	3.80	***
Personal involvement	.238	.239	2.91	***	.079	.080	0.71	n.s.
Moderating effect								
Source disclosure X Personal involvement	–	–	–	–	.408	.230	2.05	*
Model fit								
R^2 (in %)	16.4				19.2			
F-value	12.16			***	9.72			***

$***p < .001$; $**p < .01$; $*p < .05$; n.s. = non-significant.

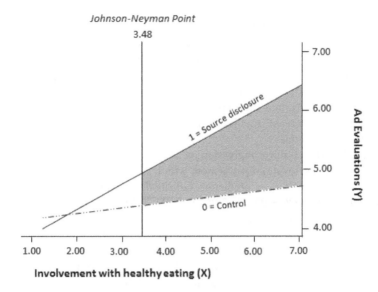

Figure 2.   Source disclosure by involvement area of interaction on ad evaluations.

Table 4.   Hierarchical regression models on attitudes towards unhealthy eating.

| | Dependent variable: attitudes toward unhealthy eating | | | | | | | |
| | Model 1 | | | | Model 2 | | | |
	B	β	t	Sig.	B	β	t	Sig.
Main effects								
Source disclosure	−.537	.304	−1.76	^	−.534	−.153	−1.80	^
Personal involvement	−.253	−.179	−2.05	*	.054	.038	0.32	n.s.
Moderating effect								
Source disclosure X	—	—	—	—	−.790	−.314	−2.66	**
Personal involvement								
Model fit								
R^2 (in %)	6.0				11.1			
F-value	3.94			*	5.12			**

$^{**}p < .01$; $^{*}p < .05$; $^{\wedge}p < .10$; n.s. = non-significant.

A floodlight analysis identified the Johnson–Neyman point at $JN_{\text{Involvement}} = 4.40$ (Spiller et al. 2013). The analysis revealed a significant positive effect of source disclosure on ad evaluations for any model where involvement was greater than 4.40 ($B_{JN} = -0.59$, SE $= .30$, $p = .05$), but not for any model where involvement was lower than 4.40. $B_{JN} = -0.59$ indicates the group difference (unstandardized effect) in terms of ad evaluations between the control and the source disclosure conditions when X equals the Johnson–Neyman point (Figure 3). These result suggest that the negative main effect of source disclosure on attitude toward unhealthy eating is enhanced (vs. no effect) under conditions of high (vs. low) involvement with healthy eating. These findings fully support H3c.

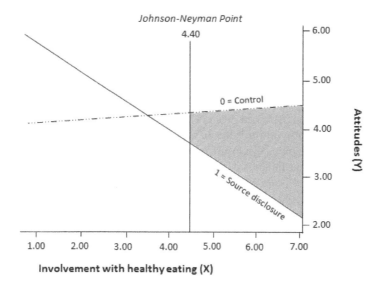

Figure 3.   Source disclosure by involvement area of interaction on attitudes.

5.   Discussion

5.1   *Summary of findings*

Commercial marketers in industries with strong social and health implications, such as food and beverages use a variety of advertising tactics to reach consumers (Royne and Levy 2015). This study set out to understand if health departments and social marketers can do the same. Within the context of unhealthy eating – a relevant issue leading to increasing obesity rates every year, despite the considerable amount of public money invested in its prevention (Krishen and Bui 2015) – we investigated the effectiveness of co-created advertising in fostering positive social change, a research domain in which the potential benefits of participatory approaches have thus far been neglected. First, the results confirm that disclosing consumer participation in ad creation leads to positive ad evaluations and decreases positive attitudes towards unhealthy eating. Second, the process of identification triggered by perceived sympathy towards the ad creator mediates the main effect of source disclosure on ad evaluations. Third, the effect of source disclosure on ad evaluations and attitudes is enhanced when the audience is highly involved with the advertised issue.

5.2   *Theoretical contribution*

This study offers a first step towards understanding consumer participation in SEA, adding to a growing body of literature on consumer responsabilization and participation in social and health care (Shamir 2008; Giesler and Veresiu 2014; Boivin et al. 2014). In particular, our findings complement and expand to the public health sector extant knowledge of commercial CGA in reference to the source disclosure effect and the identification process (Ertimur and Gilly 2012; Thompson and Malaviya 2013; Lawrence, Fournier, and Brunel 2013). Similar to Lawrence, Fournier, and Brunel (2013), we find that disclosing consumer participation in ad creation positively affects ad evaluations. It is worthwhile noting, however, that this positive effect may be partially driven by the clear specification that consumers and institutions were collaborating in the development of the advertisement. Previous studies in the commercial sector used manipulations conveying information that did not imply a collaborative effort between consumers and companies (Thompson and Malaviya 2013; Lawrence, Fournier, and Brunel 2013). We address this point in the Limitations and future research section.

Consistent with the identification path theorized by Thompson and Malaviya (2013), we find evidence of the mediating effect of sympathy towards the ad creator. Acknowledging the issues tackled by the ad creators while understanding their feelings and motivations results in sympathy towards the ad creators, which in turn accounts for a portion of the positive effect of source disclosure on ad evaluations.

Most importantly, our findings demonstrate the moderating role of personal involvement with the advertised issue in co-created SEA. Whereas previous conceptualizations of involvement considered only brand loyalty in the private sector (Thompson and Malaviya 2013), we demonstrate that involvement with a social or health issue moderates the main effect of source disclosure on ad evaluations and attitudes towards unhealthy eating.

5.3 *Implications for practice and public policy*

This study holds relevant implications for advertising practice. First, our findings confirm that the simple disclosure of consumer participation in co-created SEA is enough to cause a variation in terms of ad evaluations and attitudes towards unhealthy eating. This evaluative variation can be prompted with few, impactful lines of text. Specifically, previous research on commercial CGA demonstrates that information about the ad creator conveyed in only 38 words (i.e., a main text of 12–14 words describing the message source plus 24 words of contextual information) is sufficient to cause a significant variation in ad and brand evaluations (Thompson and Malaviya 2013). Converging with existing literature, the 44 words employed in the co-created condition to convey information about the message source (i.e., a main text of 20 words describing the message source plus 24 words of contextual information, see Appendix 1) was effective in changing ad evaluations and attitudes, in comparison to the control condition. Coherently with the constraints faced by the advertising medium employed, advertisers are advised to include 'minimum viable information' on the co-created source, balancing the available space with the need to convey a sufficiently powerful description of the source. Second, the moderating role of personal involvement suggests that targeted messages should be supported by a network of advertising initiatives aimed at increasing the baseline level of involvement in the target audience. While personal involvement with the advertised issue cannot be directly manipulated in the message format, supporting campaigns and programs can be run in parallel to gradually increase the populations' awareness and interest in specific social and health issues.

This research demonstrates the role of co-created communications for positive social change and provides preliminary validation of the effectiveness of participative approaches in public sector advertising. At the same time, our findings imply that this advertising strategy requires an infrastructure that can support its implementation in the public sector (Giesler and Veresiu 2014). The creation, implementation and maintenance of an adequate infrastructure would not only enable a horizontal collaboration between consumers, advertisers and institutional bodies, but may even serve to increase the baseline level of personal involvement discussed in the implications for advertising practice. Health departments are already using social media, health apps and interactive websites to share information and policies, and to improve governments' understanding of public attitudes (Andersen, Medaglia, and Henrikensen 2012). The co-creation of SEA would only stretch this online engagement a little further, with the added benefits of enhanced understanding of the target audience and increased message effectiveness. In addition, the broader social media network can be employed to disseminate supporting campaigns, programs and initiatives aimed at increasing the population's involvement with relevant social and health issues.

5.4 Limitations and future research

This research is not without limitations. First, the results highlight a significant complementary mediation of sympathy on the direct effect of source disclosure on ad evaluations, rather than an indirect-only mediation (Zhao, Lynch, and Chen 2010). This result suggests that potential mediators other than sympathy towards the ad creator have been omitted. Literature on CGA points towards other potential mediators, such as perceived motives of the ad creator (Berthon, Pitt, and Campbell 2008), source credibility (Thompson and Malaviya 2013), executional quality (Lawrence, Fournier, and Brunel 2013) and even advertising authenticity (Ertimur and Gilly 2012). Future research should include these variables in a comprehensive structural model to illuminate the drivers of effectiveness of co-created advertising both in the private and in the public sectors.

Second, the scope of our investigation was limited to unhealthy eating and constrained by the use of a single, static visual ad presented in an attention-getting format (i.e., structured experimental design). Additional research is required to validate the findings reported herein to different contexts within the broader health, social and environmental domains. In addition, as suggested by Escalas and Stern (2003), more engaging ads may leverage narrative transportation and potentially elicit additional cognitive and emotional reactions other than sympathy. Future research should extend this investigation to the audience's reactions to source disclosure in dynamic media, such as interactive ads and videos.

Third, our experiment was constrained by an attention getting design which resulted in longer exposure times in comparison to real life settings. The average exposure time across conditions was more than 10 seconds longer than the average gaze duration (Pieters and Wedel 2004). While controlling for the effect of exposure time returned no significant results for any of the variables of interest, it is likely that the prolonged exposure and the absence of visual distractions (e.g., other surrounding content as typical of print advertising) triggered a higher level of mental processing. The exclusion of respondents failing the treatment check further requires the interpretation of these results as stemming from conditions of high situational attention. Our findings suggest the effectiveness of co-created SEAs in situations of high attention, yet future research is warranted on how to ensure the audience is attentive both to the source and the content of the message.

Acknowledgements

The authors wish to thank the editor, the guest editors, the two anonymous reviewers and the participants to the GAMMA 2015 conference in Singapore for their constructive comments.

Disclosure statement

No potential conflict of interest was reported by the authors.

References

Amos, C., G. Holmes, and D. Strutton. 2008. Exploring the relationship between celebrity endorser effects and advertising effectiveness. *International Journal of Advertising* 27, no. 2: 209–34.

Andersen, K.N., R. Medaglia, and H.Z. Henriksen. 2012. Social media in public health care: Impact domain propositions. *Government Information Quarterly* 29, no. 4: 462–9.

Berthon, P., L. Pitt, and C. Campbell. 2008. Ad lib: When customers create the ad. *California Management Review* 50, no. 4: 6–30.

Boivin, A., P. Lehoux, J. Burgers, and R. Grol. 2014. What are the key ingredients for effective public involvement in health care improvement and policy decisions? A randomized trial process evaluation. *The Milbank Quarterly* 92, no. 2: 319–50.

Cialdini, R.B., and M.R. Trost. 1998. Social influence: Social norms, conformity and compliance. In *The handbook of social psychology*, ed. D.T. Gilbert, S.T. Fiske, and G. Lindzey, 4th ed., vol. 2, 151–92. Boston, MA: McGraw-Hill.

Dibb, S., and M. Carrigan. 2013. Social marketing transformed: Kotler, Polonsky and Hastings reflect on social marketing in a period of social change. *European Journal of Marketing* 47, no. 9: 1376–98.

D'Souza, C., and M. Taghian. 2005. Green advertising effects on attitude and choice of advertising themes. *Asia Pacific Journal of Marketing and Logistics* 17, no. 3: 51–66.

Eisenberg, N., and J. Strayer. 1987. Critical issues in the study of empathy. In *Empathy and its development*, ed. N. Eisenberg and J. Strayer, 3–16. Cambridge: Cambridge University Press.

Erdogan, B.Z. 1999. Celebrity endorsement: A literature review. *Journal of Marketing Management* 15, no. 4: 291–314.

Ertimur, B., and M.C. Gilly. 2012. So whaddya think? Consumers create ads and other consumers critique them. *Journal of Interactive Marketing* 26, no. 3: 115–30.

Escalas, J.E., and B.B. Stern. 2003. Sympathy and empathy: Emotional responses to advertising dramas. *Journal of Consumer Research* 29, no. 4: 566–78.

Giesler, M., and E. Veresiu. 2014. Creating the responsible consumer: Moralistic governance regimes and consumer subjectivity. *Journal of Consumer Research* 41, no. 3: 840–57.

Guttman, N., and C.T. Salmon. 2004. Guilt, fear, stigma and knowledge gaps: Ethical issues in public health communication interventions. *Bioethics* 18, no. 6: 531–52.

Kähkönen, P., H. Tuorila, and H. Rita. 1996. How information enhances acceptability of a low-fat spread. *Food Quality and Preference* 7, no. 2: 87–94.

Kang, Y.S., and P.M. Herr. 2006. Beauty and the beholder: Toward an integrative model of communication source effects. *Journal of Consumer Research* 33, no. 1: 123–30.

Kearney, J.M., K.F.A.M. Hulshof, and M.J. Gibney. 2001. Eating patterns–temporal distribution, converging and diverging foods, meals eaten inside and outside of the home–implications for developing FBDG. *Public Health Nutrition* 4, no. 2b: 693–8.

Kelley, H.H. 1967. Attribution theory in social psychology. In *Nebraska symposium on motivation*, ed. D. Levine, vol. 15, 192–238. Lincoln: University of Nebraska Press.

Kirmani, A., and B. Shiv. 1998. Effects of source congruity on brand attitudes and beliefs: The moderating role of issue-relevant elaboration. *Journal of Consumer Psychology* 7, no. 1: 25–47.

Kreuter, M.W., and S.M. McClure. 2004. The role of culture in health communication. *Annual Review of Public Health* 25: 439–55.

Krishen, A.S., and M. Bui. 2015. Fear advertisements: Influencing consumers to make better health decisions. *International Journal of Advertising* 34, no. 3: 473–94.

Lawrence, B., S. Fournier, and F. Brunel. 2013. When companies don't make the ad: A multimethod inquiry into the differential effectiveness of consumer-generated advertising. *Journal of Advertising* 42, no. 4: 292–307.

Office of Road Safety Western Australia. 2012 Short film competition 2012. http://www.ors-wa.com.au/Campaigns/Film-Competition (accessed September 2, 2014).

Parker, R., and S.C. Ratzan. 2010. Health literacy: A second decade of distinction for Americans. *Journal of Health Communication* 15, no. S2: 20–33.

Petty, R.E., and J.T. Cacioppo. 1986. The elaboration likelihood model of persuasion. *Advances in Experimental Social Psychology* 19: 123–205.

Petty, R.E., J.T. Cacioppo, and D. Schumann. 1983. Central and peripheral routes to advertising effectiveness: The moderating role of involvement. *Journal of Consumer Research* 10, no. 2: 135–46.

Pieters, R., and M. Wedel. 2004. Attention capture and transfer in advertising: Brand, pictorial, and text-size effects. *Journal of Marketing* 68, no. 2: 36–50.

Preacher, K.J., and A.F. Hayes. 2004. SPSS and SAS procedures for estimating indirect effects in simple mediation models. *Behavior Research Methods, Instruments, and Computers* 36, no. 4: 717–31.

Royne, M.B., and M. Levy. 2015. Reaching consumers through effective health messages: A public health imperative. *Journal of Advertising* 44, no. 2: 85–7.

Shamir, R. 2008. The age of responsibilization: On market-embedded morality. *Economy and Society* 37, no. 1: 1–19.

Spiller, S.A., G.J. Fitzsimons, J.G. Lynch Jr., and G.H. McClelland. 2013. Spotlights, floodlights, and the magic number zero: Simple effects tests in moderated regression. *Journal of Marketing Research* 50, no. 2: 277–88.

Thompson, D.V., and P. Malaviya. 2013. Consumer-generated ads: Does awareness of advertising co-creation help or hurt persuasion? *Journal of Marketing* 77, no. 3: 33–47.

Wilson, E.J., and D.L. Sherrell. 1993. Source effects in communication and persuasion research: A meta-analysis of effect size. *Journal of the Academy of Marketing Science* 21, no. 2: 101–12.

World Health Organization. 2014. Body-mass index. http://apps.who.int/bmi/index.jsp?introPage= intro_3.html (accessed March 25, 2015).

Zaichkowsky, J.L. 1994. The personal involvement inventory: Reduction, revision, and application to advertising. *Journal of Advertising* 23, no. 4: 59–70.

Zhao, X., J.G. Lynch, and Q. Chen. 2010. Reconsidering Baron and Kenny: Myths and truths about mediation analysis. *Journal of Consumer Research* 37, no. 2: 197–206.

Appendix 1. Stimuli employed in the experimental design

For each experimental condition (source disclosure: control vs. co-created), participants were provided with the corresponding information on the advertisement's source, followed by the same message content (for analogous procedures, see Thompson and Malaviya 2013; Lawrence et al. 2013).

Control condition: 'The advertisement you are about to see was created by the Department of Health. The Department of Health provided informational support and developed the final advertisement'.

Visual stimulus available upon request to the first author

Co-created condition: 'The advertisement you are about to see was created by a previously affected consumer in collaboration with the Department of Health. The consumer provided his insights and personal experience on unhealthy eating. The Department of Health provided informational support and developed the final advertisement'.

Visual stimulus available upon request to the first author

Index

Note: **Boldface** page numbers refers to figures and tables

action-related knowledge 27–8, 32–4, **33, 34**
advertisement skepticism 143, **143**
advertising expenditure and brand popularities: African American and Hispanic media 54–5, **55**; brand affinity scores *see* brand affinity scores; brand perception 44–5; childhood obesity and food marketing 44; empirical model 49; hierarchy-of-effects model 43; Kantar Media 43, 48; overview of 42–3; Persuasion Knowledge Model 56; product placement 45–8, **48**, 52, **53, 54**; Tripartite Typology of Product Placement 48
African Americans, advertising expenditure and brand popularities 54–5, **55**
analysis of variance (ANOVA) tests 80, 82, 84
astroturf organizations 136; consequences of 138–9; negative effects of 136, 144; research study 139–44; *vs.* grassroots 137–8

brand affinity scores: for children 49–51, **50**; definition 46; empirical model for 49; for mothers 49–51, **50**
brand equity 65
brand perception 44–5
brand popularity 43

carbon offsetting *see* voluntary carbon offsetting
CFC *see* consideration of future consequences
CGA *see* consumer-generated advertising
childhood obesity, food marketing toward children 44
chronic regulatory focus 9–18
co-created SEAs 151–2, 162
cognitive ability in children 45
cognitive resistance 109–10
conceptual-mediated moderation model **117, 121**
consideration of future consequences (CFC) 6–7
consumer-generated advertising (CGA) 3; definition of 150; limitations 163; measures

of 156; participants and procedure 155; personal involvement, moderating effect of 153–4, 159–61; practice and public policy, implications for 162–3; source disclosure 150–2, 155, 157, **158**; source identification, mediating effect of 152–3, 157–8; theoretical contributions 161–2
consumers' knowledge, on green consumption 23–4, 27–8
cross-gender phenomenon: brand extensions 109; of male models 106

defensive stereotyping process 139

effective knowledge 27–8, 32–4, **33, 34**
elaboration likelihood model (ELM) 153
engendering distrust process 139
environmentally responsible behavior 5–7, 9–10

fear appeals of climate change 74–80, **81, 82, 83, 84**
feminine-oriented products 106–9
food marketing: and brand perception 44–5; toward children 44
fossils fuel industries 136

gender role stereotypes: in advertising 107–8; effect of 112–13; perception of 113
Global Marketing Conference in Singapore (2014) 1
global warming 136–40, 142–3
grassroots organizations, astroturfs *vs.* 137–8
green advertising 34–5
green consumption: constructs and measurements 28, 40–1; consumers' knowledge and 23–4; full structural analysis 31, **31, 32**; green advertising 34–5; knowledge levels, effect on 27–8, 32–4, **33, 34**; model fit 29, **31**; model of goal-directed behavior 25–6, **26**; reliability and validity model 29, **30**; socio-demographic profiles 28, **29**; voluntary carbon offsetting 25

hierarchy-of-effects (HOE) model 43
Hispanic media, advertising expenditure and brand popularities 54–5, **55**
HOE model *see* hierarchy-of-effects model
Hovland's theory 78

IMC *see* integrated marketing communication
incongruent information processing 108–10, 113
Inconvenient Truth, An 74, 79, 85
integrated marketing communication (IMC) 64–5, 69
Intergovernmental Panel on Climate Change (IPCC) 135
International Journal of Advertising 1
IPCC *see* Intergovernmental Panel on Climate Change

Johnson–Neyman point 159, 160

Kantar Media 43, 48
kids' brand affinity score 49–51, **50**
knowledge and green consumption 27
Korea, environmental advertising in *see* United States *vs.* Korea, environmental advertising in

mass media, coverage of environmental issues 77
match-up hypothesis 107
mediated moderation model 115, 117–18, **126**
model of goal-directed behavior (MGB) 25–6, **26**
mothers' brand affinity scores 49–51, **50**

need for uniqueness (NFU) 111–12; conditional indirect effect by **122, 127**; interaction effect of **120, 126**; mediated moderation testing **121,** 125–7
New York City Department of Health (NYCHD) 155
NFU *see* need for uniqueness
non-conventional advertisements 108
nonprofit organizations **143**; research study of 139–44; types of 139
non-stereotypical gender role (NSGR) advertising 106; congruent and incongruent information processing 108–9; effect of 107, 110; investigations on 130; need for uniqueness 111–12; perceived novelty and cognitive resistance 109–10; research methodology 114–30; self-construal level in 110–11; stereotypes, concept of 107–8
norm-activation model 76–7
NSGR advertising *see* non-stereotypical gender role advertising
NYCHD *see* New York City Department of Health

Office for Road Safety of Western Australia 149
one-way analysis of variance tests 80, 82, 84

on-premise signs, illumination of: branding the site 65–6, 69; communicating business location 63–4, 68–9; control variables, impact of 70; integrated marketing communications 64–5, 69; level of visibility 63; for light pollution 61; marketing functions 62–3; methodology 67; profile of respondents 67–8; restrictions on 61–2; sales impact of 66–7, 70; store/business image enhancement 66, 70; visual conspicuity 63

perceived collective efficacy 79
Persuasion Knowledge Model (PKM) 56
Pledge of Allegiance 100, 101
prevention-focused individuals 2, 5, 8
primed regulatory focus 10–18
PROCESS program 115
product incongruity 108
product placement 45–8, **48**, 52, **53, 54**
pro-environmental advertising: effectiveness of 4–5; environmental concern 7–8; recycle and reduce messages 8–9; responsiveness to 9
pro-environmental behavior 6; collective efficacy 79, 85; data collection 79; descriptive statistics and correlation matrix 82, **83**; fear appeals 75–6, 79–80, 85; implications of 86–8; manipulation check 79, **80,** 81; measurement scale 80; moral obligations 76–7; organizations and mass media 77; regression analysis 84, **84**; research design 79–80; risk perception 78; self-efficacy 78–9; threat perception 75, 76
promotion-focused individuals 2, 5, 8
PSA *see* public service announcement
public distrust and disengagement 138–9
public service announcement (PSA) 96

recycle and reduce messages 8–9
regulatory engagement theory 97
regulatory focus theory (RFT) 5; chronic *vs.* primed 10–18; environmental concern 5–7, 9–10; environmentally responsible behavior 5–6; future consequences 6–7; influence of 5; prevention-focused 5, 8; pro-environmental ads *see* pro-environmental advertising; promotion-focused 5, 8–10; promotion *vs.* prevention 5; research study 9–20, **14, 15**

SC level *see* self-construal level
SEAs *see* socially empowering advertisements
self-construal (SC) level 110–11; conditional indirect effect by **118, 125**; interaction effect of **124**; mediated moderation, testing for 123–5

INDEX

SGR advertising *see* stereotypical gender role advertising
social learning theory 113
socially empowering advertisements (SEAs) 150, 153
stereotypes, concept of 106–7
stereotypical gender role (SGR) advertising 115–16, **116,** 118–19, **120,** 128
system knowledge 27–8, 32–4, **33, 34**

theory of planned behavior (TPB) 24, 25
threat perception 75, 76
TPB *see* theory of planned behavior
Tripartite Typology of Product Placement 48

United States Environmental Protection Agency 4
United States *vs.* Korea, environmental advertising in: autonomous *vs.* imposed choices 97–8; behavioral intention toward energy saving 101, **101**; environmental protection practice 95–7; limitations 102–3; overview of 93–5; pretest analysis 98–101; theoretical and managerial implications 102

VCO *see* voluntary carbon offsetting
visual conspicuity 63
voluntary carbon offsetting (VCO) 24–5

For Product Safety Concerns and Information please contact our EU
representative GPSR@taylorandfrancis.com Taylor & Francis Verlag GmbH,
Kaufingerstraße 24, 80331 München, Germany

Printed and bound by CPI Group (UK) Ltd, Croydon, CR0 4YY
01/05/2025
01858426-0013